Simon Gray

Simon Gray was born in 1936 in Hayling Island.
He lives in London with his wife, two cats and a dog.

SIMON GRAY

Key Plays

Butley
Otherwise Engaged
Close of Play
Quartermaine's Terms
The Late Middle Classes

Introduced by
Harold Pinter

faber and faber

This collection first published in 2002
by Faber and Faber Limited
3 Queen Square London WC1N 3AU
Published in the United States by Faber and Faber Inc.
an affiliate of Farrar, Straus and Giroux LLC, New York

Typeset by Country Setting, Kingsdown, Kent CT14 8ES
Printed in England by Mackays of Chatham plc, Chatham, Kent

The right of Simon Gray to be identified as author of this collection
and the works in it has been asserted in accordance with
Section 77 of the Copyright, Designs and Patents Act 1988

Introduction © Harold Pinter, 2002
This collection © Simon Gray, 2002

Butley was first published in 1971 by Methuen and Co. Ltd.
The lines from T. S. Eliot's *Collected Poems 1909-1962* are reprinted
by permission of Faber and Faber Ltd. The lines by Beatrix Potter, from
Cecily Parsley's Nursery Rhymes and *Appley Dappley's Nursery Rhymes*,
are reprinted by permission of Frederick Warne and Co. Ltd.
Otherwise Engaged was first published in 1975
in a volume (including *Plaintiffs and Defendants*)
entitled *Otherwise Engaged and Other Plays* by Eyre Methuen Ltd.
Quartermaine's Terms was first published in 1981 by Eyre Methuen Ltd.
Close of Play was first published in 1979 by Eyre Methuen Ltd.
The Late Middle Classes was first published in 1999 by Nick Hern Books Ltd.

A CIP record for this book
is available from the British Library

0-571-21634-X

2 4 6 8 10 9 7 5 3 1

Contents

Introduction

BY HAROLD PINTER

Simon Gray asked me to direct *Butley* in 1970. I found its savage, lacerating wit hard to beat and accepted the invitation. I then went on to direct another seven of his plays, finishing with *The Late Middle Classes* in 2000. Apart from the fact that, during the course of these thirty years, Simon and I formed an indissoluble friendship, my involvement in his plays represents a uniquely rich and vivid part of my professional life. It's something I remain truly thankful for.

The extraordinary thing about *Butley*, it still seems to me, is that the play gives us a character who hurls himself towards destruction while living, in the fever of his intellectual hell, with a vitality and brilliance known to few of us. He courts death by remaining ruthlessly – even dementedly – alive. It's a remarkable creation and Alan Bates as Butley gave the performance of a lifetime.

In *Otherwise Engaged* Alan Bates inhabited the other side of the coin. Simon Hench sees his obligation as one of self-protection. He will not allow himself to be known. His defensive mechanisms are almost perfect (almost but not quite). His lethal wit is of another kind to Butley's. He trips people up and lays them bare with a consummate delicacy, out of apparent compassion for them, as it were. The play is quite beautifully shaped. Alan Bates was again brilliant and Nigel Hawthorne uproarious as his brother Stephen.

Close of Play is, I suppose, the darkest of Simon's plays. It was never appreciated by the critical fraternity, which failed to understand it for what it was – a radical exploration of poetic drama. Its range of operation, its sleight of hand, its command of varying modes of language, its use of monologue and chorus – all this moved far away from its ostensible naturalism. The character of Daisy was a wonderful one. Peggy Ashcroft rehearsed the part for about a week, but then, in great pain, had to leave the company for a cartilage operation. We were left with a splendid cast and a highly professional understudy, but Peggy Ashcroft was much missed.

St John Quartermaine in *Quartermaine's Terms* is a masterly portrayal of an innocent. It is tender and unerring, never sentimental. Edward Fox's performance was memorable, a figure moving among elusive shadows, lost in alien territory – in fact the action around him might as well be taking place on Mars. But this shadow world finally proves to be only too concrete and Quartermaine finds himself up against the real, the harsh, the indifferent dark. Directing the play was both joyful and heartbreaking.

The Late Middle Classes I found a rich and beautifully wrought piece of work. Directing it was extremely satisfying but the production ran into deeply unsettling waters. The enterprise began with a miracle of casting. The central role (a thirteen-year-old boy) we found very difficult to cast. Suddenly we stumbled upon a fifteen-year-old girl (Sarah Bedi) who passed as a good-looking thirteen-year-old boy. She was wonderful; precise, contained, mysterious. Her sister (Anne Bedi) became her understudy and was almost as good. So we had two girls masquerading (very successfully) as boys. In the programme we called Sarah Sam and Anne Alex.

We opened the production at Watford, where it broke all box-office records, but theatrical politics blocked the play's presentation in London. The play, graceful, tough and poignant, deserved to be seen by many more people.

Life in the theatre hasn't brought me anything more rewarding than directing Simon Gray's plays.

BUTLEY

For Roger Gard
1936–2000

Butley was first presented by Michael Codron on 14 July 1971 at the Criterion Theatre, London. The cast was as follows:

Ben Butley Alan Bates
Joseph Keyston Richard O'Callaghan
Miss Heasman Brenda Cavendish
Edna Shaft Mary Wimbush
Anne Butley Colette O'Neil
Reg Nuttall Michael Byrne
Mr Gardner George Fenton

Director Harold Pinter
Designer Eileen Diss

Characters

Ben Butley
Joseph Keyston
Miss Heasman
Edna Shaft
Anne Butley
Reg Nuttall
Mr Gardner

Act One

An office in a college of London University. About ten in the morning. The office is badly decorated (white walls, greying, plasterboard) with strip lighting. There are two desks opposite each other, each with a swivel chair. Ben's desk, left, is a chaos of papers, books, detritus. Joey's desk, right, is almost bare. Behind each desk is a bookcase. Again, Ben's is chaotic with old essays and mimeographed sheets scattered among the books, while Joey's is neat, not many books on the shelves. On each desk there is a table lamp and in front of each desk a hard chair. There is one telephone, on Ben's desk, the flex of which is long enough to reach Joey's desk. There are a few hard-backed chairs around the walls, and one armchair, in Ben's corner of the room. On the wall is a blown-up picture (photograph) of T. S. Eliot, with a smear across it and one of its corners curled. The panels to the office door are frosted glass, behind which people, when they approach, are dimly seen.

Ben is a heavy smoker, and should smoke more frequently than the text indicates. Joey does not smoke.

As the curtain rises, Ben enters, in a plastic raincoat, which he takes off and throws into his chair. He has a lump of cotton wool on his chin, from a particularly nasty shaving cut. He goes to his chair, sits down, looks around as if searching for something, shifts uncomfortably, pulls the plastic mac out from under him, searches through its pockets, takes out half a banana, a bit squashed, then throws the raincoat over to Joey's desk. He takes a bite from the banana, removes it from the peel and drops the last piece onto his desk. Then he

7

throws the peel onto Joey's desk. He slumps into his chair – a long pause – the telephone rings.

Ben Butley, English. Hello, James, have a nice break? (*A pause – he mouths a curse.*) Sorry, James, I can't talk now – I'm right in the middle of a tutorial – 'bye. (*Then he touches the cotton wool and tries to pull it off. He lets out an exclamation. Touches his chin, looks at his finger. In an undertone*) Bugger! (*He gets up, looks under his desk, drags out a bulging briefcase from which he pulls an opened bag of cotton wool. He delves into his briefcase again and takes out a tin of Nescafé. He shines the base on his sleeve, then holds it to his chin as if it were a mirror. He tries to put the cotton wool on, then switches on the light. It doesn't come on. He sticks the cotton wool on. He shoves the Nescafé tin back into his briefcase and stuffs the cotton wool into his jacket pocket. He goes across to the main switch and flicks it on. The strip lighting flickers into brilliance. He checks the cotton wool using the glass door of his bookcase as a mirror, then, unable to bear the strip light, flicks it off again. He goes across to Joey's desk and tries the lamp. It comes on. He wipes stray wisps of cotton wool from his fingers with the banana skin, then drops it into the clean ashtray on Joey's desk. He switches off Joey's lamp and carries it across to his desk. There is a shape at the door, then a knock.*) Bugger! Just a minute! (*He carries his lamp across to Joey's. The door opens cautiously.*) A minute, I said. (*He goes to the door and checks it with his hand.*) Hello.

Student (*off*) Hello.

Ben (*after a pause*) Can I help you?

Student (*off*) Well, it's my tutorial. On Wordsworth. 'The Prelude.'

Ben Oh. No, I can't give tutorials during the first week after the break, I'm afraid. Too much administration.

Student (*off*) Oh? When should I come, then?

Ben Come at the same hour of the same day of next week.

Student (*off*) Next week?

Ben Next week. If we keep to our timetable we'll know where we are, won't we? All right?

He closes the door. He goes back to his desk, sits down and takes out of his pocket a copy of Cecily Parsley.

'The Prelude.'

He shudders, then turns a page, reaches for the light, clicks it. Nothing happens. He gets up and goes over to Joey's desk, tries the light, it comes on. He sighs. He sits down in Joey's chair, opens one of his drawers, props his feet in it, and settles down to read. Joey comes in with a briefcase. He puts it down on his desk, clears the banana peel into the waste-paper basket, picks Ben's raincoat up, carries it over to the peg, puts the desk lamps back on their respective desks. He turns on his table light – it comes on.

Good morning.

Joey Good morning.

Ben Nice to see you.

Joey Nice to be seen. What's the matter with your chin?

Ben I'm trying to cultivate cotton wool on it. Your own is shining pleasantly, what did you have to work with, a razor?

Joey What did *you* use?

Ben Anne left one behind. Behind the fridge, to be exact. So either mice have taken up shaving, or that stubble was sheared from her calves. I thought of mounting a tuft in a locket. You needn't have taken the only one we have.

Joey It also happens to be the only one I have.

Ben Couldn't you have shared Ted's? It's no pleasure slicing open my chin with my estranged wife's razor blade. The symbolism may be deft, but the memory still smarts.

Joey I didn't mean to take it, in point of fact. I put it in the bag without thinking.

Ben Lust is no excuse for thoughtlessness. And where is your bag? (*He stands up and peers round for it.*)

Joey What? Oh, I left it with Reg.

Ben Reg? Who's Reg?

He perches on the front of his own desk with his feet up on a chair and lights a cigarette. Joey hastily occupies the vacated desk chair.

Joey Reg is his name.

Ben Whose name?

Joey Ted's.

Ben Reg is Ted's name?

Joey The one you call Ted is the one I call Reg. He calls himself Reg too.

Ben How sweet.

Joey In fact, everybody calls him Reg except you. You call him Ted.

Ben Why do I do that, I wonder?

Joey To embarrass me.

Ben Oh yes, that must be it. (*Pause.*) Did you have a good weekend?

Joey It was all right. (*Pause.*) Have you seen James this morning?

Ben Ah! Our professor! He's just been hounding me on the telephone. He and Hazel spent most of the break in bed recovering from one of Hazel's gastric goulashes.

Joey Did he say anything? I mean, are there any details yet?

Ben You want details of James's diarrhoea?

Joey You know what I mean. About my board.

Ben Ah. About your board. Now when is that, exactly?

Joey A fortnight tomorrow.

Ben Indeed? A fortnight tomorrow? Mmmm. Where the hell is it?

He begins to search in his desk drawers – Joey comes over to him.

Joey What?

Ben It's no real advance. (*Sits.*) But it's got some interesting things in it. Damn! Anyway –

'How do you do, Mistress Pussy?
Mistress Pussy, how do you do?'
'I thank you kindly, little dog,
I fare as well as you!'

Joey Did he say anything?

Ben You're genuinely interested in this promotion of yours, aren't you? Why? (*Little pause.*) No, he didn't say anything. Your name didn't come up, and there's no reason that it should until, in the normal course of events and strictly according to the rules, the board is rigged, the strings are pulled, and it's passed over that of someone more closely related to the Principal, or with more distinguished qualifications. I should warn you that there are almost as many of the latter as of the former.

Cecily Parsley lived in a pen,
And brewed good ale for gentlemen;
Gentlemen came every day.

Joey goes to his shelves and takes down a book.

Till Cecily Parsley ran away.

Why? (*Ben crosses to Joey.*) Why has he got your bag?

Joey He happened to pick it up for me when we got off the train.

Ben Not many young men are as gallant these days. You haven't been home yet, then?

Joey To the flat? No. (*He sits at his desk.*)

Ben Ah. Why not?

Joey Because I didn't have time, obviously. (*He begins to correct a set of essays from his briefcase.*)

Ben I waited for you.

Joey Did you? Sorry.

Ben (*watches him*) You had a nice little mid-term break then, did you?

Joey It was all right.

Ben Well, are you going to tell me about it, or shall
I probe and pry?

Joey I'd rather let it slip out naturally, if I may?

Ben But you're much more charming under interrogation.
My natural force plays excitingly with your natural
submissiveness. Or has your holiday changed you, as we
say in the trade, radically? (*He opens Joey's briefcase.*)
Ah-hah! I thought so! (*As Joey looks up.*) Blake! Why is
your briefcase bulging with Blake! (*He opens one of the
books and takes out a piece of paper.*) What's this?

Joey I happen to be lecturing on him this half. (*He tries
to take the book and notes from him.*) Kindly don't mess
my notes up. Can I have it back, please?

Ben Notes to whom? Reg?

What immortal hand or eye
Could frame thy fearful symmetry?

Ted is certainly quite symmetrical – in a burly sort of
way.

Did he who made the lamb make thee? (*Laughs.*)

Joey All right, all right, let's *be* infantile. (*He goes across
to Ben's desk and picks up his briefcase.*)

Ben (*drops Joey's book and notes, lunges across and
grabs his own briefcase*) No, bags first go. I haven't
unpacked it for weeks.

*He opens it, as Joey returns to his marking. He pulls
out an empty Scotch bottle, then a red-covered
manuscript.*

It's laid out like a film script. It must be an American
MA thesis – ah – 'Henry James and the Crucified
Consciousness' – aaah. (*Ben wanders over to Joey's desk,*

13

pulls out a blue sock, puts the thesis down on Joey's desk, along with a few more papers, files, crumpled newspaper, the Nescafé tin and the briefcase itself.) Now where's the other? – There must be a pair –

Joey (*picks up the thesis*) You mean you forgot to give his thesis back?

Ben Not yet. So far I've forgotten to read it. Forgetting to give it back will come later. Failing Americans is a slow and intricate ritual and that's what they come here for – the ritual – aaah, here it is. (*He takes out another sock. It is red. He picks up the blue. Looks at them.*)

Joey Those are mine. Naturally.

Ben Naturally you're very welcome. (*He tosses the socks at Joey.*) Personally I wouldn't be caught dead wearing a pair like that. (*He lifts up his trousers, studies his socks.*)

Joey Those happen to be mine, too.

Ben You really must give up buying cheap socks. I can feel a hole growing around the toe.

Joey (*savagely*) Perhaps if you bothered to cut your toenails – (*He picks up the thesis and essays Ben has dropped.*)

Ben Are we going to have a tantrum?

Joey The thing is to stop your rubbish creeping across to my side of the room. (*He makes as if to stack them neatly, then crams them savagely into Ben's shelves.*) Here, anyway. (*He goes back to his desk and continues marking.*)

Ben *Are* we? I'd quite enjoy one.

Joey Would you?

Ben Then I'll know you're back, you see. You've been a little thin on presence so far.

Joey There's not enough room.

Ben sits down cross-legged on the top of Joey's desk and watches Joey. He clears his throat delicately. He smiles genteelly.

Ben (*genteel*) I was just wondering if I might enquire as to how your friend is, may I?

Joey smiles.

Hoh, h'I'm so glad.

Joey continues transcribing marks.

May h'I hask, done all those, 'ave we?

He takes the essay Joey is holding.

Ho, but you 'adn't done them last week, 'ad you? Did you do them on the train, going h'up with your friend?

Shape at the door, Ben doesn't notice.

H'I h'always say that h'if h'a job's worth doing h'it's worth h'ignoring.

Knock on the door. Ben turns, starts to move rapidly to it. When it opens, Miss Heasman, a pretty, competent-looking girl, steps in.

Miss Heasman Oh, sorry, I was just wondering when my tutorials are.

Ben Same as last term, except of course for this week.

Miss Heasman You didn't take me last term. My name is Heasman, Carol Heasman. I'm replacing Mrs Grainger.

Ben Mrs Grainger?

Miss Heasman Yes. She said she didn't get to see you often, owing to administrative tangles.

Ben Mrs Grainger got into administrative tangles?

Miss Heasman No, you were busy with them.

Ben If only they'd let us get on with it and teach. (*Laughs.*) Anyway, you'd better come at the same hours as Mrs Grainger, all right?

Miss Heasman I expect so. What were they?

Ben Could you find out from Mrs Grainger, please?

Miss Heasman I'll try.

Ben Thank you.

> *He holds the door wider. Miss Heasman goes out. Ben returns to his desk.*

I didn't care for that one at all, there was an air of mad devotion about her that reminds me of my wife's mother, the mad monk.

> *Looking at Joey, who is still transcribing marks. Joey tries to go on working. In a normal tone, after a pause:*

You're in trouble, Joey.

Joey What? (*He looks up.*)

Ben I'm sorry. I've been wondering how to tell you. But as you've still got a fortnight before the board. (*Sits. Pause.*) A member of the department has his knife out.

Joey Who?

Ben That pre-break meeting we had – the one you had to leave early – to meet Reg?

Joey Yes. Well?

Ben The contemporary books list?

Joey Yes. Well, go on.

Ben On the face of it, you were very adroit. You didn't actually support me, but you indicated a certain, attitude shall we say? By coughing into my speeches with dialectical authority. You wouldn't have thought that so genteel a rhetorical device could give offence. On the face of it. Eh?

Joey But who – who did I offend?

Ben (*gets up and perches on the front of his desk again*) First of all, who proposed that a contemporary novels list – Burroughs, Genet, Roth, etc. – be added to our syllabus?

Joey You did.

Ben And who opposed it?

Joey Everybody else. Except – me.

Ben Who won?

Joey We – you did. They gave way in the end – didn't they?

Ben (*sinisterly*) Oh yes, it was passed unanimously – but I happen to know that one person – one powerful person there – resented *our* victory and blamed you – yes, you – for it.

Joey But this is ridiculous! It's absolutely – I scarcely said anything anyway.

Ben Exactly. But this person was hoping – was *relying* – on you to oppose that book list with every cell in your body.

Joey Ben, please – eh?

Ben Think, child, think! Who had most to lose by that list being passed? Who is *most* affected?

Joey Nobody. Nobody at all. You're the one who's going to teach it, they'll be *your* lectures, *your* seminars, *your* tutorials . . .

Ben (*after a long pause, as Joey, realising, looks at him*) Exactly. Precisely. Absolutely. Fool! Imbecile! Traitor! Lackey! – I wouldn't be caught dead reading those books. And you know how it exhausts me to teach books I haven't read. Why didn't you oppose me?

Joey It's your fault. Your instructions were quite clear.

Ben Haven't you heard of a sub-text? It's very fashionable now. In fact, I remember advising you to use the word twice in every paper when I was guiding you through your finals. (*He goes to examine him.*) But what's the matter, dear? You're looking a little peaky around the gills, wherever they are? Were you frightened, a trifle? You needn't be – you played the toad to perfection. (*He returns to his desk.*)

Joey Is there a sub-text to that? Or can I take it as straight abuse?

Ben It's straight abuse. Can you take it?

Joey (*trembling slightly*) No, not any longer. (*He gets up, and begins to pack his briefcase.*)

Ben Where are you going?

Joey To the library.

Ben Why?

Joey I've got a lecture at twelve.

Ben But you're not running away from me so soon?

Joey And there are a few things on my Herrick I've got to dig up.

He goes to the door – Ben cuts him off.

Ben Dig up! (*Laughs.*)

Diggory, diggory Delvet
Little old man in black velvet
He digs and he delves
You can see for yourselves
The holes dug by Diggory Delvet.

It is velvet, isn't it, this jacket? (*fingering it*)

Joey tugs his sleeve away.

No, don't flounce.

They stand staring at each other.

You were due back last night, remember?

Joey Did it make any difference?

Ben In that I spent the evening expecting you.

Joey In point of fact, I said I'd be back either last night or this morning.

Ben Also you didn't phone.

Joey I was only in Leeds for four days. Of course I didn't phone.

Ben Why not? Language difficulties? I reserved a table at Bianchi's. I was going to take us out.

Joey (*after a pause*) I'm sorry.

Ben shrugs. They each return to their desks.

It just didn't occur to me –

Ben It doesn't matter.

Joey I'm sure I said –

Ben Yes, yes, I expect you did. I assumed you were coming back, that's all. And as I spent four days on the phone to people who weren't there – bugger! (*He sits down at his desk.*) I'm sorry. All right? And if that doesn't satisfy you, Edna thinks well of you, and James is more than happy.

Joey How do you know?

Ben These things slip out. Under my persistent questionings.

Joey Edna's actually very important, isn't she? (*He goes across to Ben and sits on the hard chair in front of Ben's desk.*)

Ben It depends rather on the context.

Joey I mean in terms of influence –

Ben You mean in terms of promotion?

Joey Well – (*Grins.*)

Ben She'll certainly sit on your board, yes. Don't worry. You'll get your lectureship. Then you'll be safe for ever.

Joey I like Edna, in point of fact. No, really. We came in on the tube together this morning. She was telling me about her Byron –

Ben Can we actually – do you mind? – not discuss either Edna or Byron but most of all Edna on Byron, for purely private reasons just at the moment. The thought of them weighs on my spirit. (*Pause.*) Tell me, while you were amusing yourselves in Leeds, I saw a film on television about a publisher who hates himself. I've been meaning to ask you – does Ted hate himself?

Joey He quite likes himself, actually.

Ben I don't blame him. He seemed an amiable sort of chap the one time I met him, even though his mouth was full of symbolic sausage and his fist around a tankard of something foaming symbolically. I had the impression that most people would like him. And as he seemed exactly like most people, only from the North, ergo, he'd be favourably disposed towards himself only more so, or not?

He smiles. Joey also smiles.

Tell me, does he ever discuss his work with you? Or does he leave it behind him at the office? When you go around for one of those little dinners, does he put his feet up, perhaps, while you slave away over a hot stove, or does he do the cooking? No, I don't mean to probe – or am I prying? For instance, in our professor's ménage Hazel rips the meat apart with saw-edged knives while James brews up sauces from *Guardian* headlines. In my ménage, when I had one – remember? – Anne under-grilled the chops and over-boiled the peas while I drank the wine and charted my dropping sugar-count. Now that you and I are sharing my life again I open the tins and you stir the Nescafé again, just as we always used to do, those evenings, at least, when you're not cooking for Reg or Reg isn't cooking for you – which, arriving where we began, does it happen to be? And if it's the former, why, now I think of it, have you never cooked for me, do you think?

Joey He does the cooking, in point of fact.

Ben Christ, I feel awful. (*Pause.*) Do you know, all the time you were away, I didn't have one telephone call. I consider that very frightening. Not even from Tom.

Joey Oh. (*Pause.*) I thought you found his company intolerable.

Ben But one likes, as they say, to be asked. Also one likes people to be consistent, otherwise one will start coming adrift. At least this one will. (*Stands up.*) Also how does one know whether Tom is still the most boring man in London unless he phones in regularly to confirm it? This is the fourth week running he's kept me in suspense. He and Reg have a lot in common, haven't they? (*Pause. He sits on the desk.*)

Joey (*drily*) Really?

Ben Didn't Ted do his National Service with the Gurkhas?

Joey I really can't remember. I've never been very interested in Ted's – Reg's – military career, which was anyway about a decade ago.

He goes back to his own desk. Ben follows him.

Ben Oh, but the experience lives on for us through our born raconteurs – and Ted is something of a raconteur, isn't he? That magnificent anecdote of his – surely you remember?

Joey No. (*He picks up his briefcase and moves towards the door.*) I really must get to the library –

Ben No, wait. (*Blocks his way.*) You repeated it to me. About the Gurkha and the bowl of soup. (*He holds up two fists.*) I don't know if I can do your imitation of his accent – woon day Chef was in ta kitchen – is that close? – stirring ta soup wi' his elbows – wan in coom a little tyke –

Joey I remember.

Ben I was sure you would. Your imitation of Reg made me laugh so much that I was prepared to overlook its cruelty. Anyway, my point was simply that Tom's a great

National Service bore, too. There's that six-volume novel he's writing about it – that's something else. Yes. He's stopped showing me his drafts. (*He goes back to his desk.*)

Joey The last time he brought one around you dropped it in the bath.

Ben It! He brought around seventeen exercise books, of which I dropped a mere three into the bath. No, I don't like his silence. It's sinister.

Joey Well, you could always phone him up. (*He starts for the door again.*)

Ben I haven't finished. (*He comes over, takes Joey's briefcase from him and sits in Joey's desk chair.*)

Joey I must do something on this bloody lecture.

Ben Why? You're looking furtive. Why are you looking furtive?

Joey I'm not looking at all furtive.

Ben Have you seen Tom recently?

Joey No. No, I haven't.

Ben When did you last hear from him?

Joey (*shrugs*) Perhaps he's busy.

Ben Of course he's busy. He's too dull to be anything else. The question is, why has he stopped being busy with me? (*He returns to his own desk and sits on the hard chair.*) Do you think he's dropped me? His attentions have been slackening since my marriage broke up, now I come to think of it.

Joey (*carefully*) He's very fond of Anne, isn't he?

Ben (*laughs*) That's an idea. I must find out whether he's been hounding her.

Joey But Anne – (*Stops.*) She likes him, doesn't she?
I mean, I always thought – had the impression that she
was fond of him?

Ben Oh, I expect she became addicted. She took up all
my vices except drinking, smoking and you. She never
cared for you. Did you know that?

Joey I had my suspicions. Thank you for confirming
them.

Ben She said that Tom became a schoolteacher because
he had to prove, after three years of being taught by me
at Cambridge, that education was still a serious affair.
Whereas you wanted to get back to your old college here
and with me because you were incapable of outgrowing
your early influences. Nursery dependence. This analysis
was based crudely on the fact that you are homosexual.
She also said you were sly and pushing, and that she
didn't trust you an inch.

Joey You never told me this before.

Ben You never asked me before.

Joey I didn't ask you now, either.

Ben I know. But I got tired of waiting. (*Pause.*) Do *you*
like *her*?

Joey I thought we were friends.

Ben I'm sure you still are. (*He sits in the armchair, Joey's
briefcase tucked under his arm.*) She just can't stand you,
that's all. Something about you gives her the creeps,
was her word. Creeps. (*Laughs.*) What's the matter? Are
you upset? (*Joey shakes his head.*) You shouldn't be.
It was just her way of getting at me. Don't you see how
I emerge? As someone whose protégé is a creep? But
I didn't take offence. I don't see why you should.

24

Pause. Joey tries to take his case – Ben clutches it to him.

Tell me, what does he do, Reg's dad?

Joey looks at him.

(*Smiles.*) But we're not ashamed, are we?

Joey (*pause*) He owns a shop.

Ben What sort of shop?

Joey Just a shop. (*He walks away from him.*)

Ben Just a shop? Just a shop like Harrods, for example. What does he sell?

Joey (*after a pause*) Meat, I think.

Ben You think. Did you ever see the shop?

Joey Of course. Why?

Ben Was there meat on display?

Joey Yes.

Ben In that case he either owns a meat museum or if it was for sale you're quite right, he owns a shop that sells meat. He's what's called a butcher.

Joey (*sits on the hard chair in front of Ben's desk*) That's right, he's a butcher.

Ben Mmm-huh. And do they live over their shop?

Joey (*hesitates*) No. They live in, um, in a place just outside Leeds, in point of fact.

Ben In Point of Fact? And what sort of place is it – a Georgian terraced house, a Chippendale-style flat, a dug-out, a rural cottage; a bungalow?

Joey Yes. A bungalow.

Ben A bungalow, eh? Now let's see, starting with the garden, do they have, say, plaster gnomes in the garden?

Joey And also much to your satisfaction, say, an electric fire with coals in it, and a sofa decorated with doilies and a revolving bookcase with the collected works of Mazo de la Roche –

Ben In the garden? How witty!

Joey And their front doorbell plays a tune, can you believe that?

    Pause.

They happen to be very nice people, nevertheless.

Ben Nevertheless what?

Joey (*emphatically*) Nevertheless they happen to be very nice people.

Ben (*sits on the edge of his desk, leaving Joey's briefcase in the armchair*) What tune? (*Pause.*) Does Reg's mother work in the shop too?

Joey No.

Ben Oh. Where is she then, in the daytime?

Joey Out.

Ben Out where?

Joey Just out.

Ben She has a job, then?

Joey Yes.

Ben And where does she do this job? On the streets?

Joey You could put it like that, yes.

Ben What does she do? Sweep them?

Joey No.

Ben She walks them?

Joey Yes, in point of fact.

Ben The precise suburb is irrelevant. (*Pause.*) So Reg's mother is a prostitute.

Joey giggles, checks himself.

Joey No, she's a – traffic warden.

Ben She isn't! But what on earth did you do?

Joey Nothing in particular.

Ben You went to a football match?

Joey Football match?

Ben Hasn't it caught on there? Here in the South we place it slightly below music and well above theatre, in the cultural scale. Did you?

Joey What?

Ben Go to any football matches?

Joey Well done. Yes, we did. We went to a football match – and furthermore we wore rosettes, coloured scarves and special hats and carried rattles.

Ben You didn't! (*Laughs.*) Rattles and rosettes? You didn't! You poor old sod. Why in Christ did you stay? (*Pause.*) All right then, why did he take you there? Is it like bringing one's latest girl back to the folks –?

Joey His friends back. He doesn't like people to know he's queer. A lot of the time he doesn't like me to know. But I suppose he probably took me there as a kind of compliment – and perhaps as a test.

Ben To see if you could take him *au naturel*?

Joey That sounds reasonable, yes.

Ben And could you?

Joey He's much more natural as a London publisher who knows all about food, and cooks marvellously. Much more natural and much more convincing.

Ben But tell me – the butcher and the traffic warden – do they *know* –

Joey Know what?

A shape appears at the door. Ben charges out as Miss Heasman knocks.

Ben Oops! Sorry!

Miss Heasman Sorry!

Ben (*off*) Just dashing up to the Registrar's – some administrative tangle. Mrs Grainger, isn't it?

Miss Heasman (*off*) Miss Heasman! I can't find Mrs Grainger but I'm very anxious for a session on *A Winter's Tale*.

Ben Good God! Are you really? Well, keep trying and perhaps by next week . . . I go up here. Goodbye.

Ben dodges back and surprises Joey as he tries to leave.

– that you and Reg have it off together?

Joey Of course not. (*Shuts the door.*) And now I think I'd like to stop talking about it if you don't mind. I'm beginning to feel queasy.

Ben Recollections of tripe and stout?

Guilt Lord, I pray
Answer thy servant's question!
Is it guilt I feel
Or is it indigestion?

Don't worry, *rognons au vin* at Bianchi's will calm the
unsettled soul. (*He sits on his desk – lights a cigarette.*)

Joey Tonight you mean? For dinner?

Ben I hardly fancy them for tea.

Joey Um, the thing is, I'm, um, going around to Reg's
tonight. (*Pause.*) I – I didn't – I'm sorry, it just seemed
impossible not to go, under the circumstances.

Ben Mmm-huh. (*Little pause.*) I'm willing to treat Reg
if necessary.

Joey Well, you see Reg has already got our dinner.

Ben Oh? And what's he got for your dinner?

Joey (*laughs*) Well, kidneys, as a matter of fact. His father
gave him some special – English kidneys. As a treat.
Lamb's kidneys.

Ben Mmm-huh.

Little pause.

Joey Sorry.

Ben There's no problem. I'll get some more and Ted can
cook them for me.

Joey goes back to his desk. Pause.

What's the matter?

Joey I'd rather you didn't.

Ben Mmm-huh. May one ask why?

Joey It might be awkward.

Ben Oh? May one wonder why?

Joey Perhaps he doesn't like you very much.

Ben You surprise me. I thought he'd taken rather a fancy, on our one meeting.

Joey (*sits*) On your one meeting you pretended you thought he was an Australian and addressed him as 'Cobber'. You also pretended you thought he was an interior decorator, in order to remind him of Ted, whom he knew to be his predecessor. You were also sick over his shoes. It was a terrible evening. He hated you.

Ben You never told me this before.

Joey You never asked me before.

Ben *That* was creepy. (*Pause.*) Anyway, you exaggerate. The confusion over his national identity and profession lasted a mere twenty minutes at the beginning of the evening. It took me some twenty seconds to be sick over his shoes at the evening's end. The intervening hour was an unqualified success, in spite of the odd misunderstanding that developed into the occasional quarrel. Also you know very well that I'd taken up drinking again because I was still brooding over Anne's departure. I had what is called a drinking problem. I no longer have it.

Joey Let's face it, Ben, you drink every night. Very heavily.

Ben Exactly. There's no problem. I'm used to it again.

Pause.

Well, Joey?

Joey shrugs awkwardly.

I might also be glad of a chance to make it up. I enjoy being on terms with your chaps. (*Pause.*) Also I don't fancy a fifth night of eating alone. (*Pause.*) Well?

Joey He won't want you to come.

Ben Have you asked him?

Joey No.

Ben Then why don't you? Come on. Let's find out. (*He picks up the telephone, and hands it to him.*) Well?

Joey He's not there.

Ben How do you know, unless you try?

Joey He said he wouldn't be there until after lunch.

Ben stares at him.

He told me he had some things to do.

There is a shape at the door, not noticed by Ben and Joey, followed by a knock, and simultaneously Edna comes in. She is in her late forties and carries a small pile of folders.

Edna Hello, Ben. Joey.

Ben Hello, Edna.

Joey Hello.

Edna Am I barging in on something?

Joey No, not at all, in fact I was just on my way to the library. (*He picks up his briefcase and stands up.*)

Edna Oh, it's no good going there. It's closed while they instal a new security device. It won't be opened until this evening.

Joey Oh.

He sits down again. Ben goes to his desk.

Edna Isn't that a comment on our times? Do you know, I found a couple of students in the canteen. They actually pretended to have heard from some source or another that there were no tutorials during the first week of the half. What do you think of that?

Ben (*sits at his desk*) *Folie de grandeur.* They must learn to leave such decisions to us.

Edna Exactly. I wonder what they'd have to say if we started putting them off for any nonsensical reason that came into our heads.

Ben Yes, I often wonder that. There's so much about them one never finds out. I mean they come, they go away –

Edna (*sits opposite Ben*) Do you know anything about my particular black sheep, by the way? His name's Gardner.

Ben Gardner? Gardner, Gardner.

Joey Yes, he comes to the odd lecture, aloof in feathers.

Ben Feathers?

Joey He wears a kind of hat with feathers in it.

Edna Yes, that dreadful hat. I wish there was some action we could take about that, too. You don't remember him, Ben?

Ben I certainly can't place the hat.

Joey Isn't Gardner the one you had a conversation with just before the break? In a pub? You mentioned –

Ben A feathered youth? In a public house? Certainly not.

Edna Actually, the reason I asked whether you remember him, Ben, is that you interviewed him for his place here.

I've just looked him up in the files. (*She hands Ben Gardner's open file.*)

Ben Possibly. I only remember the ones we manage to reject, like Father O'Couligan.

Edna I must say, Ben, his headmaster's report was very unfavourable.

Ben I'm not surprised. Father O'Couligan was in his forties. The headmaster must have had him in the sixth form for a couple of decades at least. And frankly five minutes of O'Couligan was as much as I –

Edna No, I was talking about Gardner. I simply can't help wondering what made you take him.

Ben Well, Edna, I suppose I must have decided he wasn't fit for anything else.

Edna A university isn't a charity, you know.

There is a silence.

Ben Do you mean for me, Edna? Or for the students?

Edna I'm not in the mood to be flippant about the more loutish of our students today. Not with the committee's report on the Senate House fresh in my mind.

Ben Sorry, what report?

Edna It was in *The Times* this morning.

Joey I read it. In *The Guardian*. It was very disturbing.

Ben looks at him.

Edna Disturbing! They completely destroyed the Velium Aristotle. Completely destroyed it. *That* was their way of protesting about South Africa.

Joey I thought it was about Rhodesia. The University maintaining relationships –

Edna Well, one excuse is as good as another, of course.

Ben James said it was the Greek Colonels. But perhaps we're underestimating their capacity for direct logical connections. Perhaps they were protesting about the Velium Aristotle.

Edna It wouldn't surprise me. I had one or two last term who were mutinous about *The Faerie Queene*.

Ben You mean the Principal? He really should learn discretion.

Edna (*after a short pause, releases a burst of ghastly laughter*) No, Ben, you mustn't say things like that. (*Laughs again.*) Besides, the Velium Aristotle is no laughing matter. But I intend to nip Gardner in the bud before he gets completely out of hand. I'm not having any bomb-throwing hooligan skipping *my* seminars!

Ben Any bomb-throwing hooligan has permission to skip mine. (*He gets up and moves towards the door.*)

Edna (*retrieves Gardner's file from Ben's desk*) Well, there's no point in my haranguing you. I suppose I'd better take it to James.

Ben To James?

Edna Certainly. Gardner is ripe for a Dean's Report. Oh, I meant to say, you and Anne must come around soon, if you could bear an evening in my poky little flat. And Joey, of course.

Ben Thanks.

Joey (*enthusiastically*) I'd love to.

Edna How's the baby?

Ben Oh, very well. As far as one can tell. With babies, I mean.

34

Edna Yes, they are indecipherable, aren't they? How old is he now?

Ben He's (*thinks*) six or seven months, about.

Edna It's wretched of me, but I've forgotten his name. Though I do remember him as a bonny little thing.

Ben Miranda.

Joey Marina.

Ben Yes. (*Laughs.*) Marina. He's called Marina.

Edna Oh dear, oh Ben, I'm sorry. I always think of babies as 'hims' or 'its'.

Ben Well, it's probably safer these days. Our ends never know our beginnings.

Edna Any teeth yet?

Ben Just the – uh – (*Wags his finger around his mouth.*) – *gums*, you know, and a few wisdom . . . or whatever they're . . .

Edna That sounds most satisfactory. Are you all right for baby-sitters?

Ben Baby-sitters. (*Laughs.*) Oh, no problem. Marina's mother is a marvellous baby-sitter. Anne has simply added a contemporary skill to Goethe's ideal woman. (*After a pause.*) I'm afraid we are going through what we professionals know as a sticky patch.

Edna Oh dear. Ben, I'm sorry. I don't know what to say. You must both be desperately unhappy. (*Pause.*) I do hope she's not in that flat all by herself.

Ben Oh, we sorted that out. She told me that if I was half a man I'd leave. But on discovering that *she* was, she left herself. She's with her mother. Together they make up two pairs. I imagine Marina is the odd man out.

Edna I see. Oh dear. (*Pause.*) It's always so sad for the children.

Ben Yes, we do suffer the most.

Edna Where are *you* now, Joey, are you still in that bedsitter?

Joey (*little pause*) No. (*Another pause.*) I've moved back in with Ben again, in point of fact.

Edna Oh, so you're both back where you were then.

Ben Exactly.

Edna By the way, did I mention that the little office next to mine's going begging at last? So if either of you wants a place of your own . . .

Ben Thanks, Edna, but we're used to roughing it down here.

Edna It's up to you, of course . . . Well, I must leave you two to get on with it. (*She goes to the door.*) If you should clap eyes on young Gardner, please send him straight up to me on pain of a Dean's Report.

She goes out. There is a silence.

Ben I enjoyed that. It was so graceful. In a little office next door to Edna. Christ. What does she want him for? (*He returns to his desk.*) She's got her own coterie – all those boys and girls that look as if they've got the curse permanently. (*Little pause.*) Her obsession with Byron is one of the more *triste* perversions. But she shouldn't be allowed to practise it with students. She's got her bloody book for therapy.

Joey She's finished her book. That's what she was telling me on the tube this morning.

Ben Well done, Edna. I suppose it means another two decades while she finds a publisher.

Joey She's found one.

Ben She never did understand her role. Which is not to finish an unpublishable book on Byron. Now the centre cannot hold. Mere Edna is loosed upon the world. (*Pause. Sits in the armchair.*) Bloody woman! (*Pause.*) Bugger! (*Pause.*) Bugger! The Dean's Report!

Joey It *was* Gardner you told me about, then? The boy who complained about Edna's seminars in a pub.

Ben Edna holds her seminars in a pub? I shall have to report this.

Joey The one you said was interesting.

Ben I don't find anything interesting about a student who complains of Edna's seminars. You did it yourself years ago, and you're as dull as they come.

Joey Did you encourage him?

Ben As far as I remember, which is frankly nothing, we had a perfectly respectable conversation about Edna's vagina, its length and width.

Joey Oh God!

Ben You mustn't be jealous, Joseph. The young are entitled to the importunities that you once enjoyed.

Joey (*gets up and walks towards Ben*) I can't afford to quarrel with Edna. Besides, I've got to like her.

Ben Because you've got to, doesn't mean I've got to.

Joey She thinks of us as allies. If you upset her, she'll blame me too.

Ben What the hell are you doing here anyway? You're not lecturing until later. You could have gone straight home and tidied up your room. It's in a disgusting state.

Joey The only room in the flat that isn't in a disgusting state is mine.

Ben Really? Then can you explain why it looks as if a large, dignified and intelligent man has been going to seed in it?

Joey (*after a pause*) Did you have to use my room?

Ben Do you think I could put up with the mess every-where else? You're out most evenings, it's easy for you to keep your room clean. I don't see why you shouldn't learn what it's like to stay at home and fret your way into a drunken coma.

Joey, after a moment, goes back to his desk and sits down.

Is *that* your tantrum? How piffling.

Joey Look, Ben, I've got this lecture. Can I do some work, please? As I can't go to the library – please?

Ben (*goes to him*) When will you phone Reg up, then?

Joey I told you. After lunch.

Ben Why are you lying about his being out? (*He points Joey's desk lamp directly into his face in interrogation.*)

Joey I don't make a habit of lying.

Ben Which is why you go on being so bad at it.

There is a shape at the door. Ben looks towards it, hurries to his feet, as there is a knock. He goes over to the door, opens it a fraction.

(*jovially*) Good morning, good morning, good morning.

Student (*off*) I just wanted to find out about my tutorials.

Ben Good. Good. Have you got an essay, please!

Student (*off*) Well no, I mean you haven't set one.

Ben Well, do me one for next week, all right?

Student (*off*) Well, what on?

Ben You must decide for yourself, can't expect spoon-feeding. Righto. (*He shuts the door, comes back rubbing his hands.*) I think that's the lot –

As a shape comes to the door, there is a knock. The door opens as Ben spins around.

Miss Heasman I found Mrs Grainger, she says she would have come to you on Tuesdays at two if you'd been able to see her.

Ben So be it. Tuesdays at two with our fingers crossed. (*He crosses them.*)

Miss Heasman Today is Tuesday.

Ben Ah well, I wouldn't have been able to see her again today, I'm afraid, as she would have needed a week in which to do me an essay.

Miss Heasman Poor Mrs Grainger. But I'm all right, as I've done one.

She takes one out of her file, and hands it to Ben, who takes it reluctantly.

I haven't put a title on, but I thought: 'Hate and Redemption in *A Winter's Tale*'.

Ben Needs work. (*He hands the essay back.*) That title.

Miss Heasman Don't you want to read it before the tutorial?

Ben No, you'll have to read it aloud to me. Unless, I tell you what, give it to me now and I'll do my damnedest to get it read before next week.

SIMON GRAY

Miss Heasman (*her eyes go to Ben's desk*) No, I'll read it aloud. Two o'clock, then. (*She turns and goes out.*)

Ben (*imitates her walk and slams the door*) Bugger! (*He comes back to his desk.*) 'Hate and Redemption' – I told you she was mad. She must be a secret agent, in Edna's employ . . . (*He picks up a handful of essays from the desk then drops them one by one on the floor.*) Hate and Redemption, Pity and Terror, Sin and Salvation. (*dropping more essays onto the floor*) Faith and Despair in *Pride and Prejudice*, *The Mill on the Floss*, Appley and Dappley, Cecily Parsley. (*liturgically, as he is dropping essays. He looks at his desk.*) Why don't those cleaning women do their job properly? Standards are declining everywhere. Ruskin's char threw Carlyle's *History of the French Revolution* out with the other rubbish. But then they took a pride in their work in those days. (*He picks up another essay, looks at it, laughs and sits down.*) I should think Reg would enjoy cooking my kidneys. It sounds worse than settling my hash. Anne's mother, the mad monk, settles the hash of bus-conductors, milkmen, postmen, anyone stupid enough to waste their time insulting her. 'Oh, I settled his hash all right.' She probably got the taste for it after she killed off her husband. I wonder if there was any reference in the coroner's report to the state of his hash. This hash, my life . . . this long disease my . . . (*He begins to read, then lets it slip from his fingers, leans back, picks reflectively at the cotton wool.*) Why the hell did we call her Marina?

I made this, I have forgotten
And remember.
The rigging weak and the canvas rotten
Between one June and another September.

Born in June, May . . . April . . . February . . . November . . . Conceived in September . . . So sometime in early

40

September there was what you might call a seminal
fuck . . . Where? In the park once we . . . let me think,
beneath the trees.

> Beneath the trees there is no ease.
> For the dull brain, the sharp desires
> And the quick eyes of Woolly Bear.

It must have been our last, we were already fallen into the
sere, the yellow leaf, a flash of thigh in the yellow leaf.

> What seas what shores what granite islands towards
>   my timbers
> And woodthrush calling through the fog
> My daughter.

Joey You do miss her then?

Ben (*goes over to Joey*) You know, what marks you out
as a repressed as well as a practising pervert is your
sentimentality over children. Marina doesn't need a
mother or father, she needs a pair of hands, to pick her
up, change her, put things to her mouth, put her down
again.

Joey But later on she might need a father.

Ben You generally have the taste to let *me* raise the
subject of my ruined marriage.

Joey I can't help wondering whether you miss it.

Ben Only the sex and violence. And these days one can
get those anywhere.

Joey So there's absolutely no chance . . .

Ben Chance of what?

Joey Of your marriage reviving. You don't want it to?

Ben Reviving? It's never died. I consider it inviolate. I'm
a one-woman man and I've had mine, thank God.

Joey But things can't just go on as they are.

Ben Can't they? Why not? (*He takes the telephone directory from his desk and begins to look up a number.*)

Joey But supposing she wants to marry again.

Ben Good God! Who would want to marry *her*?

Joey You did.

Ben That was before she'd been through the mill . . . (*He begins to run his finger down the column.*)

Joey (*standing* up) Listen, Ben, you could be making a mistake about Anne. If you really don't want to lose her –

Ben (*goes to the telephone on Joey's desk*) Your conversation is beginning to sound as if it's been stitched together from song titles of the fifties. (*He begins to sing.*) Making a mistake about Anne . . . If you really don't want to lose her . . .

Joey Look, Ben, I'm trying to tell you something.

Ben Haylife and Forlings . . .

Joey looks at Ben. Ben sings as he dials.

Three-four-eight – owe-seven-two-owe.

Joey What are you doing?

Ben (*sits down and speaks into the telephone*) Ah, hello – can I speak to Mr Nuttall, Reg Nuttall, please?

Joey (*hurrying over to the telephone*) He's not there.

Ben Thank you.

He waits, humming and smiling at Joey. Joey seizes the telephone, they wrestle over it, Ben hangs on to it.

(*into the phone, crouched away from Joey*) No, I'm waiting for Mr Nuttall, please.

Joey All right. All right. I'll do it.

Ben hands him the receiver. Joey puts the receiver down and holds on to telephone. There is a pause.

Ben Well?

Joey Do you intend to stay in the room while I find out if he'll have you to dinner?

Ben Certainly. But you needn't stay while I find out. (*He goes to pick up the telephone.*)

Joey (*shouts*) I said I'd do it!

Ben (*a long pause*) But what *are* you afraid of? He can only say no, in which case I'll only make your life a living hell.

Joey Perhaps I'm afraid he'll say yes.

Ben Well, you do worry for him, don't you, dear?

Joey Why do you think it's him I'm worried for?

Ben Oh, we all know how you worry for yourself. (*He reaches for the telephone.*)

Joey holds it tight, and looks at Ben. Ben laughs and reaches for it.

Joey (*runs away with it followed by Ben*) You're a fool, Ben. A bloody fool!

Ben stops. The telephone rings. Ben takes the telephone and puts the base down on his desk. Joey sits down at his desk.

Ben Butley, Nursery. (*Laughs.*) Oh hello, James, what? Ah, well, I was just pondering those lines –

His rhythm was present in the nursery bedroom,
In the rank ailanthus of the April dooryard –

(*Pause.*) No, no, I'm quite free. (*Little pause. He mouths a curse.*) Gardner? Gardner, Gardner, Gardner. No I don't recall a student called Gardner – What year is she? Ah! *He!*

He grimaces at Joey. A shape appears at the door.

Oh God, poor Edna.

There is a knock on the door. He claps his hand over the mouthpiece.

(*to Joey*) Block that student! (*into the receiver*) He says I *what*? No he must have misunderstood me. I don't recall telling a student . . .

Joey has gone to the door, opens it, then steps back. Anne comes in. Ben sees Anne, gapes at her and turns back to the telephone.

Look, I appear to have miscalculated, I've got a student after all, speak to you later, eh? 'Bye. (*He hangs up. There is a silence.*) How are you?

Anne Thank you. And you?

Ben Coping with Edna. Do you remember Edna? The one you called a human contraceptive? Do you remember?

Anne Actually, I called her a pill.

Ben Well, I updated you.

He laughs. Another silence.

Anne How are *you*, Joey?

Joey Oh. Um, very well thanks. Um, how's Miranda?

Anne Marina. She fills her belly and her nappy. She grows the odd tooth. She cries.

Ben How adult. Except for the odd tooth, one loses that. (*Pause.*) Actually, I've been thinking of finding a new dentist. I know you dote on Tonks, darling, but he's terribly camp. One sits in that chair with one's whole body at his mercy. (*to Joey*) Who do you go to?

Joey A man in Pimlico.

Anne Joey's teeth are always in marvellous condition.

Ben Are they? Let's see.

Joey What?

Ben Let's see your teeth.

Joey grimaces. Ben goes close, inspects them.

You're quite right. (*to Anne*) They sparkle. Although from time to time I've noticed – (*He hums 'Christ the Lord is risen today'.*)

Anne (*laughs, to Joey*) One of Ben's marriage jokes. I'm surprised you haven't heard it.

Joey Well, I haven't.

Anne How flattering for me.

Joey (*after a pause*) Well, I think it'd be better if I – I'd better get along. (*He picks up his briefcase.*)

Ben Why?

Anne Because he's embarrassed.

Ben Are you?

Joey I've got a lecture.

Ben He has. On Blake.

Anne Ah. Then he'd better go.

Joey goes out.

Ben He's very sensitive. You frighten him.

Anne Because he's creepy, and he knows I know it.

Ben Yes. I've told him. He took it surprisingly badly.

Anne (*pause*) You've settled down nicely together again, then, have you?

Ben We have our ups and downs.

Anne That's all right then. May I sit? (*She sits on the hard chair in front of Ben's desk.*)

Ben I went to see you over the weekend, as arranged, but you were out.

Anne Yes, I'm sorry.

Ben Grounds for a scene, though, don't you think?

Anne Oh, I should wait. (*Little pause.*) I had to see Tom's headmaster about a job.

Ben And did you get one?

Anne Yes.

Ben Good. (*He stares at her.*) But you look a trifle peaky around the gills – wherever they are. I can never locate them on Joey. Are you all right?

Anne I'm fine.

Ben Good. I saw Marina instead. I expect your mother the mad monk told you.

Anne She said it was very quick. Like a visit from the postman.

Ben I was there for twenty minutes. You'd better check on the postman. Ah! (*He sits at Joey's desk.*) Well, this is almost as delightful as it's unexpected, to what is it owed?

Anne I came to find out whether you wanted us back.

Ben (*after a pause*) Is that an offer?

Anne No. It's a question. I'd like the truth, please. Do you want us back?

Ben Frequently. (*Little pause.*) But not permanently. Do you want to come back?

Anne No.

Ben We've cleared that up, then. I think we're going to get on very well from this time forth, don't you?

Anne (*pause*) Joey hasn't told you, then?

Ben Told me what?

Anne He's known for weeks. His – what's his name – friend Reg must have told him.

Ben Reg?

Anne Tom told him. At least, he told me he had.

Ben Tom? Tom and Reg? What on earth have Tom and Reg got to do with us?

Anne He's asked me to marry him.

Ben (*after a pause*) Which one? (*Pause.*) You're not. (*Laughs.*) You can't be.

Anne Yes I am. Do you mind?

Ben Yes, yes, I mind very much. (*Pause, he pulls himself together.*) After all, a man's bound to be judged by his wife's husband. The most boring man in London – you said yourself he was the dullest man you'd ever spent an evening with.

Anne That was before I got to know him properly.

47

Ben And what do you call him now?

Anne The dullest man I've ever spent the night with. But I don't mind. Why should you?

Ben Because – because I shall miss old Tom, that's why. I'm too old to make mature new friendships with bores, far too impatient. (*He walks round to his own desk.*) They have to grow on you steadily, hours by hours through years on years, until they're actually doing their bit towards holding you together. Like ivy around crumbling walls. (*Little pause.*) Is that why you want him?

Anne Are you going to make difficulties?

Ben What?

Anne About the divorce?

Ben Divorce?

Anne You see, I'm not allowed to marry him until I'm divorced from you. It's the law of the land. Are you going to make difficulties?

Ben This is humiliating.

Anne But deserved. By both of us.

Ben (*laughs*) I'll bloody make difficulties all right. After all, this is liable to be the only phase of our marriage that I shall enjoy. At least since the moment in the registry office when the clerk who handled our contract was under the impression that he was supposed to bind me for a year or two to the mad monk your mother. (*He gets up and faces her across his desk.*) I'll have to have my fun somewhere, won't I? Because, after all, one moment of pleasure isn't much out of a whole year, is it?

Anne It's a moment more than I had.

Ben And how many moments do you expect from your next?

Anne I shan't count them. I'm not in it for fun, you see. I never was. And nor were you.

Ben Oh. What *was* I in it for?

Anne Perhaps you wanted a break.

Ben Well, I'm certainly getting one, aren't I?

Anne Or perhaps you were frightened. But it doesn't matter any more because you're not any more. And I suppose you needn't ever try again, now that you've found out whatever it is you were determined to learn. (*Pause.*) I don't care. Not at all.

Ben Then you're halfway there. And Tom will certainly teach you to sit still. (*He walks round behind her and comes to face her.*) If you must get married again, surely we can do better for you than that. After six weeks you'll be the two most boring men in London. There are signs already. You're developing a new tone – a combination of the didactic and the enigmatically stoic – that's more than halfway towards Tom's prose style. By the way, does he know that you greet spring and its signs of life with wheezing and sneezes from your hay fever? Tom endorses spring. He admires it for its moral exuberance. (*Pause.*) Do you still make little popping sounds when you drink your coffee? No, it's your nose – your nose I've always taken exception to, or is it your mouth? You can't marry Tom.

Anne I can.

Ben All right, you probably can. You can probably do a lot of hideous things. You're tough, versatile and brutal. What I mean is, don't.

Anne Why not?

A shape appears at the door.

Well?

A pause.

Edna (*knocks, steps in*) Can I have a word? (*She is obviously distraught.*)

Ben By all means. (*He gestures to Anne.*)

Edna Oh, I'm sorry, I didn't realise – I'll look back later, if I may. (*She goes out.*)

Anne He's asked me to live with him until we get married. Are you going to make trouble?

Ben Tell me, when did we last have it off? Was it that time in the park, beneath the trees, or did we have a quick go subsequently, in bed or under the kitchen table, Joey and I were trying to work it out –

Anne rises. He jumps away, as if expecting a blow, shields his face, then laughs, shakily.

You're going to live with him *until* you get married, did you say? At least that's a realistic prospectus. (*He calls out, as Anne leaves.*) 'Bye, darling. 'Bye-bye, sweet princess, goodbye . . . (*He closes the door behind her and stands pulling at the cotton wool on his chin. He pulls it off.*) Ahh, Butley is himself again. (*Hums 'Christ the Lord', then sings.*) Christ your breath is bad today haa-aa-al-it-osis. Haa-aa – (*He breaks off, trembling. He sits down at his desk, puts his hand to his face, takes it away, looks at it, touches his chin, inspects his fingers.*) Bloody woman! Bloody woman! (*He feels in his pocket and takes out more cotton wool.*)

Curtain.

Act Two

The office as before. It is shortly after lunch. When the curtain rises Miss Heasman is sitting on the hard chair by Ben's desk, reading from her essay. Ben is apparently asleep in the armchair, a cigarette in his hand.

Miss Heasman (*a pause – she looks at Ben*) 'Hermione's reawakening – the statue restored to life after a winter of sixteen years' duration – is in reality Leontes's reawakening, spiritually, and of course the most moving exemplification of both the revitalisation theme and thus of forgiveness on the theological as well as the human level.'

Ben Level?

Miss Heasman Yes.

Ben The human *level*?

Miss Heasman Yes. Um, shall I go on?

Ben Mmm.

Miss Heasman 'The central image is drawn from nature, to counterpoint the imagery of the first half of the play, with its stress on sickness and deformity. Paradoxically, *A Winter's Tale* of a frozen soul –'

Ben Bit fishmongery, that.

Miss Heasman (*laughs mirthlessly*) '– is therefore thematically and symbolically about revitalisation.'

Ben Sorry. Re-whatalisation?

Miss Heasman Re-*vi*talisation.

Ben (*gets up and goes to Miss Heasman*) Thematically and symbolically so, eh?

Miss Heasman Yes. (*She looks towards him challengingly.*) 'The central image is drawn from' – no, we've had that – um. 'In this context –'

Ben Can you see?

Miss Heasman What?

Ben (*aims his desk light at Miss Heasman's essay, forgets to turn it on, goes to a hard chair in the corner of the room and sits down out of view*) There.

> *Miss Heasman, after a moment, leans over, turns on the light.*

Sorry. No irony intended. (*Pause.*) 'Context.'

Miss Heasman Um, yes. 'In this context it might be said that Leontes represents the affliction that is a universal, and so contingently human evil, and in this sense, the sense of a shared blight . . .'

Ben (*lets out a noise like a laugh, pretends to be coughing*) Sorry. Yes, a shared blight – yes, look, how much longer is it exactly?

> *Miss Heasman fumbles through the pages – Ben goes over to his desk.*

I'll tell you what, as our time together's drawing to a close, read the last two or three sentences, so we can get the feel of your conclusion.

> *Miss Heasman looks pointedly at her watch, riffles through her pages. Ben picks at the cotton wool on his chin, drums his fingers, checks these movements, smiles attentively when Miss Heasman looks at him.*

Miss Heasman Ready?

Ben Please, please.

Miss Heasman 'So just as the seasonal winter was the winter of the soul, so is the seasonal spring the spring of the soul. The imagery changes from disease to floral, the tone from mad bitterness to joyfulness. As we reach the play's climax we feel our own – spiritual – sap rising.'

Ben (*after a long pause*) Sap?

Miss Heasman Sap.

Ben Sap. Sap. Yes, I think sap's a better word than some others that spring rhymingly to mind. Good. Well, thank you very much. (*Pause.*) He had a ghastly time of it, didn't he?

Miss Heasman Who?

Ben Leontes. I mean, Shakespeare doesn't leave him alone for a minute – as you point out. He gets hold of the poor old bugger and gives it to him thematically and symbolically, he afflicts him with imagery – floral and diseasal, didn't you say?

Miss Heasman Floral was Perdita.

Ben She's an affliction, too, though, isn't she? And all those levels – as you note – so exhausting for him.

Miss Heasman I'm sorry, I don't understand.

Ben No, I'm just agreeing with you.

Miss Heasman Um, with what exactly?

Ben That he doesn't give Leontes much chance. First he sends him mad with jealousy, then he teaches him a moral lesson. And talk about free speech – (*Laughs.*) Every observation illuminating a theme or developing a symbol – we see eye to eye on all that.

Miss Heasman Actually I found it very moving.

Ben (*after a pause*) You *liked* it?

Miss Heasman Very much. Very, very much.

Ben I'm so sorry. A slight misunderstanding. (*Pause.*) What do you want to do – I mean, after your exams?

Miss Heasman Teach.

Ben English?

Miss Heasman Yes.

Ben Well, I suppose that's more radical than being a teacher of exams, for which I think you're already qualified, by the way. I hope you'll take that as a compliment.

Miss Heasman It isn't meant to be one, is it? But whatever you think of my essay, if I don't do well in the exams, I might not be able to be a teacher.

Ben Teacher of whom?

Miss Heasman Sixth forms, I hope.

Ben Isn't it more exhilarating to get them earlier? Sixth-form teachers are something like firemen called in to quench flames that are already out. Although you can never tell – recently I've enjoyed reading almost as much as I did when I was twelve. I do hope I didn't slip through their net – it makes one lose confidence. But I'm sure you'll be all right. Perhaps books are just my *madeleines*, eh?

> Gravy and potatoes
> In a big brown pot
> Put them in the oven
> And cook them very hot.

54

Miss Heasman I'm sorry?

Ben And so am I. I'm not really myself this afternoon, what do you want to do next week?

Miss Heasman We have to cover at least six Shakespeares.

Ben From what I've heard already, Shakespeare's as good as covered. (*He opens the door.*)

Miss Heasman (*holds out her essay*) Could you please write some comments on this?

Ben It's a good time to be merciless. (*taking the essay*) It comes in useful when dealing with the young.

Miss Heasman Believe it or not, you can be as rude as you like. I don't take it personally.

Ben That's another good way of taking the fun out of teaching. Good afternoon, Miss Heasman.

Miss Heasman Thank you.

> *She goes out. Ben stands at the open door, gestures obscenely after her. Then, aware that he is holding her essay, pinches his nostrils, holds the essay at a distance, makes gagging sounds, pantomimes gas-poisoning as he goes back to his desk. Miss Heasman has come back to the door, stands watching him. Ben drops the essay onto his desk, stiffens, turns slowly. He and Miss Heasman stare at each other. Miss Heasman turns and goes quickly from the room.*

Ben (*makes as if to hurry after her, stops*) Oh Christ! Bloody girl! (*He stands for a moment, then takes out an address book, looks up a name, goes over to his desk and dials the number.*) Hello, Kent Vale Comprehensive? Headmaster, please. (*Little pause.*) Ben Butley. (*Aside.*) Friend to Education. (*into the telephone*) Thank you. (*He puts the telephone on the desk, runs over to a* *carrier bag, extracts a quarter of Scotch, runs back, clamps it under his chin, unscrews the cap as he talks in a Scottish accent.*) Ahh, hello, Headmaster, sorry to trouble you on a trifling matter, but I've been trying to make contact with one of your staff, Tom Weatherley, and it's proving to be a tricky business. (*Pause.*) Ben Butley, Friend to Tom Weatherley, a member of your staff. Do you ken him? (*Little pause.*) Oh, naturally I don't want to disturb him if he's teaching, but I've got a rather delicate message for him – I'd rather entrust it to someone of authority like yourself, if I may? (*Listens.*) Thank you. It's just that could he and I have a little chin-wag – (*Little pause.*) – chin-wag some time about the proceedings – solicitors, alimony, maintenance, custody, visiting rights – always so sad when there are wee bairns to consider – we always say – property, so on, so forth. (*Pause.*) Oh, I'm Tom's fiancée's husband. I've only just heard the news. By the way, HM, quite a coincidence, my wife that was, Tom's wife to be, Anne Butley that is, might be coming to teach in your school, I believe – do keep an eye out for her, I'd be most obliged. (*He takes the telephone away from his chin, feels his chin, makes a face.*) Oh, and there is one other thing, could you tell Tom that he'll have to foot the bill for any ops this time unless he can get it on the National Health, I've got enough blood on my hands – (*Looks at his fingers.*) – at the moment, and it's all my own, ha ha ha, if you see what I mean. (*Little pause.*) Oh you don't, well never mind, HM, I don't really think we educationalists should be expected to see anything but the clouds into which we thrust our heads, eh?

There is a shape at the door. Ben looks towards it.

Love to Tom and Anne when you see them, eh? Goodbye. (*He puts down the telephone, stares towards the door, then takes a swig of Scotch, goes to the door, peers through the frosted glass. He drops the Scotch into his pocket and knocks gently against the glass.*)

Tap tappit, tap tappit, he's heard it before.
But when he peeps out there is nobody there

Opens the door.

But packets and whimsey put down on the stair.

(*He walks over to his desk.*) Or is something frightening him again? Is that why he's peeping through the frosted glass with his whiskers twitching and his paws to his nose, eh?

Joey, after a pause, enters – goes to his desk, puts down his briefcase and turns on the desk lamp.

If it's Anne you were hiding from, she's gone. If it's Edna, she hasn't arrived.

Joey I heard voices. I thought perhaps you and Anne were still –

Ben What? Thrashing it out? Having it off? What would Anne and I still be doing, together in a small room, after two hours? She was always succinct, even with her knickers down.

Joey I saw Edna in the common room. She was just leaving when I went in.

Ben And how did she seem? Jovial?

Joey No, very upset.

Ben Ah.

Joey Was that Miss Heasman I passed in the corridor?

Ben How did she look? Jovial?

Joey She had her face averted. As if she were in tears.

57

Ben Then that was certainly Miss Heasman, yes. Everything seems to be running smoothly, doesn't it? (*He stares at Joey.*) Tell me, what did you make of old Anne turning up in that enterprising fashion?

Joey I don't know.

Ben You don't?

Joey looks at him.

She was under the impression that you've known for some time.

Joey (*a pause*) I did try to warn you.

Ben Yes, and thank you. But tell me, how come that you've known for some time?

Joey Well, actually I got it from Reg.

Ben From Reg? Yes? (*Pause.*) You know I think we're building up a case here for a conspiracy theory of personal relationships. Go on.

Joey (*sits*) Tom's meeting Reg had nothing to do with me. It was something professional, I don't know what, but they got on very well and Tom told Reg and Reg told me, and then Tom phoned Reg and told Reg not to tell me or if he *had* told me to ask me not to tell you until he or Anne had told you.

Ben Yes, I recognise Tom's delicate touch there in your sentence structure. It must have been amusing to hear me chatter mindlessly on about my marriage, eh?

Joey I tried to warn you.

Ben But was it amusing? Was it fun? (*Pause.*) Are you going to answer me?

Joey Sorry. I took the question to be rhetorical.

Ben (*going over to him*) All right. Let me ask you, then, *why* you promised not to mention to your best friend – is that presuming? – that his wife was being screwed by, while contemplating marriage to, the most boring man in London? Is that question sufficiently unrhetorical?

Joey Because I didn't think it was my business.

Ben Not your business? And how many personalities and dramas over which we've gossiped and whinnied in the past years have been our business? There have been some pretty sticky silences between us recently, and here you were, my dear, in possession of a piece of information that was guaranteed to raise at the very least an amused eyebrow.

Joey All right, because I'm a coward, that's why. I'm sorry. (*Pause.*) I *am* sorry, in point of fact.

Ben Matters of fact and points of fact have been cluttering your syntax since you started going steady with that butcher's boy.

Joey I'm sorry because I hoped it wouldn't happen. Now it's a fact and I wish it weren't.

Ben laughs, tugs at the cotton wool on his chin and pulls it off. His hand is trembling.

I'm – I'm sure you could get her back.

Ben How far back?

Joey To live with you. She and Marina.

Ben That's too far back. Far too far back.

Joey Then what will you do?

Ben Grab my quota of fun, that's all. (*He returns to the telephone.*) I'm working to a very tight schedule. I've given myself a mere week to get the most boring – and

tenacious – man in London out of his job and home.
I'm moving on to his landlady now.

Joey Fun?

Ben Or trouble. I can't remember which I've promised
myself.

Joey But what's the point of making trouble?

Ben Fun. (*He dials again.*) Because hounding them from
job and home is no trouble. Local councils, the police,
whole governments do it. Why shouldn't a private citizen
be allowed to join in?

*He waits, then slams down the phone. Joey goes to
the door.*

Where are you going? (*He dials another number.*)

Joey The library's open now. I thought I'd go up –

Ben And hide again? Who from this time?

Joey shrugs.

From Edna. Yes, it must be Edna.

Joey Well, I'm not going to be here when she comes to
have it out with you.

Ben laughs.

I can't help it. *I'm* not going to antagonise her.

Ben OK, I'll do it for you. You run along.

Joey looks at him, hesitates, then makes for the door.

(*into the telephone*) Ah, Haylife and Forling, I must say
you do drag out your lunch, some of which, by the way,
appears still to be in your mouth, from the sound of you.

As Joey hurries to him from the door:

This is Joseph Keyston, friend to Reg Nuttall, if you take my meaning – may I speak to him, please?

> *He hands the telephone to Joey. Joey takes the telephone and puts it down. There is a pause.*

You see how life repeats itself, with diminishing climaxes. (*Little pause.*) Well? Is he still out, have you some more moralising to do, or are you simply welching on a promise?

Joey All right. If you want, I'll cancel Reg. We can go to Bianchi's. Just the two of us.

Ben (*in an American accent*) Cancel Reg? Cancel him? (*Laughs.*) This is a human bean you're talking about here, kid, not a cheque, or an order of groceries, but a human *bean*! And frankly, dear, he's more of an attraction than your shy self, at the moment. All our games together are going a trifle stale, Reg and I may be able to find some new ones.

Joey Reg won't be very playful.

Ben Don't worry. I shall get my fun. Besides, in this bag here, kidneys! Yes, kid, kidneys! (*He waves the carrier bag at Joey.*)

Joey (*after a pause*) I'm sorry, Ben. Not tonight.

Ben Mmm, huh. So *you're* not inviting me.

Joey I'm not going. We can either eat at the flat or at Bianchi's. It's up to you.

Ben Well, if you're really not coming then there'll be all the more kidneys for Reginald and myself. What do you think he'll say to that, for an offer? (*A pause.*) Don't you care then?

Joey No. Not any more.

Ben You're not breaking off with him, you competitive child you? Is that what you're trying to tell me?

Joey No. I'm trying to tell you that it'll be much better if you leave that side of my life alone. (*his voice shaking*) I can't stop you from phoning him up, you can do it any time, Ben, I'm just advising you, because I don't think you'll get much fun from him, I really don't. I know you've had a bad day already, with Tom and Anne, but you're making it worse.

Ben (*makes as if to dial, hesitates, dials*) You're passing up a chance for a Lawrentian-type wrestle. Can't I interest you?

Joey Just remember that I warned you. (*He sits quite still at his desk.*)

Ben Two warnings in one day.

   Joey watches tensely.

Haylife and Forlings? This is Ben Butley, friend to Joseph Keyston, friend to Reg Nuttall, with whom I'd like to speak, please. (*Little pause.*) Thank you. (*He looks at Joey, grinning, is suddenly stopped by his expression.*) What is it? (*Little pause.*) Joey? (*He starts to put the telephone down, checks himself.*) Hello, is that Reg – (*Little pause.*) Ah, his secretary. (*He hesitates, then makes up his mind.*) May I speak to him, please?

   Pause, Ben watches Joey, then offers Joey the telephone. He shakes his head. Ben listens again.

I see. Thank you very much. (*He puts the telephone down, looks at Joey.*) He's out. (*Smiles.*) Is that a relief?

Joey In a sense.

Ben You'd better tell me about it.

Joey What?

Ben Whatever it is you're warning me about.

Joey No. It's nothing.

Ben Come on, Joey.

Joey It doesn't matter. Let it go.

There's a knock on the door. Ben drops the Scotch bottle into his pocket. Edna puts her head in.

Edna Are you free now, please?

She comes in. Ben sits down. Very calmly, smiling.

Now, would you kindly tell me what transpired between yourself and this Gardner?

Joey (*earnestly*) I don't know anything about it, Edna.

Edna (*still calm*) My teaching, it appears, isn't up to his standard.

Ben Indeed. Well, I can assure you, Edna, that it's more than up to mine. I know our society has become insolently egalitarian, but I refuse to believe that the gardener's verdict on your teaching will be given too much weight. I didn't know we had a garden – let alone –

Edna This is the first time in twenty years' teaching that I've been complained about.

Joey It's preposterous. You're a very good teacher, Edna.

Ben All right. Well, let's get this sorted out. To whom did he complain?

Edna To James.

Ben And what did James say?

Edna He said you'd promised Gardner he could have tutorials with you. This conversation apparently took place in a pub.

63

Ben What? I've had no – well, there was a student,
now I come to think of it, but, my God, I'd completely
forgotten – I suppose it might have been Gardner,
I scarcely took him in. He wasn't wearing feathers in his
cap. (*Little pause.*) Previously you talked of a plumed
youth, wasn't it? (*Laughs.*)

Edna And you said nothing to him about coming to you
for Eliot?

Ben I have an idea he told me he'd become keen on
Eliot. That's all.

Edna Keen on Eliot.

Ben Something of the sort. I suppose I assumed he was
after a few tutorials – but really I haven't given him a
thought.

Edna And did you discuss whether these tutorials are to
replace his seminars with me?

Ben Certainly not.

Edna And did you tell him to go to James and explain
the circumstances – that he wasn't getting anything out
of my seminars.

Ben Is that what James said?

Edna He tried so hard not to tell me what Gardner had
said that it was perfectly obvious. He had his diplomatic
smile on – the one that makes him look exactly like a
rabbit. But I suppose I should be grateful that he didn't
encourage that lout to throw my furniture out of the
window, or burn my notes. I work very hard for those
seminars.

Joey We know you do, Edna.

Edna I don't expect gratitude, far from it. But I do expect
a minimum of civilised behaviour. And I expect to be

backed up by the Head of the Department and the other members of the staff when I'm unlucky enough to have a bolshy troublemaker in my group.

Joey But of course we'll back you up.

Edna What happened at the Senate House – it's beginning here. The Aristotle is just the beginning. (*She sits down, fumbles in her handbag, closes it.*) But why did they pick on me?

Ben I don't think anybody would want to pick on you, Edna.

Edna Because I'm a woman, that's why. It's always easier to get at a woman. They think we're more vulnerable. Well, in my case, they've got another think coming. I haven't finished with Gardner and like ilk. Not by a long shot. (*Pause.*) How dare he! How dare he complain!

Ben (*stands up*) Look, perhaps the best thing *is* to let me take him on.

Edna There's not the slightest question of that, Ben. Not the slightest. He stays in my seminars. That's all there is to it.

Ben Of course. If that's the way you want it. The only trouble is, you may not see much of him.

Edna In that case, it will be my pleasure to get him suspended. I've already started a Dean's Report.

Ben As you wish. It's certainly your privilege. I just don't see what'll be gained.

Edna The satisfaction of causing him trouble.

Ben Yes, I can see that might be fun.

Edna I don't care. (*She opens her handbag, takes out a handkerchief.*) So you two *are* on his side then?

Ben looks at Joey – they both go over to her.

Joey Certainly not. I think Edna's got every right –

Ben puts his hand on her shoulder.

Edna Leave me alone. (*She pulls her arm away.*)

Ben Edna. (*gently*) I'm sorry, Edna. It's my fault for not taking young Gardner seriously.

Edna Nobody takes anything seriously any more. But universities were serious once, yes they were. But now they despise them, yes they do, just as they despise me. Just as you two despise me.

Joey Despise you!

Ben I just didn't want you to be hurt – or worry too much.

Edna That's precisely what I mean.

The telephone rings.

Ben Sorry – (*He answers the telephone.*) Butley, English. Oh, um, hello, actually no, this isn't too good a time. I'm in the middle of something –

Edna (*stands up*) If that's James, please tell him that I'm going home. As education has become optional in this college, I've chosen to cancel my classes for the rest of the day. (*She goes out.*)

Ben Sorry, James. Could we talk later? (*He puts the telephone down, sits on the edge of the desk, has a swig of Scotch, stares at Joey.*) Bloody woman!

Joey So you did agree to take Gardner in, then.

Ben One of us took the other in, all right. I shall find out later which way around it is.

Joey You'll enjoy that, I'm sure.

Ben I deserve it, after all this.

Joey And what about Edna?

Ben Bloody woman, that's all about Edna. She's lucky to be rid of him. It's not my fault she's too vain to admit it.

Joey And all you had to do just now was to keep quiet, and then tell Gardner it couldn't be managed.

Ben But I *am* managing it.

Joey Oh Christ! But what for? What the hell for?

Ben Perhaps I had a sense of vacancies opening up in my life. I needed to fill them, perhaps.

Joey Then why don't you do it from your legitimate students, instead of fobbing them off and refusing to teach them?

Ben (*sitting in armchair*) I haven't got any legitimate students. They're all bastards. Which is my term of endearment for bores. Gardner's interesting. He actually interests me. At least, I think he does, I can't remember him clearly and I'll have to see the hat. You interested me once, dear, and look where it's got you. An assistant lectureship. Of course I don't know if my interest can carry you through your board –

Joey You mean he'll have a relationship with you, don't you? While all poor Edna can offer him is a relationship with Byron, in a properly conducted seminar.

Ben (*hums 'Christ the Lord has risen today'*) Well, Joseph, what chance your lectureship now? Edna says you despise her. And she's quite right. Toadying is the sincerest form of contempt.

Pause. They stare at each other.

I remember when you stood in this room, darkly dressed to colour up your melancholy, and I had you read a little Eliot to me. Do you remember? (*Little pause.*) Little did we know that a long time away, far into the future, we would be worrying and fretting together about your promotion. Our beginnings never know our ends. They're always so sad, so sad.

Joey turns to go.

Don't flounce, Dappley. It doesn't suit your mousey hindquarters.

Joey It's not my fault you buggered everything up with Anne. You don't have to bugger everything up for me, too.

Ben No, I don't. I'm doing it as a favour and for fun.

Joey I'm sick to death of your fun! (*He goes to the door.*)

Ben Bum-twitch, bum-twitch, bum-twitch, bum-twitch!

He laughs and Joey slams the door. He runs after him and shouts down the corridor:

Teacher's pet!

He comes back – has a swig of Scotch, takes the telephone over to Joey's desk, starts to dial, changes his mind, takes another drink. Little pause.

Appley Dappley, little brown mouse
Goes to the cupboard in somebody's house
In somebody's cupboard there's everything nice
Pot, scotch, french letters
For middle-aged mice.

The telephone rings. Ben answers it.

Woolly Bear, English. (*Pause.*) What? (*Little pause.*) Who would like to see Mr Keyston? (*Little pause.*) Indeed? Yes, yes he's here, just a minute. (*He puts his hand over*

the receiver, then speaks into it.) Mr Keyston says kindly
send him along to the office. Thank you.

*He puts the telephone down, puts the Scotch into a
drawer, goes to the desk, sits down, takes out a pen.
Feels the cotton wool on his chin. There is a knock.
He pores over an essay as there is another knock.*

Come.

*The door opens. Reg enters. Ben goes on working at
his essay.*

Minute, please. (*Then looks up.*)

Reg Is Joey here?

Ben Good God, it's Reg, isn't it? Of course it is.

*He gets up, goes over, holds out his hand. As they
shake hands:*

I'm terribly sorry, do come in.

Reg Your porter said he was here.

Ben And so he will be. He just went off to have a brief
word with a colleague in distress. How are you?

Reg Very well, thanks. And you?

Ben (*gestures towards his desk*) As you see. (*Laughs.*)

Reg Yes. (*He glances at the desk, appalled.*) Look,
you're obviously very busy. If you just tell Joey I'm at the
porter's desk –

Ben Don't be silly. You sit yourself down over there –
(*He offers him a chair.*) – and I'll just finish this off,
I won't be a minute.

*Reg hesitates, glances at Joey's desk and bookshelves
and lights a cigarette. Ben pretends to go on marking,
makes a few exclamations under his breath.*

(*Not looking up*.) What brings you down here, anyway?

Reg I just thought I'd look in.

Ben (*writes furiously*) Have to make my script illegible so that they don't find out about my spelling. There. (*He pushes the essay away*.) To check up, eh?

Reg Check up?

Ben Joey's always saying that if you got your hands on our little room, which is an everywhere, or rather on me, eh? As I'm responsible for the mess we're in – (*Laughs*.) But you should see our flat. Even Joey's room is like a pigsty – naturally, I'm the pig that made it that way. You really must come around and help us out. He says you've done wonders with your little kitchen.

Reg I'm in publishing.

Ben (*puzzled*) Yes?

Reg Not in interior decorating. (*He sits on the hard chair by Joey's desk*.)

Ben Oh God yes. (*Laughs*.) I'm sorry about that. No, I don't get your job wrong any more. It would be inexcusable. I'm always making Joey tell me about it, in fact.

Reg I know. He's always telling me about having to tell you about it.

Ben He says you're a marvellous cook.

Reg I'm glad he eats well.

Ben And keeps his figure, lucky sod. (*Little pause. Gets up and sits on hard chair opposite Reg*.) You know, Reg, I'm very glad to have the chance to speak to you privately – I behaved abominably the last time we met.

I do hope – well, you've forgiven me for your shoes.
I never apologised properly.

Reg It's all right. These things happen.

Ben But your shoes survived, did they?

Reg They were suede.

Ben Oh dear. Suede. (*Pause.*)

Reg Look, you must want to get on. I'll go back to the
porter – (*He gets up.*)

Ben No, you mustn't do that. (*He gets up.*)

Reg I don't mind. In point of fact we were doing a little
business together. He's an Arsenal supporter.

Ben Good God. Is he really? In point of fact?

There is a pause.

Reg So I can let you get on with –

Ben Have a drink? (*He goes to his desk, opens the
drawer.*)

Reg I don't think I ought to.

Ben (*coming back with the Scotch and two soiled
glasses.*) You are lucky. Then you'll really enjoy it.

*He pushes one of the glasses into Reg's hand. Reg
peers down into the glass, winces at its condition. Ben
dashes Scotch into it, then into his own.*

I understand you've met my friend Tom. Tom Weatherley,
by the way.

Reg I know Tom, yes.

Ben You know all my domestic news, too, I gather. I only
heard it myself today.

Reg Yes, I heard something about it. I'm sorry.

Ben Do you detest warm Scotch? I don't know how you drink it in your part of the world?

Reg This is fine.

Ben Good. Cheers.

Reg Cheers.

Ben Thanks.

He drinks. Reg goes to Joey's bookshelves.

It's nice to have some company. These last few hours I've felt quite like Antony at his close – the air is full of the gods' departing musics. So do forgive any tendency to babble, eh?

Reg No, that's all right. I understand.

Ben Cheers. (*He sits on the hard chair by his desk.*) Actually what this whole business has brought home to me is how dependent I am on my past.

Reg (*turning to him*) But it was – excuse me – but it was quite a short marriage, wasn't it?

Ben No, I was talking about Joey.

Reg Oh.

Ben It's as if my marriage were an intermission, if you see. Now I'm catching up with my past again, which is where I suppose my future is also.

Reg Really?

Ben Sorry. I'm being literary. But I always think of *you* as a born romantic. From Joey's descriptions of *your* past. A touch of the butterfly, eh?

Reg Really? And what does Joey say to make you think that?

72

Ben Oh, I don't know – the way you've pulled up your roots in the North, what I imagine to be your emotional pattern, your love of the bizarre.

Reg (*pause*) And how does that express itself?

Ben Joe's always recounting your experiences – for example with the Gurkhas. You were with them, weren't you?

Reg I was stationed with them, yes. About ten years ago, during my National Service.

Ben Exactly. And I scarcely knew what a Gurkha was – I still tend to think he's something you get with a cocktail.

Reg Do you?

Ben They must be tough little towsers.

Reg They are. (*He sits at Joey's desk.*) You didn't do your National Service I take it.

Ben Oh Christ! Sorry, I mean no.

Reg How come?

Ben I got took queer.

There is a pause. Reg puts his glass down.

Oh! You're ready for another one.

Reg No, I – in point of fact, I'd rather not.

Ben This is an altogether different suburb. (*He refills Reg's glass.*)

Reg Sorry? What suburb?

Ben Oh, it's a little joke of Joey's. Almost impossible to explain out of context. (*He pours himself a drink and leans on the front of his desk.*) But how is the world of fiction?

Reg Can't complain.

Ben Cheers. What have you got coming out at the moment?

Reg At the moment I'm doing two cookery books, an authoritative guide to bird-watching in Lincolnshire, the only intelligent account of the farce of El Alamein – by an NCO, needless to say – and a New Testament commentary.

Ben That's your fiction list?

Reg No, that's our list for next month.

Ben No novels at all then?

Reg Well, just one of those historical romances where the hero shoves his sword into assorted villains and his cock into assorted ladies. It won't get the reviews but it'll make us money.

Ben If he did it the other way around you might get both.

Reg (*laughs briefly*) But the point is, you see, by putting that one through we can afford to do something worthwhile later. For instance, I've just made a decision about a novel on National Service life.

Ben Oh, one of those. I thought that vogue was eight years dead.

Reg No, not one of those. This is something special, in my opinion. Of course, it mightn't interest you as you didn't do National Service, but personally I found it moving, witty, gracefully organised – genuinely poetic.

Ben The National Service? Good God! Those qualities are hard enough to come by in art. It's never occurred to me to look for them in life, especially as run by the armed forces. Cheers.

Reg Nevertheless I expect you *will* be curious in this case. Theoretically I can't tell you our author's name as the board doesn't meet until tomorrow, but if I just mention that he's a comprehensive school teacher – (*He raises his glass slowly.*) Cheers.

Ben (*after a pause*) Well, well. (*He sits in the armchair.*) The most boring man in London strikes again.

Reg I'm sorry.

Ben Why?

Reg It must be painful for you.

Ben Why?

Reg Because of his relationship with you. It was wrong of me to have mentioned it.

Ben On the contrary. It was the correct move. Has Joey read it?

Reg Not yet. It was offered to me in strict secrecy – at least until I'd made up my mind. But I can tell him about it now. I think he'll like it.

Ben That's because you don't know him very well, perhaps. He may be something of a dilettante in personal relationships, but he holds fast to standards on important matters. We once drew up a list of the five most tedious literary subjects in the world. National Service came fifth, just behind the Latin poems of Milton.

Reg Really? And what occupied the other three places?

Ben The English poems of Milton.

Reg When I was at Hull I chose Milton for my special subject.

Ben That sounds an excellent arrangement. The thing is to confine him to the North. Down here we can dally with Suckling and Lovelace.

Reg And Beatrix Potter? Joey says you've got great admiration for the middle-class nursery poets.

Ben With reservations. I find some of the *novellae* a trifle heavy going. (*A pause.*) I call Joey Appley Dappley, did you know?

Reg Do you?

Ben And he calls me Old Mr Prickle-pin. After

Old Mr Prickle-pin, with never a coat to
Put his pins in.

Sometimes I call him Diggory Diggory Delvet, when he's burrowing away at his book.

There is a pause.

Reg What did you mean by being took queer?

Ben (*coyly*) Oh, you know, I'm sure. (*laughing*) You do look shocked, Reg.

Reg That's surprising, because I'm not surprised even.

Ben You don't think there's anything shameful in it, then?

Reg In what?

Ben Dodging the draft.

Reg There are thousands of blokes from working-class homes who couldn't. They didn't know the tricks. Besides they'd rather have done ten years in uniform than get out of it that way.

Ben Then you think there's something shameful in being taken queer?

Reg I'm talking about people pretending to be what they're not.

Ben Not what?

Reg Not what they are.

Ben But if people do get taken queer, it's nature we must blame or their bodies, mustn't we? Medicine's still got a long way to go, Reg.

Reg Why do you use that word?

Ben What word?

Reg 'Queer.'

Ben Does it offend you?

Reg It's beginning to.

Ben Sorry. It's an old nursery habit. One of our chars used to say it. Whenever I came down with anything it would be, 'Our Ben's took queer again, poor little mite.' (*There is a silence.*) Although I can see it's a trifle inappropriate for a touch of TB –

Reg TB?

Ben They found it just in time. At my board medical, in fact. Why *do* you object to the phrase, though?

Reg No, no, it doesn't matter. A misunderstanding. I'm sorry.

Ben Oh, I *see. Queer!* – of course. Good God, you didn't think I'd sink quite so low, did you? (*Laughs.*)

Reg I'm sorry.

Ben It's all right. (*There is a pause.*) Cheers. (*He raises his glass.*)

Reg Cheers.

Another pause.

Ben Homosexual.

Another pause.

Reg What?

Ben Homosexual. I was just wondering – should one say that instead of 'queer' – in your sense of the word. Homosexual.

Reg It doesn't really matter at all. I don't really care –

Ben Do you feel the same about 'fairies' as you do about 'queers'?

Reg Yes, in point of fact. Since you ask.

Ben Right, I've got that. (*He gets up and moves towards Reg.*) Of course they've almost vanished anyway, the old-style queens and queers, the poofs, the fairies. The very words seem to conjure up a magical world of naughty thrills, forbidden fruits – sorry – you know, I always used to enjoy them enjoying themselves. Their varied performances contributed to my life's varieties. But now the law, in making them safe, has made them drab. Just like the heterosexual rest of us. Poor sods. (*Little pause.*) Don't you think?

Reg (*stands up and puts his glass on the desk*) Oh, there's enough affectation and bitchiness in heterosexuals to be getting on with. (*He glances at his watch.*) Don't you think?

Ben Oh, don't worry. He'll be here in a minute. (*Pause.*) How are things between you two, by the way?

Reg What things?

Ben No complications?

78

Reg What kind of complications would there be?

Ben In that our routine doesn't interfere with your – plural meaning – routine.

Reg Plural meaning? Meaning what?

Ben Yours and his. Your routines together.

Reg Ah. Well, it has done, frankly, yes. Now you ask. But I don't think it will from now on.

Ben (*sits on the hard chair opposite Reg*) Then you're beginning to get the hang of it? Good. Because sometimes I've suspected that our friendship – going back so far and including so much – so much of his history and so much of my history which has really become *our* history – singular meaning this time – must make it difficult for any new people we pick up on the side.

Reg Like your wife, do you mean?

Ben Well done. Yes, like poor old Anne. She must have felt her share amounted to a minor infidelity, really. I speak metaphorically, of course, but then I suppose marriage is the best metaphor for all our intense relationships. Except those we have with our husbands and wives. (*Laughs.*) Naturally.

Reg So you think of yourself as married to Joey, do you?

Ben Metaphorically.

 A pause. The telephone rings. Ben picks it up.

Butley, English. Oh, hello, James – no, I'm afraid I still can't talk properly. I'm in the middle of a tutorial. (*He winks at Reg.*) OK. Yes. Goodbye.

Reg What metaphor would you use when you learned that Joey was going to move in with someone else? Would that be divorce, metaphorically?

Ben (*after a long pause*) What?

Reg (*laughs*) Sorry. I shouldn't do that. But I was thinking that it must be odd getting news of two divorces in the same day.

Ben (*pause*) Joey hasn't said anything.

Reg No. I'm giving the news. You might say that when he comes to me our Joey will be moving out of figures of speech into matters of fact. Ours will be too much like a marriage to be a metaphor.

Ben (*little pause*) I thought you didn't admit to being – what? – different?

Reg There are moments when frankness is necessary. No, our Joey's just been waiting for the right queen, fruit, fairy, poof or homosexual to come along. He's come.

Ben (*after a pause*) Well, isn't he lucky?

Reg Time will tell. I hope so. But I'm tired of waiting to make a proper start with him. I'm tired of waiting for him to tell you. You know our Joey – a bit gutless. No, the truth of the matter is, I've been trying to get Joey to bring you around to dinner one evening and tell you straight, so we could get it over with. I knew he'd never find the nerve to do it on his lonesome. But he's kept dodging about, pretending you were busy, one excuse after another. It's worked out quite well, though, hasn't it?

The door opens. Joey comes in. Sees Reg.

Hello. We've just been sorting things out. Ben and I.

Ben (*to Joey*) Cheers.

Joey stands staring from one to the other.

Yes, our Reg has just been giving me the second
instalment of the day's news. But then traditionally,
because metaphorically, I should be the last to hear.

Joey (*after a pause*) I wanted to tell you myself.

Ben Wanted to, did you? And were you looking forward
to a subsequent scene?

Joey No.

Ben How unlike each other we are. I would have
enjoyed it.

Reg (*after a pause*) How did your lecture go?

Joey All right.

Reg Grand. Any more teaching today?

Joey No.

Reg Come on then. (*He moves over to Joey.*) Let's go
move your things.

Joey No, I can't, until later.

Reg Why not?

Joey Because there's something I've got to do. (*He
glances at Ben.*)

Ben Oh, don't stay on my account.

Joey No. It's something I promised Edna I'd –

Reg Oh. Well, have you got time for a cup of tea?

Joey Yes.

They move towards the door.

Ben Reg.

Reg turns.

Are you coming back after tea?

Reg (*looks at Joey*) I don't see any reason to. Why?

Ben I think you're pretty bloody good, Reg. In your way. It's not my way, but it seems to get you what you want.

Reg So far. But thanks.

> *Ben goes across to the carrier bag, scrambles in it, comes back with a package, hands it to Reg. Reg takes it.*

What's this? (*opening the package*)

Ben My kidneys. Best English lamb.

Reg You've been done. They're New Zealand, thawed.

Ben The small, dapper irony is that I've been trying to join you for supper all day – not to say for the last month. May I anyway?

Joey Of course.

Reg I'm sorry. We can't.

Joey Why not?

Reg Because I've just bought two tickets for the match tonight. From one of your porters. (*to Ben*) I'm sorry. Perhaps some other time.

> *He passes the bag of kidneys to Joey, who passes them to Ben.*

Ben Thank you. (*He drops the kidneys on his desk.*)

Joey Do we have to go to the match?

Reg Yes. It's an important one. (*to Ben*) But some other time. Now I'd like that tea, please.

> *Joey looks at him and leads the way to the door.*

Ben (*watches them*) Reg!

Reg turns.

I didn't know you supported a London club too, Reg? (*He picks up the whisky bottle.*)

Reg Leeds are away to Arsenal.

Ben Ah. Well, enjoy it.

Reg Thanks. (*He turns to the door.*)

Ben Reg. (*Reg turns again.*) Will you wear it all, then?

Reg Sorry? What? Wear what?

Ben Your gear and tackle and trim. Have you got it with you?

Reg What? (*Puzzled, he looks at Joey.*)

Ben Your scarf and cloth cap and rattle. Your rosettes and hobnail boots. Isn't that your road, any road, up your road?

Reg I'm parched. Can we compare customs some other time? (*He turns.*)

Ben Reg!

As Reg seems to go on.

Reg!

Reg steps back in.

No, it's not customs, Reg, it's you, old cheese. Personally I don't give a fuck that moom and dud live oop Leeds and all, or that the whole tribe of you go to football matches looking like the back page of the *Daily Mirror* and bellow 'Ooop ta Rovers' and 'Clobber busturds' or own a butcher's shop with cush on ta side from parking tickets.

Joey laughs – Reg sees him.

I really don't, old cheese. No, what's culturally entertaining is yourself. I'm talking about your hypocrisy, old darling.

Reg Is that what you're talking about?

Ben (*making a circle round Joey's desk through the speech*) Because you're only good at getting what you want because you're a fraction of a fake, old potato, you really are. You don't show yourself north except twice a year with your latest boy or sommat in tow, do you? And I bet you get all your football out of ta *Guardian* and television except when you flash a couple of tickets at some soft southern bugger – do you object to that word, old fruit? – like me, to show some softer southern bugger like him – (*gestures at Joey*) – how tough you are. Did you cling consciously on to funny vowels, or did you learn them all afresh? I ask, because you're not Yorkshire, you're not working class, you're just a lucky parvenu fairy, old fig, and to tell you the truth you make me want to throw up. Pardon, ooop! All over your characteristically suede shoes.

Joey (*shuts the door*) Shut up, Ben!

Ben (*walking round Reg*) Why, have I upset him? What's the matter, Reg? I thought you liked plain talk and straightforward blokes, brass tacks, hard dos and no bloody metaphors. *I* don't blame you for being ashamed of ta folks, except when you want to come the simple sod – sorry, homo – sorry, bloke. I'd feel ta same in thy clogs.

Joey Ben!

Reg Anything else?

Ben Yes, tell me. (*Comes back to confront him.*) Have you had plain talk and brass tacks about thyself with

moom, when she's back from pasting tickets on cars,
lud, eh, or with dud while he's flogging offal, lud?
Thou'd get fair dos all right then, wouldn't thee? From
our dud with his strup? Or would he take thee down to
local and introduce thee round to all t'oother cloth caps?
'This is our Reg. He's punsy. Ooop, pardon, Reg lud.
Omosexual. Noo, coom as right surprise to moother und
me, thut it did, moother joost frying oop best tripe and
garbuge and me settling down with gnomes to a good
read of Mazo de la Roche.'

*He laughs in Reg's face. There is a pause. Then Joey
makes a spluttering sound, as with laughter.*

Reg (*turns, looks at Joey*) Oh, I see. The information for
all this drollery comes from you. Perhaps you'd better
sort him out. (*He walks back to the door.*)

Ben Reg! Coom 'ere, lad! You coom and sort me out.
Coom on, lud, it's mun's work!

Reg stops, walks slowly towards Ben.

Cloomp, cloomp, cloomp, aye, tha's they moother's feet,
Reg!

*Joey lets out another gasp. There is a silence, Reg
standing in front of Ben.*

Reg I don't like these games, Joey. You know that.

Joey (*spluttering*) I'm sorry, I didn't mean . . .

Ben Going to cook my kidneys after all then?

Reg Is that what you want?

Ben Ah coom on –

Reg No, I'm not playing with you. So don't say one
more word, eh? Not a word. (*He turns to go.*)

Ben (*steels himself*) Ah Reg, lud –

Reg turns around.

Coom on then.

Joey Ben!

Ben Owd sod, feery, punsy –

Reg hits Ben in the stomach, not very hard – he falls to the ground.

Joey Don't!

There is a silence, then a shape at the door.

Reg There. Is that what you wanted?

Edna knocks, puts her head in.

Edna Oh sorry.

Ben Living theatre. Next time around in Polish.

Edna Oh. (*to Reg*) I'll come back later. (*She goes out.*)

Ben For a kick at my balls. Why should she be left out?

Reg (*calmly*) But you're pitiful, pitiful. This man you've given me all the talk about. That you made me jealous of. (*He turns, goes to the door.*)

Ben Still, couldn't take it, could you, butcher's boy!

Reg (*to Joey*) It was silly. You'll have to outgrow that kind of thing, Joey.

He smiles at Ben, and goes out, closing the door quietly. There is a long moment. Then Ben goes and leans on the edge of the desk, smiles at Joey.

Ben (*touches his chin*) Your bugger's made me bleed again. (*Laughs.*) You're beginning to get little wrinkles around your eyes. Are they laughter wrinkles, or is it age, creeping up, you on little crow's feet? (*Pause.*) You'll be one of those with a crêpe neck, I'll be one of the fat ones with a purple face, Reg will be . . . (*Pause.*) I was watching you while you were shaving the morning you were going to Leeds. If you'd moved your eyes half an inch you'd have seen me in the mirror. I was standing behind you studying your neck and my jowels.

Joey I saw you.

Ben Ah! Well, what did you think of all that, with our Reg, eh?

Joey I thought it was creepy.

Ben I wonder what your next will be like? Don't be afraid to bring him home, dear, will you? (*genteel*) I do worry so.

Joey There isn't going to be a next one. At least, not for some time.

Ben Ho, reely? I think that's a good plan, h'abstinence makes the 'eart grow fonder. (*He sits on desk.*)

Joey I'm moving in with Reg.

Ben (*after a pause*) I don't think he'll have you, dear, after your indiscretions and sauciness.

Joey Yes he will.

Ben You'll go running after him, will you? How demeaning!

Joey Possibly. But it's better than having him run after me. I've been through that once, I couldn't face it again.

Ben You love him then, your butcher's boy?

Joey Actually, he's not a butcher's boy, in point of fact. (*He picks up his briefcase and returns to his desk. Little* *pause.*) His father teaches maths at the university. His mother's a social worker. They live in an ugly Edwardian house . . .

Ben (*after a pause, nods*) Of course. Quite nice and creepy. Creepy, creepy, creepy, creepy!

Joey I'm sorry.

Ben Well, thank you anyway for the fiction. (*He sits on the hard chair by his desk. There is a pause.*) So you love him then?

Joey No. But I've got to get away from you, haven't I?

Ben Really? Why?

Joey (*sits at desk.*) For one thing, I'd like to get some work done. During your married year I did quite a bit. I'd like to finish it.

Ben What?

Joey My edition of Herrick.

Ben If the consequence of your sexual appetites is another edition of unwanted verse then you have an academic duty to control yourself. Could I also mention, in a spirit of unbecoming humility, that if I hadn't taken over your studies when you were an averagely dim undergraduate, you'd never have got a first. Your nature is to settle for decent seconds – indecent seconds, in Reg's case.

Joey I know. But those were in the days when you still taught. Now you spread futility, Ben. It creeps in, like your dirty socks do, into my drawers. Or my clean ones, onto your feet. Or your cigarette butts everywhere. Or your stubble and shaving cream into our razor. Or your voice, booming out nursery rhymes into every corner of this department, it seems to me. Or your –

Ben Shut up! That's rehearsed.

Joey Thousands of times.

* [**Ben** (*after a pause*) He's going to get it published for you, isn't he?

Joey (*shrugs, after a pause*) Yes. He said he'd help.

Ben (*laughs*) And Appley Dappley has sharp little eyes. And Appley Dappley's so fond of pies.

Joey I can't help it. It's the only way I'll get ahead.

Ben Into what? There's nothing left for you to get ahead in, it's all in the past, and that thins out as the years go by. You'll end up like Edna, sending out Dean's Reports on any student you haven't killed off, and extinguishing a poet or two in the library. While it all rots away around you.

Joey Perhaps it won't rot away if – (*Pauses.*) I'd rather end up like Edna than like you. Once you talked to me of literature as the voice of civilisation, what was it, the dead have living voices –

Ben I hope not. I may have quoted . . .

> the communication
> Of the dead is tongued with fire beyond the language
>   of the living.

I can still quote it when the moment's right.

---

* The passage in brackets was cut from the production the night before we opened. I am re-instating it because it now seems to me a passage that, whether it should be played in performance or not, conveys a great deal of useful information about Butley's relationship with Joey and about his sexual nature. In the first performance and all subsequent productions, this passage was replaced by the following stage direction:

> *A long pause – during which Ben goes to his desk chair and sits – the whisky bottle in his hand.*

Joey And when will it be right again? It hasn't been with me since your marriage – since before it, really. It's been Beatrix Potter and passages and pastiches from Eliot . . .

Ben I adjust my selection to the context. Why did you move back into the flat with me, then?

Joey Habit, I suppose. I'm fairly feeble, as both you and Reg point out to me. I don't like being alone, and I couldn't resist – I was actually quite pleased when your marriage broke down.

Ben That's called friendship. (*Laughs.*)

Joey You should have stuck it out. With Anne.

Ben Should I?

Joey But at least you slept with her. You sleep with women –

Ben Not when I can help it. Mankind cannot stand too much reality. I prefer friendship.

Joey But it's the sort of friendship people used to have with me at school. Abuse, jokes, games . . .

Ben It's only a language, as good as any other and better than some, for affection.

Joey But I've got these wrinkles around my eyes, and my neck will crêpe, just as you said. And you're fattening and thirty-five, just as you said, and we don't belong in a school or nursery any more. Reg is right. We're pitiful. We're pitiful together.

Ben We're all pitiful, together or apart. The thing is to be pitiful with the right person, keep it from everybody else. And from yourselves whenever you can.

Joey Well then – well then – I can't keep it from myself any longer. I've been trying to keep you and Reg apart because I knew this would happen. But I've been longing for it, all the same. (*Pause.*)]

I'm sorry it had to be today, what with Anne and Tom. I would have waited . . .

Ben (*in senile professional tones*) Which shows you have no sense of classical form. We're preserving the unities. The use of messengers has been quite skilful. (*Pause.*) All right. All right. It doesn't really matter very much.

Joey What will you do?

Ben (*after a pause*) Could you, do you think, staunch the flow of blood? (*He lifts his chin back.*)

Joey (*comes over reluctantly, takes the piece of cotton wool Ben holds out to him.*) It's just a bubble. (*He hesitates, then bends forward with the cotton wool.*)

Ben The trouble with – all these confessions, revelations, clean breaks and epiphanies – shouldn't we call them these days? – is that – cluttered contact goes on. For instance, we still share this room. (*as Joey steps away*) You're going to have to live with your past, day after day and as messily as ever. I'll see to that.

Edna (*knocks, opens the door, smiles*) May I?

Ben Of course. (*Laughs.*) Of course you may, Edna. It's your turn.

Edna Now you'll really be able to spread yourself. It's much more sensible. (*to Joey*) I've moved out all my files. What can I do now?

  A pause – Ben sinks into the chair in realisation of the news.

Joey I can manage down here. (*He moves away, goes to the shelves, takes down his books.*)

Edna I'm glad I made one of you take advantage.

Joey goes out with a load of books.

I've quietened down, Ben, you'll be glad to hear. But I'd like to say I'm sorry about my – my little outburst just now. I must learn not to be so sensitive. I suspect it's the only way, with this new generation.

Ben They are rather frightening.

Edna Oh, I don't imagine you're frightened of them.

Ben I haven't enough pride. I shall continue to throw myself on their mercy. (*He goes to Joey's shelves – takes down a pile of books and puts them on the desk.*)

Edna They weren't very merciful to Aristotle in the Senate House.

Ben He had too many advantages. They couldn't be expected to tolerate that.

Edna (*laughs*) Well . . .

Ben (*watches her*) I haven't congratulated you on your book.

Edna Wouldn't it have been awful if someone had got in ahead of me? Twenty years – I'm really rather ashamed.

Ben Will you go on to someone else now?

Edna I don't know. (*She sits on the hard chair by Ben's desk.*) You know, last night I played a little game – I closed my eyes and turned over groups of pages at a time – and then I looked at a page. It was in the commentary on a letter from his sad wife. And I remembered immediately when I started working on it. It was in Ursula's cottage in Ockham, Surrey. I was still working on it when the summer term of the following year was over. I finished it during my first week back at Ursula's.

I can even remember the weather – how's the book on Eliot, by the way?

Ben It has a good twenty years to go.

Edna I'm sure that's not true. James is always saying that you get through things so quickly. I'm sure you'll be finished with Eliot in no time. Anyway, don't dally with him. Let me be a lesson to you –

Ben (*watching her*) Do you still go to Ursula's cottage?

Edna Oh, not in the same way. Ursula got married during chapter six. (*She laughs and goes to the door, stops.*) Oh hello. No, don't run away. (*She puts her head back in.*) Mr Gardner's here.

Ben Oh! Right.

Edna Will you go in, Mr Gardner?

She goes out. Gardner comes in. He is wearing a hat with feathers in it, a white Indian shirt, sandals, no socks.

Ben (*stares blankly ahead, then looks at him*) Well, Mr Gardner – you're here for your Eliot.

Gardner Yes, please.

Ben Tell me, what *did* I say in the pub?

Gardner Well, I told you I couldn't stand Miss Shaft's seminars and you told me I was interesting enough to do Eliot, and that I ought to go and see James. You said he'd pass the buck back to you because whenever he had a problem he converted it straight into a buck and passed it. Actually, you called him Cottontail.

Ben Did I? (*After a pause, he smiles.*) And here we both wonderfully are.

Gardner Yes. (*Smiles.*) Thank God.

Ben Well, let's get going. (*He goes to the shelf, gets a copy of Eliot, brings it back.*) Can you start by reading me a passage, please? Don't worry if you can't understand it yet. (*He hands him the book, open.*) There. Do you mind?

Gardner No, I'd like that. (*He sits on the hard chair by Ben's desk.*)

Joey (*comes in*) Oh, sorry. (*He goes to his desk and begins to pack the contents of the drawers.*)

Ben This is Mr Gardner, celebrated so far for his hat. Do you like it?

Joey Of its style.

Ben Once – some years ago – I taught Mr Keyston. During our first tutorial we spent a few minutes discussing his clothes. Then he read me some Eliot. Today I'm actually wearing his socks. Those are the key points in a relationship that now goes mainly back.

Joey (*opening drawers*) So you see, Mr Gardner, you'd better be careful. If you value your socks.

Gardner looks at his feet: he is not wearing socks. Ben and Joey look at Gardner's feet, then Joey goes on putting papers into his briefcase.

Ben Please begin.

Gardner (*reads*)
'In that open field.
If you do not come too close, if you do not come
  too close,
On a summer midnight, you can hear the music
Of the weak pipe and the little drum
And see them dancing around the bonfire
The association of man and woman

94

In daunsinge, signifying matrimonie –
A dignified and commodious sacrament.

Joey, finished clearing, looks at Gardner.

Two and two, necessarye coniunction,
Holding eche other by the hand or the arm
Whiche betokeneth concorde. Round and round the fire.

*Joey looks towards Ben, they exchange glances, then
Ben looks away. Joey goes out, closing the door gently.*

Leaping through the flames, or joined in circles,
Rustically solemn or in rustic laughter
Lifting heavy feet in clumsy shoes,
Earth feet, loam feet, lifted in country mirth
Mirth of those long since – '

Ben So you're Gardner, are you?

Gardner (*stops, looks at him in surprise, smiles*) Yes.

Ben
Ninny Nanny Netticoat,
In a white petticoat,
With a red nose –
The longer he stands,
The shorter he grows.

Gardner What?

Ben I'm moving on, Mr Gardner. I'm breaking new ground.

Gardner Oh. (*He laughs.*)

Ben Furthermore, I hate your hat.

Gardner I'm sorry.

Ben Did you wear it when you bombed the Velium Aristotle? And are you going to wear it for your raids on *Dappley* and *Parsley*, eh?

Gardner What?

Ben It won't do you any good. Aristotle in his Velium stood alone, vulnerable, unreadable and so unread. But *Dappley* and *Parsley* are scattered in nursery consciousnesses throughout the land. They can still be tongued with fire.

Gardner What are you talking about? – I wasn't anywhere near the Senate House when that happened. I don't even know what it was about, properly.

Ben No, you're a personal relationships type of chappie, I can sense that. Please go away. Go back to Miss Shaft.

Gardner What? But I can't – after all that trouble –

Ben Trouble for you, fun for me. Go away, Gardner, and take your plumage with you, I don't want to start again. It's all been a ghastly mistake. I don't find you interesting, any more. You're not what I mean at all, not what I mean at all. I'm too old to play with the likes of you.

> *Gardner puts the Eliot down, goes out. Ben puts the book back, sits at the desk, turns off the desk lamp and tries feebly three times to turn it on again.*
> *Curtain.*

OTHERWISE ENGAGED

For Harold
Two summers, 1971 and 1975

Otherwise Engaged was first presented by Michael Codron on 30 July 1975, at the Queen's Theatre, London. The cast was as follows:

Simon Alan Bates
Dave Ian Charleson
Stephen Nigel Hawthorne
Jeff Julian Glover
Davina Jacqueline Pearce
Wood Benjamin Whitrow
Beth Mary Miller

Director Harold Pinter
Designer Eileen Diss
Lighting Leonard Tucker

Characters

Simon
Dave
Stephen
Jeff
Davina
Wood
Beth

Act One

The living room of the Henches' house in London. It is both elegant and comfortable, but not large. Two sofas, two armchairs, a coffee table, a telephone with an answering machine, an extremely expensive and elaborate hi-fi set, and around the walls shelves to accommodate a great range of books (which are evidently cherished) and an extensive collection of records, in which Wagner and other opera sets can be distinguished. Stage left is a door that leads onto a small hall, at one end of which is the front door, and at the other a door which, in its turn, when opened, reveals a passage that goes on to stairs going down to the basement. More stairs lead up from the hall to another section of the house. The house has, in fact, recently been divided into two, so that there is a top flat. Stage right has a door that leads to the kitchen, and, as becomes evident, there is a door that opens from the kitchen into the garden. When the curtain goes up, Simon is unwrapping a new record. He takes it out with the air of a man who is deeply looking forward to listening to it – there are several records, in fact – the complete Parsifal. *He goes to the hi-fi, puts the first record on, listens, adjusts the level, then goes to the sofa and settles himself in it. The opening chords of* Parsifal *fill the theatre. The door opens, left. Dave enters. Simon turns, looks at him, concealing his irritation as Dave wanders into the kitchen, returns, and sits restlessly in the armchair. A pause in the music.*

Dave What's that, then?

Simon gets up and switches off the record.

Simon Wagner. Do you like him?

Dave (*standing up*) No, well, I mean, he was anti-Semitic, wasn't he. Sort of early fascist, egomanic type.

Simon What about his music, do you like that?

Dave Well, I mean, I'm not likely to like his music if I don't like his type, am I?

Simon (*concealing his impatience*) Everything all right? In the flat, that is. No complaints or other urgencies?

Dave No, no, that's all right. Oh, you mean about the rent?

Simon Good God no, I wasn't thinking about the rent.

Dave It's all right if it waits a bit then, is it?

Simon Good God yes, pay us this week's when you pay us last week's – next week, or whenever.

Dave OK. I'm a bit short, you know how it is. Your wife out again, then?

Simon Yes, she's gone to . . . (*thinks*) Salisbury. She left last night.

Dave That girl in the first year came round last night for something to eat. I dropped down to borrow a chop or something, fish fingers would have done.

Simon Would they really?

Dave But she wasn't here, your wife.

Simon No, she wouldn't have been, as she was either in, or on her way to, Salisbury.

Dave So I had to take her out for a kebab and some wine. Then I had to get her to come back.

Simon Ah, she stayed the night, then? Good for you!

Dave No, she didn't.

Simon Oh. You managed to get rid of her, then, instead, well done!

Dave She just left by herself.

Simon Before you had a chance to get rid of her, oh dear, why?

Dave Said she didn't fancy me.

Simon Good God, why ever not?

Dave I don't know. I mean, I asked her if she'd like a screw and she said no. Then I asked her why not, and she said she didn't fancy me, that was why not.

Simon Still, she's left the door open for a platonic relationship.

Dave Yeah, well, then she went off to see something on television with some friend. I haven't got a television.

Simon Well, I'm afraid I can't help you there, nor have we.

Dave Anyway she said she might be going to that Marxist bookshop down the road today.

Simon What time?

Dave About lunchtime, she said.

Simon But good God, lunch will soon be on you, hadn't you better get going? It would be tragic to miss her.

Dave Yeah, well that's it, you see. I'm a bit short, like I said. I mean we can't do anything –

    Pause.

Simon Can I lend you some?

Dave What?

Simon Can I lend you some money?

Dave Yeah, OK.

Simon (*giving him a fiver*) Is that enough?

Dave Yeah. Right. (*Takes it.*) That's five.

Simon Well, I'll get back to my music while you're making your own.

Stephen (*enters, through the kitchen door*) Hello. Oh, hello.

Simon (*concealing his dismay*) Oh, Stephen. This is Dave, who's taken over the upstairs flat. Dave, my brother Stephen.

Stephen Oh yes, you're at the poly, aren't you?

Dave That's right.

Stephen What are you studying?

Dave Sociology.

Stephen That must be jolly interesting. What aspect?

Dave What?

Stephen Of sociology.

Dave Oh, the usual stuff.

Stephen Psychology, statistics, politics, philosophy, I suppose.

Dave We're sitting in at the moment.

Stephen Really? Why?

Dave Oh, usual sort of thing. Well – (*Goes towards the door and out.*)

Stephen What is the usual sort of thing?

Simon No idea.

Stephen (*after a pause*) Well, I must say!

Simon Oh, he's not as thick as he seems.

Stephen Isn't he? He certainly seems quite thick. (*Sits down.*) I'm surprised a student could afford that flat, what do you charge him?

Simon Two pounds a week, I think.

Stephen But you could get, good heavens, even through the rent tribunal, ten times that.

Simon Oh, we're not out to make money from it.

Stephen Well, *he* seems rather an odd choice for your charity, with so many others in real need. Beth's not here, then?

Simon No, she's taken some of her foreign students to Canterbury.

Stephen Did she go with that teacher she was telling Teresa about?

Simon Chap called Ned?

Stephen Yes.

Simon Yes.

Stephen What do you think of him?

Simon Oh, rather a wry, sad little fellow. Bit of a failure, I'd say, from what I've seen of him.

Stephen A failure? In what way?

Simon Oh, you know, teaching English to foreigners.

Stephen So does Beth.

Simon True, but Beth isn't a middle-aged man with ginger hair, a pigeon-toed gait, a depressed-looking wife and four children to boot.

Stephen You know, sometimes I can't help wondering how people describe me. A middle-aged public school teacher with five children to boot. A bit of a failure too, eh? Anyhow, that's how I feel today.

Simon Why, what's the matter?

Stephen That damned interview.

Simon Interview?

Stephen For the assistant headmastership. You'd forgotten then!

Simon No, no of *course* I hadn't. When is it exactly?

Stephen (*looks at him*) Yesterday.

Simon Good God! Was it really? Well, what happened?

Stephen I didn't get it.

Simon Well, who did?

Stephen A chap called MacGregor. And quite right too, as he's already assistant headmaster of a small public school in Edinburgh, very capable, written a couple of textbooks – in other words he's simply the better man for the job.

Simon I don't see what that's got to do with it. I don't know how your headmaster had the face to tell you.

Stephen Oh, he didn't. Nobody's had the face or the grace. Yet.

Simon Then how do you know he's got it?

Stephen It was written all over MacGregor. I've never seen anyone so perky after an interview.

Simon Oh good God, is that all? Of course he was perky. He's a Scot, isn't he? They're always perky. Except when they're doleful. Usually they're both at once.

Stephen If you'd seen him come bouncing down the library steps.

Simon In my experience a bouncing candidate is a rejected candidate. No, no, Steve, my money's on your paddle feet. (*He sits.*)

Stephen Even though my interview lasted a mere half-hour although his lasted fifty-seven minutes? Even though I fluffed my mere half-hour, and before a hostile board? Do you know, one of the governors couldn't get over the fact that I'd taken my degree at Reading. He was unable to grasp that Reading was a university even, he referred to it as if it were some cut-price institution where I'd scraped up some – some diploma on the cheap. MacGregor went to Oxford, needless to say.

Simon Did he? Which college?

Stephen And then another governor harped on the number of our children – he kept saying *five* children, eh? Like that. Five children, eh? As if I'd had – I don't know – five – five –

Simon Cheques returned.

Stephen What?

Simon That's what you made it sound as if he sounded as if he were saying.

Stephen Anyway, there were the two governors manifestly hostile.

Simon Out of how many?

Stephen Two.

Simon Ah, but then your headmaster was on your side.

Stephen Perhaps. (*Pause.*) At least until I succeeded in putting him off.

Simon How?

Stephen By doing something I haven't done since I was twelve years old.

Simon (*after a pause*) Can you be more specific?

Stephen You will of course laugh, for which I shan't of course blame you, but I'm not sure that I can stand it if you do laugh at the moment. It was something very trivial, but also very embarrassing. (*Pause.*) You see, the governor who didn't feel Reading was up to snuff had a rather low, husky voice, and towards the end I bent forward rather sharply, to catch something he said, and this movement caused me to fart.

> *They stare levelly at each other. Simon's face is completely composed.*

Simon You haven't farted since you were twelve?

Stephen In public, I meant.

Simon Oh. Loudly?

Stephen It sounded to me like a pistol shot.

Simon The question, of course, is what it sounded like to Headmaster.

Stephen Like a fart, I should think.

Simon Oh, he probably found it sympathetically human, you've no grounds for believing he'd hold anything so accidental against you, surely?

Stephen I don't know, I simply don't know. (*He gets up.*) But afterwards, when he had us around for some of his wife's herbal coffee –

Simon Herbal coffee?

Stephen They paid far more attention to MacGregor than they did to me. I had to struggle to keep my end up. Headmaster was distinctly aloof in his manner – and MacGregor, of course, was relaxed and I suppose a fair man would call it charming.

Simon What herbs does she use?

Stephen What? What's that got to do with it? How would I know?

Simon Sorry, I was just trying to imagine the – the setting, so to speak.

Stephen You know, what really hurts is that I can't complain that it's unfair. MacGregor really is better qualified, quite obviously an admirable bloke. But what I do resent, and can't help resenting, is the edge Oxford gives him – the simple fact that he went there improves his chances – but I suppose that's the way of the world, isn't it? Almost everybody goes along with it, don't they?

Simon Oh, I don't know –

Stephen Of course you know. You subscribe to it yourself, don't you?

Simon Certainly not. Why should I?

Stephen Because you went to Oxford yourself.

Simon Good God, so what?

Stephen Well, how many other members of your editorial board also went there?

Simon Only five.

Stephen Out of how many?

Simon Eight.

Stephen And where did the other three go, Cambridge?

Simon Only two of them.

Stephen And so only *one* of the nine went elsewhere?

Simon No, he didn't go anywhere. He's the Chairman's son.

Stephen I think that proves my point.

Simon It proves merely that our editorial board is composed of Oxford and Cambridge graduates, and a half-wit. It proves absolutely nothing about your chances of beating MacDonald to the assistant headmastership. And it's my view that poor old MacDonald, whether he be Oxford MacDonald or Cambridge MacDonald or Reading MacDonald or plain Edinburgh MacDonald –

Stephen MacGregor.

Simon What?

Stephen His name happens to be MacGregor.

Simon Absolutely. Has no chance at all. Even if they do believe you have too few qualifications and too many children, even if they suspect that your single fart heralds chronic incontinence, they'll still have to appoint you. And if they've been extra courteous to MacDonald it's only to compensate him for coming all the way from Edinburgh for a London rebuff. (*Stands up.*)

Stephen Actually it would be better, if you don't mind, not to try and jolly me along with reasons and reassurances. I shall have to face the disappointment sooner or later, and I'd rather do it sooner – wouldn't you?

Simon No, I have a distinct preference for later, myself. I really do think you'll get it, you know.

Stephen Yes, well thanks anyway. I'd better get back. What time's your friend coming?

Simon What friend?

Stephen When I phoned and asked whether I could come round, you said it mightn't be worth my while as you were expecting a friend.

Simon Good God! Yes. Still, he's one of those people who never turns up when expected. So if I remember to expect him I should be all right.

Stephen You mean you don't want him to turn up? Who is he anyway?

Simon Jeff Golding.

Stephen Oh *him*! Yes, well, I must say that piece he wrote in one of last week's Sundays, on censorship and children – I've never read anything so posturingly half-baked.

Simon Oh, I doubt if he was posturing, he really is half-baked.

Stephen I shall never forget – never – how he ruined the dinner party – the one time I met him – his drunkenness and his appalling behaviour. And I shall particularly never forget his announcing that people – he meant me, of course – only went into public school teaching because they were latent pederasts.

Simon Good God, what did you say?

Stephen I told him to take it back.

Simon And did he?

Stephen He offered to take back the latent, and congratulated me on my luck. That was his idea of badinage. By God, I don't often lose control but I made a point of cornering him in the hall when he was leaving. I got him by the lapels and warned him that I'd a good mind to beat some manners into him. If Teresa hadn't happened to come out of the lavatory just then – she'd rushed in there in tears – I might have done him some damage. I've never told you that bit before, have I?

Simon You haven't told me any of it before, it's very amusing. Tell me, who gave this memorable dinner party?

Stephen You did.

Simon Did I really? I don't remember it. It must have been a long time ago.

Stephen Yes, but I have a feeling your friend Jeff Golding will remember it all right.

The front door slams and Jeff Golding enters left.

Jeff Simon – ah, there you are. (*There is a pause.*) Weren't you expecting me?

Simon I most certainly was. Oh, my brother Stephen – Jeff Golding. I believe you know each other.

Stephen We do indeed.

Jeff Really? Sorry, 'fraid I don't remember.

Stephen A dinner party Simon gave – some years ago.

Jeff (*clearly not remembering at all*) Nice to see you again. (*to Simon*) Could I have a Scotch, please?

Simon Of course. (*Goes to the drinks table.*) Steve?

Stephen No thank you.

Jeff (*collapses into a chair*) Christ! Christ! I've just had a session at the Beeb, taping a piece with Bugger Lampwith. I've got the goods on him at last.

Stephen Lampwith. Isn't he a poet?

Jeff Not even. He's an Australian. A closet Australian. Went to Oxford instead of Earl's Court. Thinks it makes him one of us. Still, I got him out of his closet with his vowels around his tonsils, once or twice. Thrice, actually. (*Laughs at the recollection.*)

Stephen What exactly have you got against him?

Jeff Isn't that enough?

Stephen Simply that he's an Australian?

Jeff They're all right as dentists.

Stephen But could you please explain to me why you have it in for Australians?

Jeff Once you let them into literature they lower the property values.

Stephen Really? How?

Jeff They're too fertile, scribble, scribble, scribble like little Gibbons. They breed whole articles out of small reviews, don't mind what work they do, go from sports journalists to movie critics to novelists to poets to television pundits, and furthermore they don't mind how little they get paid as long as they fill our space. So you see, if there weren't any Australians around, sods like me wouldn't end up having to flog our crap to the *Radio Times* and even the *Shiterary Supplement,* let alone spend Saturday morning interviewing buggers like Bugger Lampwith.

Stephen We've got half-a-dozen Australian boys in our school at the moment. They're not only friendly, frank and outgoing, they're also intelligent and very hard-working.

Jeff Exactly, the little buggers. Hey! (*to Simon*) Roger's been going around telling people I can't face him since my review of his turgid little turd of a novel. Have you read it?

Simon Which?

Jeff My review – first things first.

Simon Yes, I did.

Jeff Well?

Simon Some good jokes, I thought.

Jeff Weren't there? And what did you honestly, frankly and actually think of his turd?

Simon I haven't read it.

Jeff Didn't you publish it?

Simon Yes.

Jeff Well, if you ask me, the bloke you got to write the blurb hadn't read it either, bloody sloppy piece of crap, who did it anyway?

Simon Actually I did.

Jeff D'you know what it bloody is – I'll tell you what it bloody is – I wish I'd come out with it straight when I wrote about it – it's a piece of – *literature*, that's what it bloody is!

Stephen You don't like literature?

Jeff (*a pause*) I don't like literature, no.

Stephen Why not?

Jeff Because it's a bloody boring racket.

Stephen You think literature is a *racket*?

Jeff Are you in it too?

Stephen I happen to teach it, it so happens.

Jeff Does it, Christ! To whom?

Stephen Sixth formers. At Amplesides.

Jeff What's Amplesides?

Stephen It happens to be a public school.

Jeff Does it? Major or minor?

Stephen Let's just say that it's a good one, if you don't mind.

Jeff I don't mind saying it even if it's not. It's a good one. Christ, I can't remember when I last met a public school teacher.

Stephen Probably when you last met me.

Jeff But I don't remember that, don't forget.

Stephen Would you like me to remind you? I'm the latent pederast.

Jeff (*after a pause*) Then you're in the right job.

Stephen (*to Simon*) I think I'd better go. Before I do something I regret. (*Turns and goes out through kitchen.*)

Simon Oh, right. (*making an attempt to follow Stephen*) Love to Teresa and the kids. (*calling it out*)

> *Sound of door slamming. Jeff helps himself to another Scotch.*

Jeff Seems a real sweetie, what's he like in real life?

Simon Not as stupid as he seems.

Jeff That still leaves him a lot of room to be stupid in.

Simon He is my brother.

Jeff I'm very sorry.

Simon Actually, the last time he met you, he offered to fight you.

Jeff Then he's matured since then. Where's Beth?

Simon Gone to Canterbury.

Jeff With her woggies?

Simon Yes.

Jeff Never seem to see her these days. You two still all right, I take it?

Simon Yes, thanks.

Jeff Christ, you're lucky, don't know how you do it. She's so bloody attractive, of course, as well as nice and intelligent. I suppose that helps.

Simon Yes, it does really.

Jeff And she's got that funny little moral streak in her – she doesn't altogether approve of me, I get the feeling. Even after all these years. Christ, women! Listen, there's something I want to talk to you about, and I'll just lay down the guidelines of your response. What I want from you is an attentive face and a cocked ear, the good old-fashioned friendly sympathy and concern for which you're celebrated, O bloody K?

Simon Well, I'll do my best.

Jeff Remember Gwendoline?

Simon Gwendoline, no. Have I met her?

Jeff Hundreds of times.

Simon Really, where?

Jeff With me.

Simon Oh. Which one was she? – To tell you the truth, Jeff, there've been so many that the only one I still have the slightest recollection of is your ex-wife.

Jeff Are you sure?

Simon Absolutely.

Jeff Well, that was Gwendoline.

Simon Oh, I thought her name was Gwynyth.

Jeff Why?

Simon What?

Jeff Why should you think her name was Gwynyth?

Simon Wasn't she Welsh?

Jeff No, she bloody was not Welsh.

Simon Well, I haven't seen her for years, don't forget, not since the afternoon you threw your drink in her face and walked out on her.

Jeff And that's all you remember?

Simon Well, it *did* happen in my flat, a lunch party you asked me to give so that you could meet the then Arts Editor of the *Sunday Times*, and you did leave her sobbing on my bed, into my pillow, with the stink of Scotch everywhere –

Jeff Don't you remember anything else about my Gwendoline days, for Christ's sake? What I used to tell you about her?

Simon (*thinks*) Yes. You used to tell me that she was the stupidest woman I'd ever met.

Jeff *You'd* ever met.

Simon Yes.

Jeff And was she?

Simon Yes.

Jeff Well, you've met some stupider since, haven't you?

Simon Probably, but fortunately I can't remember them either.

Jeff So you rather despised my poor old Gwendoline, did you?

Simon Absolutely. So did you.

Jeff Then why do you think I married her?

Simon Because of the sex.

Jeff Did I tell you that too?

Simon No, you told her that, once or twice, in front of me.

Jeff Christ, what a bloody swine of a fool I was. (*Pours himself another drink*.) Well, now I'm suffering for it, aren't I? Listen, a few months ago I bumped into her in Oxford Street. I hadn't given her a thought in all that time, and suddenly there we were, face to face, looking at each other. For a full minute, just looking. And do you know something, she cried. And I felt as if we were – Christ, you know – still married. But in the very first days of it, when we couldn't keep our hands off each other. In a matter of minutes.

Simon Minutes?

Jeff Minutes. Bloody minutes. All over each other.

Simon In *Oxford* Street?

Jeff I'll tell you – I put my hand out, very slowly, and stroked her cheek. The tears were running down, her mouth was trembling – and she took my hand and pressed it against her cheek. Then I took her to Nick's flat – he's still in hospital by the way.

Simon Really? I didn't know he'd gone in.

Jeff They're trying aversion therapy this time, but it won't do any good. He's so bloody addictive that he'll come out hooked on the cure and still stay hooked on the gin, poor sod. Saline chasers. Anyway, I took her to Nick's, and had her, and had her, and had her. Christ! And when she left, what do you think I did?

Simon Slept, I should think.

Jeff I cried, that's what I did. Didn't want her to leave me, you see. I'm in love with her. I think I love her. And since then there have been times when I've thought I even liked her. Well?

Simon Well, Jeff, that's marvellous. Really marvellous.

Jeff Oh yes, bloody marvellous to discover that you want to marry your ex-wife.

Simon But why ever not? It just confirms that you were right the first time. Why not marry her?

Jeff (*taking another drink*) Because she's got a new bloody husband, that's why. In fact not so new, five years old. A bloody don in Cambridge called Manfred. Christ knows why he had to go and *marry* her!

Simon Perhaps he likes sex too.

Jeff According to Gwen he likes TV situation comedies, football matches, wrestling, comic books, horror films and sadistic thrillers, but not sex.

Simon What does he teach?

Jeff Moral sciences.

Simon Then there's your answer. Philosophers have a long tradition of marrying stupid women, from Socrates on. They think it clever. Does she love him?

Jeff Of course she does, she loves everyone. But she loves me most. Except for their bloody child. She bloody dotes on the bloody child.

Simon Oh. How old is it?

Jeff Two – three – four – that sort of age.

Simon Boy or girl?

Jeff Can't really tell. The one time I saw it, through my car window, it was trotting into its nursery school with its arm over its face, like a mobster going to the grand jury.

Simon Haven't you asked Gwen which it is?

Jeff Yes, but only to show interest. Anyway, what does it matter? What matters is she won't leave Manfred because of it. She's *my* wife, not his, I had her first, and she admits as much, she'll always be mine, but all I get of her is two goes a week when I drive up to Cambridge – Tuesdays and Thursdays in the afternoon, when Manfred's conducting seminars. In the rooms of some smartie-boots theologian.

Simon (*pacing up and down*) Do you mean Manfred conducts his seminars in the rooms of some smartie-boots theologian or you have Gwen in the rooms of some smartie-boots theologian?

Jeff I have Gwen there. He's a friend of Manfred's, you see.

Simon So Manfred's asked him to let you use his rooms?

Jeff Oh no, Manfred doesn't know anything about it. Or about me. No, smartie-boots seems to have some idea that it's part of his job to encourage what he calls sin. Oh Christ, you know the type, a squalid little Anglican queen of a pimp, the little sod. Turns my stomach. (*Adds more Scotch.*) Christ, you know, Simon, you want to know something about me?

Simon What? (*Sinks into an armchair.*)

Jeff I'm English, yes, English to my marrow's marrow. After years of buggering about as a cosmopolitan *littérateur*, going to PEN conferences in Warsaw, hob-nobbing with Frog poets and Eyetye essayists, German novelists and Greek composers, I suddenly realise I hate the lot of them. Furthermore I detest women, love men, loathe queers. D'you know when I'm really at bloody peace with myself? When I'm caught in a traffic jam on an English road, under an English heaven – somewhere between London and Cambridge, on my way to Gwen, on my way back from her, rain sliding down the window, engine humming, dreaming – dreaming of what's past or is to come. Wrapped in the anticipation or the memory, no, the anticipation *of* the memory.

Pause.

Oh Christ – it's my actual bloody opinion that this sad little, bloody little country of ours is finished at last. Bloody finished at last. Yes, it truly is bloody well actually finished at last. I mean that. Had the VAT man around the other day. That's what we get now instead of the muffin man. I remember the muffin men, I'm old enough to remember the muffin men. Their bells and smells and lighting of the lamps – do you remember? Sometimes I even remember hansom cabs and crinolines, the music halls and Hobbes and Sutcliffe . . . (*Smiles.*) Or the memory of the anticipation, I suppose. Stu Lampwith. Christ, the bugger!

Pause.

Well, Christ – I suppose I'd better go and write my piece. (*He gets to his feet.*) Did I tell you what that cold-hearted bitch said last night, in bed? Christ!

Simon Who?

Jeff What?

Simon What cold-hearted bitch?

Jeff Davina. (*Takes another Scotch.*)

Simon Davina?

Jeff You don't know about Davina?

Simon (*wearily*) No.

Jeff You haven't met her?

Simon No, no – I don't think –

Jeff But Christ, I've got to tell you about bitch Davina. (*Sits down.*)

Simon Why?

Jeff Because she is actually and completely the most utterly and totally – (*Lifts his hand.*)

There is a ring at the doorbell.

What?

Simon Just a minute, Jeff. (*Goes to the door, opens it.*)

Davina Hello, is Jeff here, by any chance?

Jeff groans in recognition and sits down on the sofa.

Simon Yes, yes, he is. Come in.

Davina enters. Jeff ignores her.

Davina I'm Davina Saunders. (*to Simon*)

Simon I'm Simon Hench.

Davina I know.

There is a pause.

Simon Would you like a drink?

Davina Small gin and bitters, please.

Simon goes across to the drinks table.

Jeff How did you know I was here?

Davina You said you would be.

Jeff Why did I tell you?

Davina Because I asked you.

Jeff But why did I tell you? Because, you see, I wanted a quiet conversation with my friend, Simon, you see.

Davina You're all right then, are you?

Jeff What?

A pause. Simon brings Davina her drink.

Davina How did the interview go?

Jeff All right.

Davina What's he like?

Jeff Who?

Davina Bugger Lampwith.

Jeff OK.

Davina What's OK about him?

Jeff He's all right.

Davina Good.

Jeff What do you mean, good?

Davina That he's all right. (*Sits down.*)

Jeff Well, what d'you want me to say? You follow me across bloody London, you turn up when I'm having a private bloody conversation with my old friend Simon, you're scarcely in the room before you ask me whether I'm drunk –

Davina As a matter of sober precision, I did not ask you whether you were drunk. I asked you whether you were all right.

Jeff Then as a matter of drunken precision, no, I'm not all right, I'm drunk.

Davina That's surprising, as with you being all right and being drunk are usually precisely synonymous.

Jeff But now you're here, aren't you, and that alters everything, doesn't it?

Davina Does it?

Jeff I thought you were going to spend the morning at the British bloody Museum. I thought we'd agreed not to see each other for a day or two, or even a year or two –

    There is a pause.

Simon What are you doing at the BM, some research?

Jeff That's what she's doing. On Major Bloody Barttelot. Got the idea from *my* review of that *Life of Stanley* – naturally.

Simon Really, and who is Major Bloody Barttelot?

Davina Major Barttelot went with Stanley to the Congo, was left in a camp to guard the rear column, and ended up flogging, shooting, and even, so the story goes, eating the natives.

Jeff Pleasant work for a woman, eh?

Simon Major Barttelot was a *woman*?

Davina He was an English gentleman. Although he did find it pleasant work from what I've discovered, yes.

Simon Really? And are you planning a book?

Jeff Of course she is – cannibalism, sadism, doing down England all at the same time, how can it miss? Why do you think she's on to it?

Simon I must say it sounds quite fascinating. Who's your publisher?

Davina I haven't got one yet.

Jeff Is that what summoned you away from the BM, the chance of drawing up a contract with my old friend, the publisher Simon? (*Refills his glass.*)

Davina Actually, I haven't been to the BM this morning. I've been on the telephone. And what summoned me here was first that I wanted to give you your key back. (*Throws it over to him.*)

Jeff (*makes no attempt to catch it*) Thank you.

Davina And secondly to tell you about the telephone call.

Jeff What? Who was it?

Davina Your ex-wife's husband. Manfred.

Jeff What did he want?

Davina You.

Jeff Why?

Davina He wanted you to know the contents of Gwendoline's suicide letter.

Jeff (*after a pause*) What? Gwendoline – what – Gwen's dead!

Simon Good God!

Davina No.

Jeff But she tried – tried to commit suicide?

Davina Apparently.

Jeff What do you mean apparently, you mean she failed?

Davina Oh, I'd say she succeeded. At least to the extent that Manfred was hysterical, I had a wastefully boring morning on the telephone, and you look almost sober. What more could she expect from a mere bid, after all?

Jeff For Christ's sake, what happened, what actually happened?

Davina Well, Manfred's narrative was a trifle rhapsodic.

Jeff But you said there was a letter.

Davina He only read out the opening sentences – he was too embarrassed by them to go on.

Jeff Embarrassed by what?

Davina Oh, Gwendoline's epistolary style, I should think. It was rather shaming.

Jeff Look, where is she?

Davina In that hospital in Cambridge probably. And if you're thinking of going up there, you should reflect that Manfred is looking forward to beating you to a pulp. A *bloody* pulp was his phrase, and unlike yourself he seems to use the word literally, rather than for rhetorical effect or as drunken punctuation. I like people who express themselves limpidly – (*to Simon*) – under stress, don't you?

Jeff (*throws his drink at her, splashing her blouse, etc.*) Is that limpid enough for you?

Davina No, tritely theatrical, as usual. But if you're absolutely determined to go – and you might as well because what else have you to do? I advise you not to drive. Otherwise you may have to make do with one of the hospitals *en route*.

Simon Yes, you really shouldn't drive, Jeff . . .

Jeff turns, goes out, left, slamming the door. There is a pause.

I'll get you something to wipe your shirt –

Davina Don't bother, it's far too wet. But another drink please. (*Hands him her glass.*)

Simon Of course.

Takes it, goes to the drinks table. Davina takes off her shirt and throws it over a chair. She is bra-less. She goes to the large wall mirror, and dries herself with a handkerchief from her bag. Simon turns with the drink, looks at Davina, falters slightly, then brings her her drink.

Davina God, what a stupid man, don't you think?

Simon Well, a bit excitable at times, perhaps.

Davina No, stupid really, and in an all-round way. You know, when I was at Oxford one used to take his articles quite seriously – not very seriously but quite. But now of course one sees that his facility, though it may pass in the Arts pages as intelligence and originality, was something merely cultivated in late adolescence for the examination halls. He hasn't developed, in fact his Gwendoline syndrome makes it evident that he's regressed. Furthermore his drunken bravado quickly ceases to be amusing, on top of which he's a fourth-rate fuck.

Simon Oh well, perhaps he's kind to animals.

Davina (*sitting on the sofa*) To think I thought he might be of some use to me. But of course he's out of the habit, if he was ever in it, of talking to women who like to think and therefore talk concisely, for whom intelligence does actually involve judgement, and for whom judgement concludes in discrimination. Hence the appeal, I suppose, of a pair of tits from which he can dangle, with closed eyes and infantile gurglings. Especially if he has to get to them furtively, with a sense of not being allowed. Yes, stupid, don't you agree?

Simon Did you really go to Oxford?

Davina Came down two years ago, why?

Simon From your style you sound more as if you went to Cambridge.

Davina Anyway, he's nicely gone, you will admit, and four bad weeks have been satisfactorily concluded.

Simon Aren't you a little worried about him, though?

Davina Why should I be?

Simon Well, Manfred did threaten to beat him to a bloody pulp, after all. And it may not be an idle boast. Men whose wives attempt suicide because of other men sometimes become quite animated, even if they are moral scientists.

Davina Oh, I think the wretched Manfred will be more bewildered than belligerent. I composed that fiction between Great Russell Street and here. Of course I didn't know until I met his glassy gaze and received his boorish welcome whether I was actually going to work it through. It was quite thrilling, don't you think?

Simon You mean, Gwendoline didn't try to commit suicide?

Davina Surely you don't imagine that *that* complacent old cow would attempt even an attempted suicide?

Simon Why did you do it?

Davina Spite, of course. Well, he told me he wanted to bring it all to a climax, although he wanted no such thing of course, prolonged and squalid messes that lead least of all to climaxes being his method, so my revenge has been to provide him with one that should be exactly in character – prolonged, squalid and utterly messy even by Cambridge standards, don't you think? *You're* married, aren't you? To Beth, isn't it?

Simon That's right.

Davina I've only just realised she isn't here, is she?

Simon Well, I suppose that's better than just realising she was, isn't it?

Davina I'd like to have met her. I've heard a great deal about you both, you mainly, of course. Are you two as imperturbably, not to say implacably, *married* as he and everyone else says?

Simon I hope so.

Davina And that you've never been unfaithful to Beth, at least as far as Jeff knows.

Simon Certainly never that far.

Davina Don't you even fancy other women?

Simon (*sits in the armchair*) My not sleeping with other women has absolutely nothing to do with not fancying them. Although I do make a particular point of not sleeping with women I don't fancy.

Davina That's meant for me, is it?

Simon Good God, not at all.

Davina You mean you do fancy me?

Simon I didn't mean that either.

Davina But do you fancy me?

Simon Yes.

Davina But you don't like me?

Simon No.

Davina Ah, then do you fancy me *because* you don't like me? Some complicated set of manly mechanisms of that sort, is it?

Simon No, very simple ones that Jeff, for instance, would fully appreciate. I fancy you because of your breasts, you see. I'm revolted by your conversation and appalled by your behaviour. I think you're possibly the most ego-centrically unpleasant woman I've ever met, but I have a yearning for your breasts. I'd like to dangle from them too, with my eyes closed and doubtless emitting infantile gurglings. Furthermore they look deceptively hospitable.

Davina If they look deceptively hospitable, they're deceiving you. (*Comes over and sits on the arm of his chair.*) You're very welcome to a nuzzle.

Pause.

Go on then. And then we'll see what you can do.

Simon sits, hesitating for a moment, then gets up, gets Davina's shirt, hands it to her.

Because of Beth?

Simon This is her house, as much as mine. It's *our* house, don't you see?

Davina Fidelity means so much to you?

Simon Let's say rather more to me than a suck and a fuck with the likes of you. So, come to that, does Jeff.

Davina Yes, well, I suppose that's to be expected in a friend of his. He doesn't begin to exist and nor do you.

Simon That's excellent. Because I haven't the slightest intention of letting you invent me.

Davina And what about my Barttelot book?

Simon There I'm sure we shall understand each other. If it's any good, I shall be delighted to publish it. And if you've any sense, and you've got a hideous sight too much, you'll be delighted to let me. I shall give you the best advance available in London, arrange an excellent deal with an American publisher, and I shall see that it's edited to your advantage as well as ours. If it's any good.

Davina That means more to me than being sucked at and fucked by the likes of you.

> *They smile. Davina turns and goes out. Simon,
> with the air of a man celebrating, picks up the keys
> and glasses, puts them away. Makes to go to the
> gramophone, stops, goes to the telephone answering
> machine.*

Simon (*records*) 348 0720, Simon Hench on an answering machine. I shall be otherwise engaged for the rest of the day. If you have a message for either myself or for Beth, could you please wait until after the high-pitched tone, and if that hasn't put you off, speak. Thank you.

*Puts the button down, then goes over to the gramo-
phone, bends over to put a record on. Dave enters.
Simon freezes, turns.*

Dave She didn't show.

Simon What?

Dave Suzy. My girl. She didn't show. You know what I'd
like to do now, I'd like to get really pissed, that's what
I'd like to do.

Simon I don't blame you, and furthermore, why don't
you? You'll still catch the pubs if you hurry –

Dave Well, I'm a bit short, you see.

Simon But didn't you have a few pounds –?

Dave Yeah, well I spent those.

Simon Oh, what on?

Dave Usual sort of stuff.

Simon Well then, let me.

Pause.

I've got just the thing. (*Goes to the drinks table, fishes
behind, takes out a bottle of Cyprus sherry.*) Here. Go
on, one of Beth's students gave it to her – it's yours.
(*Hands it to Dave.*) A Cyprus sherry. Nice and sweet.
Now you settle down in some dark corner, with a
receptacle by your side, and forget yourself completely.
That's what I'd want to do if I were you. (*Points him
towards the door.*)

*Dave goes out. Simon turns back to the hi-fi. Voices
in the hall.*

Dave (*opens the door*) Bloke here for you. (*Withdraws.*)

Simon What? (*Turns.*)

Wood (*enters*) Mr Hench?

Simon Yes.

Wood Can you spare me a few minutes? My name is Wood. Bernard Wood.

Simon (*as if recognising the name, then checks it*) Oh?

Wood It means something to you, then?

Simon No, just an echo. Of Birnam Wood, it must be, coming to Dunsinane. No, I'm very sorry, it doesn't. Should it?

Wood You don't recognise me either, I take it?

Simon No, I'm afraid not. Should I?

Wood We went to school together.

Simon Did we really – Wundale?

Wood Yes. Wundale. I was all of three years ahead of you, but I recall you. It should be the other way around, shouldn't it? But then you were very distinctive.

Simon Was I really, in what way?

Wood (*after a little pause*) Oh, as the sexy little boy that all the glamorous boys of my year slept with.

Simon (*after a pause*) But you didn't?

Wood No.

Simon Well, I do hope you haven't come to make good, because it's too late, I'm afraid. The phase is over, by some decades. (*Little pause, then with an effort at courtesy.*) I'm sure I would have remembered you, though, if we had slept together.

Wood Well, perhaps your brother – Stephen, isn't it – would remember me as we were in the same year. How is he?

Simon Oh, very well.

Wood Married, with children?

Simon Yes.

Wood And you're married?

Simon Yes.

Wood Good. Children?

Simon No.

Wood Why not?

Simon There isn't enough room. What about you?

Wood Oh, as you might expect of someone like me. Married with children.

There is a pause.

Simon Well . . . um – you said there was something –

Wood Yes, there is. It's of a rather personal – embarrassing nature.

Pause.

Simon (*unenthusiastically*) Would a drink help?

Wood Oh, that's very kind. Some sherry would be nice, if you have it.

Simon Yes, I have it.

Wood Then some sherry, if I may.

Simon Yes, you may. (*Pours Wood a sherry.*)

Wood My many thanks. Your very good health. I thought you might have heard my name the day before yesterday.

Simon Oh, in what context?

Wood From my girl, Joanna. In your office, at about six in the evening.

Simon Joanna?

Wood She came to see you about getting work in publishing. She's only just left art school, but you were kind enough to give her an appointment.

Simon Oh yes, yes. I do remember a girl – I'm terrible about names – a nice girl, I thought.

Wood Thank you. How did your meeting go? Just between us?

Simon Well, I thought she was really quite promising.

Wood But you didn't make her any promises.

Simon Well, no, I'm afraid I couldn't. What work of hers she showed me struck me as a – a trifle over-expressive for our needs. (*Pause.*) Why, is her version of our, um, talk different, in any way?

Wood She hasn't said anything about it at all.

Simon I see. And you've come to me to find out about her potential?

Wood Not really, no. I've come to ask you if you know where she is.

Simon Have you lost her, then?

Wood She hasn't been home since I dropped her off at your office.

Simon Well, I'm very sorry, but I haven't seen her since she left my office.

Wood I only have one rule with her, that she come home at night. Failing that, that at least she let me know where or with whom she is spending the night. Failing that,

that at least she telephone me first thing in the morning. Could I be more unreasonably reasonable? So before doing the rounds among her pals, from Ladbroke Grove to Earls Court, I thought it might be worth finding out from you if she let anything slip about her plans.

Simon Nothing that I can remember.

Wood She didn't mention any particular friend or boyfriend?

Simon Just the usual references to this drip and that drip in the modern manner. Look, from what one makes out of today's youth, isn't it likely that she'll come home when she feels in the mood or wants a good meal, eh?

Wood I suppose so.

Simon I can quite understand your worry –

Wood Can you? No, I don't think you can.

Simon No, perhaps not. But I really don't see how I can help you any further.

Wood Did you have it off with her?

Simon What? *What?*

Wood Did you have it off with her?

Simon Look, Wood, whatever your anxiety about your daughter, I really don't think, old chap, that you should insinuate yourself into people's homes and put a question like that to them. I mean, good God, you can't possibly expect me to dignify it with an answer, can you?

Wood In other words, you did.

Simon (*after a long pause*) In other words, I'm afraid I did. Yes. Sorry, old chap.

    Curtain.

Act Two

Curtain up on exactly the same scene, Wood and Simon in exactly the same postures. There is a pause.

Wood Tell me, does your wife know you do this sort of thing?

Simon Why, are you going to tell her?

Wood Oh, I'm not a sneak. Besides, Joanna would never forgive me. She'd have told me herself, you know. She always does. She thinks it's good for me to know what she and her pals get up to. Do you do it often? (*smiling*)

Simon Reasonably often. Or unreasonably, depending on one's point of view.

Wood And always with girls of my Joanna's age?

Simon There or thereabouts, yes.

Wood Because you don't love your wife?

Simon No, because I do. I make a point, you see, of not sleeping with friends, or the wives of friends, or acquaintances even. No one in our circle. Relationships there can be awkward enough –

Wood It's a sort of code, is it?

Simon No doubt it seems a rather squalid one, to you.

Wood So that's why you chose my Joanna, is it?

Simon I didn't really choose her, you know. She came into my office, and we looked at her work, and talked –

Wood Until everybody else had gone. You decided, in other words, that she was an easy lay. And wouldn't make any fuss, afterwards.

Simon I also realised that I couldn't possibly do her any harm.

Wood What about the clap? (*Pause.*) I think I have a right to know.

Simon I keep some pills at my office.

Wood So your post-coital period together was passed gobbling down anti-VD pills.

Simon One doesn't exactly gobble them – one swallows them, as one might digestive tablets.

Wood What about going back to your wife, reeking of sex?

Simon What?

Wood What do you do about the stench of your adulteries?

Simon I confess I find this enquiry into method rather depressing. I'd willingly settle for a burst of parental outrage –

Wood And I'd far rather satisfy my curiosity. Won't you please tell me?

Simon Very well. I stop off at my squash club, play a few points with the professional, then have a shower.

Wood But you don't suffer from any guilt afterwards? No post-coital distress, no angst or even embarrassment?

Simon Not unless this counts as afterwards.

Wood So really, only your sexual tastes have changed, your moral organism has survived intact since the days when you were that lucky sod, the Wundale Tart?

Simon Look, are you here because I slept around at thirteen, with the attractive boys of your year, or because I sleep around with attractive girls of your daughter's generation, at thirty-nine? Good God, Wood, I'm beginning to find something frankly Mediterranean in this obsession with your child's sex-life – and mine – after all, let's face it, in the grand scheme of things, nothing much has happened, and in the Anglo-Saxon scheme of things, your daughter's well over the age of consent. That may sound brutal, but it's also true.

Wood Except in one important point. She's not my daughter.

Simon What? What is she then?

Wood My – (*hesitates*) – fiancée.

Simon Is it worth my saying sorry over again, or will my earlier apologies serve? (*Pause.*) But I thought you said her name was Wood –

Wood Yes.

Simon And your name is Wood.

Wood Yes. I changed my name as she refuses to change hers, and won't marry me.

Simon In that case you're not Wood of Wundale.

Wood No, I'm Strapley – Strapley of Wundale. Known as Wanker Strapley. Now do you remember me?

Simon Strapley – Strapley, Wanker Strapley. No.

Wood Well, your brother certainly would. He was known as Armpits Hench. We were two of a kind, in that we were both considered drips – what was the Wundale word for drip?

141

Simon I really can't remember.

Wood It was 'plop'.

Simon Plop.

Wood Those of us who were called it are more likely to remember it than those of you who called us it. Plop. Yes, I'm a plop, Hench. Whom one can now define, after so many years ploppily lived, as a chap who goes straight from masturbation to matrimony to monogamy.

Simon Oh, now there I think you're underestimating yourself. After all you have a wife, didn't you say, and now Joanna –

Wood I haven't got my wife any more. I doubt if I've got Joanna any more. But it's only appropriate that you should be the last common factor in our relationship. The first time I set eyes on her she reminded me of you.

Simon Where was that?

Wood At our local amateur theatricals. Joanna was playing in *The Winslow Boy*. She came on the stage in grey flannel bags, a white shirt and starched collar. She walked with a modest boy's gait, her eyes were wide with innocent knowledge. So did you walk down the Wundale Cloisters, that first year of yours. So I watched you then as I watched her. And there, on my one side, were my two poor old sons, who've never reminded me of anyone but myself. And on the other, my poor old wife, the female plop, who from that second on ceased even to remind me that we shared a ploppy past. The years we'd spent together brooding over her mastoids, my haemorrhoids and the mortgage on our maisonette, watching over our boys' sad little defeats, their failure to get into Wundale, their scrabbling for four O-Levels and then two A-Levels, their respective roles as twelfth man and scorer – they haven't even the competitiveness for sibling rivalry, poor old boys – all seemed, it all seemed such a waste, such a waste.

Simon But still you did succeed, to some extent at least, in breaking free. And you did succeed, to some extent I take it, with Joanna – so not altogether a case for predestination, when you think of it.

Wood Free meals, lots of gifts, little loans by the usual ploppy techniques of obligation and dependence – not that she felt dependent or obliged. She took what I offered and then asked for more. A generous nature. Did she get anything from you?

Simon She didn't ask for anything.

Wood Just as you never asked for anything from those boys – Higgens, Hornby, Darcy.

Simon It's true that Darcy was very kind with his tuck, but I hope I never took it as payment, nor did he offer it as such.

Wood (*pause*) What was it like with Joanna?

Simon Well, it was, um, I'm sure you know – she's a very uninhibited, um –

Wood It was, then, satisfactory?

Simon Well, as these things go.

Wood They don't for me. I'm incapacitated by devotion.

Simon But you live together?

Wood She allows me to share the flat I've leased for her. We have different rooms – I sometimes sit on the side of her bed when she's in it. More often when she's not.

Simon You're obviously in the grip of a passion almost Dante-esque in the purity of its hopelessness. You know,

I really feel quite envious – for you every moment has its significance, however tortured, I just have to get by on my small pleasures and easy accommodations, my daily contentments –

Wood So she actually talks of me as a drip, does she?

Simon The ignorance of youth. Drips have neither your capacity for ironic self-castigation, nor more importantly your gift for the futile grand gesture.

Wood If she comes back, do you know what she'll do? She'll tell me about the boys she's slept with, the adults she's conned, the pot she's smoked. She'll tell me what a good time she had with you on your office floor –

Simon Sofa, actually.

Wood If she comes back. And I'll sit listening and yearning and just occasionally I'll soothe myself with the thought that one day she'll be dead or, even better, old and unwanted and desperate – what I resent most about you, little Hench, is the way you seem to have gone on exactly as you promised you would at Wundale. If life catches up with everybody at the end, why hasn't it with you?

Simon But I haven't got to the end yet, thank God. I'm sure it will eventually.

Wood Sweet little Hench from Wundale, who picks off my Jo in an hour at his office, munches down a few pills, and then returns, without a worry in his head, the whole experience simply showered off, to his wife, who is doubtless quite attractive enough – is she?

Simon I find her quite attractive enough for me. Though taste in these matters –

Wood I'd like to kill you, Hench. Yes – kill you!

Stephen (*enters through the kitchen*) Si – (*Sees Wood.*) Oh sorry, I didn't realise . . . Good God, it is, isn't it? Old Strapley, from Wundale?

Wood The name's Wood.

Stephen Oh, sorry. You look rather like a chap who used to be at school with us, or rather me, in my year. Strapley.

Wood Really? What sort of chap was he?

Stephen Oh, actually, a bit of what we used to call a plop, wasn't he, Simon? So you're quite lucky not to be Strapley, who almost certainly had a pretty rotten future before him. (*Laughs.*)

Wood Thank you for the sherry. (*Turns quickly, goes out.*)

Simon Not at all.

Stephen I hope I haven't driven him off.

Simon Mmmm. Oh no, it's not you that's driven him off.

Stephen What did he want?

Simon He was looking for somebody I once resembled. A case of mistaken identity, that's all.

Stephen Well, if he had been Strapley, he'd hardly have changed at all, except that he's a quarter of a century older. Poor old Wanker Strapley.

Sits down. There is a pause.

Well, Si, you were quite right, of course.

Simon Mmmm?

Stephen I got it.

Simon Got what?

Stephen The assistant headmastership.

Simon Oh. Oh good! (*Pause.*) Goody.

Stephen You can imagine how stunned I was. I was so depressed when I got home, not only because I thought I'd lost the appointment, but because of that friend of yours –

Simon What friend?

Stephen Golding. Jeff Golding. That he didn't even remember me, let alone what I'd threatened to do to him – and I could hear the children quarrelling in the garden, the baby crying in her cot, and when I sat down in the sitting room there was a piece in *The Times* on the phasing out of public schools and private health, lumped together, and it all seemed – well! Then Teresa called out. I couldn't face her, you know how lowering her optimism can be – but I managed to drag myself into the kitchen – she had her back to me, at the oven, cooking up some nut cutlets for the children's lunch – and she said: 'Greetings, Assistant Headmaster of Amplesides.' Yes, Headmaster's wife had phoned while I was here, isn't that ironic? I could hardly believe it. So. I crammed down a nut cutlet –

Simon What was it like?

Stephen What?

Simon The nut cutlet.

Stephen Oh, it was from one of Headmaster's wife's recipes. They're semi-vegetarian, you know.

Simon What did it *taste* like?

Stephen Rather disgusting. But she's going to give us some more recipes if we like this one. Perhaps they'll be better.

Simon But you didn't like this one.

Stephen (*pause*) Aren't you pleased or even interested in my news?

Simon Of course I am.

Stephen In spite of thinking MacDonald the better man? Well, you needn't worry about him, he's been offered a job too. As head of sixth form English.

Simon But you're head of sixth form English.

Stephen Not any more. Headmaster reckons that with my new responsibilities I should step down from some of my teaching. I shall be head of fifth form English.

Simon Ah, fewer hours then.

Stephen Actually more hours, but at fifth-form level.

Simon Ah, less cerebration. That's even better. So . . . (*Loses thread, picks it up.*) So justice has been done to two excellent candidates.

Stephen I shall still be senior to MacDonald, you know.

Simon Isn't his name MacGregor?

Stephen Yes. (*Little pause.*) Thanks, Si. (*Ironically.*)

Simon What for?

Stephen Sharing my triumph with me.

Simon Why don't you – have a drink?

Stephen No, thank you. Headmaster's asked Teresa to ask me to look in after lunch for a celebration glass.

Simon Oh. Of what?

Stephen Pansy wine, I expect, as that's their favourite tipple.

Simon (*after a pause*) Do they make it themselves?

Stephen Headmaster's wife's aunt's husband does.

Simon Does he? (*Little pause.*) What's it like?

Stephen You know what it's like.

Simon No, I don't. What's it like?

Stephen Why do you want to know what it's like?

Simon Because I can't imagine what it's like, I suppose.

Stephen Oh yes you can. Oh yes you can.

Turns, goes out through the kitchen. Dave enters left.
He's slightly drunk. There is a pause.

Dave (*swaying slightly*) She's come. She's upstairs. She came all by herself.

Simon Who?

Dave That girl. Suzy. She dropped in for a cup of Nescafé.

Simon That's very good news, Dave. But should you, now you've got her, leave her to have it all by herself. She sounds a highly strung creature –

Dave Yeah, well, the only thing is, I'm out of Nescafé.

Simon Oh.

Dave Well, have you got any, man?

Simon No, I'm sorry, we don't drink it.

Dave Anything else?

Simon Nothing at all like Nescafé, I'm afraid.

Dave What, no coffee at all?

148

Simon Oh yes, we've got coffee. But we use beans, a grinder, and a rather complicated filter process. Metal holders, paper cones –

Dave That'll do. Is it in the kitchen? (*He moves towards kitchen.*)

Simon Actually, it's rather a precious set.

Dave (*returning*) What?

Simon It's one of those few things I feel rather specially about.

Dave You mean you've got something against lending it to me?

Simon Not at all. The beans are in a sealed bag in an airtight tin –

Dave Oh yes you have. I can tell by your – your tone.

Simon My tone? Oh come now, Dave, that's only one possible gloss of my tone. No, you take the grinder, take the filters, the jug, the paper cones and the metal holders, and the coffee beans which come from a small shop in Holborn that keeps uncertain hours and can therefore be easily replaced with a great deal of difficulty, and don't addle your head with questions about my tone, good God! (*Pause.*) Go ahead. Please. (*wearily*)

Dave No thanks. No thank you! Because you do mind all right, you bloody mind all right.

Simon No, I don't.

Dave No, you don't, no, you don't bloody mind, do you? Why should you, you've got it all already, haven't you? Machines for making coffee, a table covered with booze, crates of wine in your cellar, all the nosh you want, all the books you want, all the discs, the best hi-fi on the bloody market, taxis to work every morning, taxis home in the evening, a whole bloody house just for you and your sexy little wife – oh, you don't bloody mind anything, you don't, what's there for you to mind, you shit you!

Simon Now that's not quite fair, Dave. It's not really a whole house, you know, since we converted the top floor at considerable expense and turned it over to you at an inconsiderable rent which you don't pay anyway. But then I don't mind that either.

Dave 'Course you bloody don't, why should you? You bloody like to run a pet, don't you, your very own special deserving case.

Simon I swear to you, Dave, I've never once thought of you as my pet or as a deserving case. If we'd wanted the former to occupy our upstairs flat we'd have got a monkey, and if we'd wanted the latter we'd have selected from among the unmarried mothers or the dispossessed old-age pensioners. We thought quite hard about doing that, in fact.

Dave Then why didn't you?

Simon Because unmarried mothers mean babies, and babies mean nappies, and crying. While old-age pensioners mean senility and eventual death.

Dave So I salve your bloody conscience without being a nuisance, eh? Right?

Simon Wrong. You salve my conscience by being a bloody nuisance. Your manners irritate me, your smell is unusually offensive, you're extremely boring, your sex-life is both depressing and disgusting, and you're a uniquely ungrateful cadger. But you really mustn't mind, because the point is that I don't, either. You have your one great value, that you run a poor third to recent births and imminent deaths.

Dave I'm not staying – I'm not staying – I'm not staying in the fucking top of your fucking house another fucking minute. You – you –

Makes as if to hit Simon. Simon remains impassive. Dave turns, goes out left. Noise of door slamming. Simon closes door left. As he does so, Stephen enters right.

Stephen It's sugary and tastes of onions. And it's quite revolting, just as you imagine.

Simon Well, I did imagine it would be revolting and probably sugary, but it never occurred to me it would taste of onions. But you can't have come back to report on its flavour already, you've only just left.

Stephen I've been sitting in the car, thinking.

Simon What about?

Stephen You, and your sneers. Oh, I don't altogether blame you, but I wish – (*Sits down, looks at Simon.*) – you'd had the guts to say it outright.

Simon Say what?

Stephen That it's taken me twenty-four years to advance from Second Prefect of Wundale to Assistant Headmaster of Amplesides.

Simon (*sitting down*) But that seems very respectable progress to me. At that rate you should make it to Eton, if it still exists, by your mid-fifties. And as that's what you want, why should I have a word to say against it?

Stephen Nor against the way I'm doing it? My stuffing down nut cutlets, and herbal coffee and pansy wine. And then coming back for seconds.

Simon But you do rather more than eat the inedible and drink the undrinkable. You're among the best Junior Colts football managers in the country.

Stephen You despise my job.

Simon You've a family to support.

Stephen So you do despise my job, and despise me for doing it. Why don't you say it? That's all I'm asking you to do.

Simon But I don't want to say it! I can't remember when you were last as you've been today, or what I said then to make you feel any better. I wish I could, because that's what I'd like to say now.

Stephen The last time I felt like this was eleven years ago, after Teresa had broken off our engagement, and you didn't say anything to make me feel any better. What you did say was that I was well out of it.

Simon Well, as you've been back in it for eleven years, you'll agree that it has little relevance now.

Stephen It had little relevance then, either. As I was desperately in love with her.

Simon Good God, all I probably meant, and I don't even remember saying it, was that if she didn't want to marry you then it was better to be out of it before the wedding.

Stephen Oh no, oh no, all you meant was that *you* were relieved to be out of it.

Simon Out of what?

Stephen Out of having for your sister-in-law a girl you thought tedious and unattractive. And still do. And still do.

Simon Look, Stephen, this is really rather eccentric, even in the English fratricidal tradition. First you hold it against me that I won't join you in abusing yourself, and then you hold it against me that not only did I fail to abuse your intended wife eleven years ago, but won't join you in abusing her now that she is your wife and has borne you seven children –

Stephen Six children.

Simon Nearly seven.

Stephen Nearly six.

Simon Well, straight after the sixth, it'll be nearly seven. (*He gets up*.)

Stephen Teresa's absolutely right about you. She always has been. You're just indifferent. Absolutely indifferent!

Simon In what sense? As a wine is indifferent, or prepositionally, as in, say, indifferent to –

Stephen Imbeciles like Teresa. Go on, say it!

Simon But I don't want to say it.

Stephen Not to me, no. But that's what you tell your clever-clever metropolitan Jeff Goldings, isn't it? That Teresa and I are imbeciles.

Simon I swear to you, Stephen, I've never told a soul.

Stephen Answer me one question, Simon. One question! What have you got against having children?

Simon Well, Steve, in the first place there isn't enough room. In the second place they seem to start by mucking up their parents' lives, and then go on in the third place to muck up their own. In the fourth place it doesn't seem right to bring them into a world like this in the fifth place, and in the sixth place I don't like them very much in the first place. OK.

Stephen And Beth? What about her?

Simon (*after a little pause*) Beth and I have always known what we're doing, thank you, Stephen.

Stephen You think she's happy, do you?

Simon Yes, I do. And let's not let you say another word about her, because I don't want to hear it. Have you got that, Steve? *I don't want to hear it.* (*with low emphasis*)

Stephen No, I'm sure you don't. I'm sure you don't. The last thing you want to hear is how unhappy she is.

Simon Steve!

Stephen Well, she is! So unhappy that last week she came around to Teresa and sobbed her heart out!

Simon Steve!

Stephen She's having an affair, Simon. An affair with that Ned whom you so much despise. That's how unhappy your happy Beth is.

There is a long pause.

Simon With Ned. (*Pause.*) Beth's having an affair with Ned? (*Pause.*) Really? With Ned? Good God! (*Sits down.*)

Stephen It's time you knew.

Simon No it isn't.

There is a pause.

Stephen I had to tell you.

Simon Now that's a different matter.

There is the sound of a door opening left. Beth enters.

Beth Hello. Hello, Stephen.

Stephen Hello, Beth.

Simon (*goes over, gives Beth a kiss*) You're back nice and early, aren't you?

Beth Yes, I got an earlier train.

Simon Ah, that explains it. How was it, then, old Salisbury?

Beth Old *Canterbury*, actually. Much as it ever was, except for the parts they've turned into new Canterbury.

Simon But the Cathedral's still there?

Beth Although the French students were more interested in the new Marks and Spencers.

Simon And Ned?

Beth Oh, he preferred the Cathedral.

Stephen I really must be getting along. Headmaster will be wondering what's happening to me.

Simon Oh, but first you must tell Beth your news. (*There is a slight pause.*) The assistant headmastership, Steve.

Stephen Oh. Oh yes. I got it.

Beth Steve – how marvellous! (*Comes over, gives him a kiss.*) Congratulations – Teresa must be thrilled!

Stephen Yes, she is. I've had some black moments since the interview, but she was absolutely sure – and old Si jollied me along a bit this morning. It's all a great relief, more than anything. Well, I really must dash – see you both very soon – (*Goes towards the kitchen door.*) Oh, by the way, Si – I was a bit carried away just now, spoke a lot of nonsense, don't know why I said it.

Simon Don't you?

Stephen Yes, well I suppose I meant to hurt, but I didn't mean harm, if you see.

Simon Well then, that's fine, because no harm's been done. I didn't take it seriously.

Stephen Good. (*Hesitates, turns, goes out.*)

Beth What did he say? (*Sits and lights a cigarette.*)

Simon Actually I could hardly make out – he was in a post-success depression, I think, suddenly realising that what he's got can therefore no longer be striven for. He'll be all right the moment he sets his sights on a full headmastership. Or Amplesides is abolished. Triumph or disaster – you know, like a drug. What about tea or coffee?

Beth No, I've had some, thanks.

Simon Where?

Beth On the train.

Simon Oh, then you're probably still trying to work out which it was.

Beth Did you enjoy your Wagner?

Simon I enjoyed some things about it, very much. The picture on its cover for example, its glossy and circular blackness when unsheathed, its light balance – and if the sound is any good it'll be quite perfect.

Beth You haven't managed to play it, then?

Simon Very nearly, very nearly. But what with Dave and Stephen, Jeff and Davina, the odd bod and sod, you know –

Beth Oh, you poor thing, and you'd been looking forward to it all week.

Simon Still, one mustn't snatch at one's pleasures, nor over-plan them, it seems. (*He puts the record away in its box.*)

Beth (*pause*) How was Jeff?

Simon Oh, in excellent form, really. He got drunk, threw his Scotch in his girl's face, dashed off to Cambridge where he's been having it off with his ex-wife, Gwynyth. Did you know Gwynyth, or was she a little before your time?

Beth Isn't it Gwendoline?

Simon Yes, yes, Gwendoline. Anyway, usual sort of Jeff saga, quite droll in its way.

Beth And what's his girl like?

Simon She's got good tits and a nasty sense of humour.

Beth And did she try to get you to bed?

Simon She did.

Beth And how did you get out of it?

Simon Rudely, I'm afraid, as she's on to rather a good book, from the sound of it. Ah well –

Beth Ah well, you can play your records now, can't you?

Simon Oh no. Wouldn't dream of it.

Beth Why not?

Simon Well, for one thing, you hate Wagner.

Beth Well, I'm going to have a bath.

Simon A four-hour bath?

Beth Afterwards I've got to go along to the school – sort out the fares and docket them, that sort of thing.

Simon Ah! Well, in that case –

Simon moves to hi-fi and takes out record. Beth rises, hesitates, and moves towards him.

Beth (*stops, looks at Simon*) Stephen told you, didn't he? About me. At least I hope he has.

Simon Why?

Beth So I shan't have to tell you myself.

Simon You don't have to.

Beth What?

Simon Tell me.

Beth What?

Simon Tell me anything you don't want to tell me. Stephen said nothing of significance about anything.

Beth But you see, I may not want to tell you, but I do want you to know.

Simon Why?

Beth Because there's an important problem we shall have to discuss. And I want you to understand. (*Sits on sofa.*)

Simon In my experience, the worst thing you can do to an important problem is discuss it. You know – (*sitting down*) – I really do think this whole business of non-communication is one of the more poignant fallacies of our zestfully over-explanatory age. Most of us understand as much as we need to without having to be told – except old Dave, of course – now I thought he had quite an effective system, a tribute really to the way in which even the lowest amongst us can put our education (or lack of it, in Dave's case) and intelligence (or lack of it, in Dave's case) to serving our needs. He's done really remarkably well out of taking the metaphors of courtesy literally, as for example when he asks for a loan that is in fact a gift, and one replies, 'Of course, Dave, no trouble, pay it back when you can.' *But* this system completely collapses when he's faced with a plainly literal reply, as for example when he asks to borrow our coffee set, and he's told that it'll be lent with reluctance and one would like him to be careful with it. Weird, isn't it, he can take one's courteous metaphors literally, but he can't take one's literals literally, he translates them into metaphors for insults, and plans, I'm reasonably happy to inform you, to move out at once. So I've managed one useful thing today, after all. When we come to think of his replacement, let's narrow our moral vision slightly, and settle for a pair of respectably married and out of date homosexuals who still think they've something to hide. They'll leave us entirely alone, and we can congratulate ourselves on doing them a good turn. We'll have to raise the rent to just this side of exorbitant, of course, or they'll smell something fishy, but we'll pass the money straight on to charities for the aged, unmarried mothers, that sort of thing, and no one need be the wiser, what do you think?

Beth In other words, you do know.

Simon In other words, can't we confine ourselves to the other words?

Beth What did Stephen tell you, please, Simon?

Simon Nothing. Nothing, except for the odd detail, that I haven't known for a long time. So you see it's all right. Nothing's changed for the worse, though it might if we assume we have to talk about it.

Beth (*long pause*) How long have you known for?

Simon Oh – (*Sighs.*) – about ten months it would be, roughly. (*Pause.*) How long has it been going on for?

Beth For about ten months, it would be. (*Pause.*) How did you know?

Simon There's no point, Beth –

Beth Yes, there is. Yes, there is. How did you know?

Simon Well, frankly, your sudden habit, after years of admirable conversational economy on such day-to-day matters as what you'd done today, of becoming a trifle prolix.

Beth You mean you knew I was having an affair because I became boring?

Simon No, no, over-detailed, that's all, darling. And quite naturally, as you were anxious to account for stretches of time in which you assumed I *would* be interested if I knew how you'd *actually* filled them, if you see, so you sweetly devoted considerable effort and paradoxically imaginative skill to rendering them – for my sake, I know – totally uninteresting. My eyes may have been glazed but my heart was touched.

Beth Thank you. And is that all you had to go on?

Simon Well, you have doubled your bath routine. Time was, you took one immediately before going out for the day. These ten months you've taken one immediately on return, too. (*Pause.*) And once or twice you've addressed me, when in the twilight zone, with an unfamiliar endearment.

Beth What was it?

Simon Foxy. (*Little pause.*) At least, I took it to be an endearment. Is it?

Beth Yes. I'm sorry.

Simon No, no, it's quite all right.

Beth You haven't felt it's interfered with your sex life then?

Simon On the contrary. *Quite* the contrary. In fact there seems to have been an increased intensity in your –

(*Gestures.*) – which I suppose in itself was something of a sign.

Beth In what way?

Simon Well, guilt, would it be? A desire to make up –

Beth (*after a pause*) And did you know it was Ned, too?

Simon Ned *too*? Oh, did I also know it was Ned? No, that was the little detail I mentioned Stephen did provide. Ned. There I *was* surprised.

Beth Why?

Simon Oh, I don't know. Perhaps because – well, no offence to Ned, whom I've *always* as you know thought of as a very engaging chap, in his way, no offence to *you* either, come to think of it, I'd just imagined when you did have an affair it would be with someone of more – more –

Beth What?

Simon Consequence. *Overt* consequence.

Beth He's of consequence to me.

Simon And *that's* what matters, quite.

Beth What did you mean, when?

Simon Mmmm?

Beth *When* I had an affair, you said.

Simon A grammatical slip, that's all. And since the hypothesis is now a fact –

Beth But you used the emphatic form – when I *did* have an affair – which implies that you positively assumed I'd have an affair. Didn't you?

Simon Well, given your nature, darling, and the fact that so many people do have them these days, I can't see any reason for being *bouleversé* now that you're having one, even with Ned, can I put it that way?

Beth Given what about my nature?

Simon It's marvellously responsive – warm, a warm, responsive nature. And then I realised once we'd taken the decision not to have children – and the fact that you work every day and therefore meet chaps – and pretty exotic ones too, from lithe young Spanish counts to experienced Japanese businessmen – not forgetting old Ned himself – it was only realistic –

Beth From boredom, you mean? You know I'm having an affair because I'm boring, and you assumed I'd have one from boredom. That's why I'm in love with Ned, is it?

Simon I'm absolutely prepared to think of Ned as a very, very lovable fellow. I'm sure *his* wife loves him, why shouldn't mine?

Beth You are being astonishingly hurtful.

Simon I don't want to be, I don't want to be! That's why I tried to avoid this conversation, darling.

Beth You'd like to go back, would you, to where I came in, and pretend that I'd simply caught the early train from Salisbury, and here I was, old unfaithful Beth, back home and about to take her bath, as usual?

Simon Yes, I'd love to. (*Little pause.*) I thought it was Canterbury.

Beth It was neither. We spent the night in a hotel in Euston, and the morning in Ned's poky little office at the school, agonising.

Simon Agonising? Good God, did you really?

Beth About whether we should give up everything to live together properly.

Simon Properly?

Beth We want, you see, to be husband and wife to each other.

Simon Husband *and* wife to each other? Is Ned up to such double duty? And what did you decide?

Beth Do you care?

Simon Yes.

Beth His wife isn't well. She's been under psychiatric treatment for years. And his daughter is autistic.

Simon Oh. I'm sorry. I can quite see why he wants to leave them.

Beth But I could still leave you.

Simon Yes.

Beth But you don't think I will. Do you?

Simon No.

Beth And why not?

Simon Because I hope you'd rather live with me than anybody else, except Ned, of course. And I know you'd rather live with almost anyone than live alone.

Beth You think I am that pathetic?

Simon I don't think it's pathetic. I'd rather live with you than anyone else, including Ned. And I don't want to live alone either.

Beth But do you want to live at all?

Simon What?

163

Beth As you hold such a deeply contemptuous view of human life. That's Ned's diagnosis of you.

Simon But the description of my symptoms came from you, did it?

Beth He says you're one of those men who only give permission to little bits of life to get through to you. He says that while we may envy you your serenity, we should be revolted by the rot from which it stems. Your sanity is of the kind that causes people to go quietly mad around you.

Simon What an elegant paraphrase. Tell me, did you take notes?

Beth I didn't have to. Every word rang true.

Simon But if it's all true, why do you need to keep referring it back to Ned?

Beth It's a way of keeping in touch with him. If I forgot in the middle of a sentence that he's there and mine, I might begin to scream at you and claw at you and punch at you.

Simon But why should you want to do that?

Beth Because I hate you.

> *The telephone rings. Simon makes a move towards it. After the fourth ring, it stops.*

Simon Oh, of course. I've put on the machine.

> *Pause.*

Beth (*quietly*) You know the most insulting thing, that you let me go on and on being unfaithful without altering your manner or your behaviour one – one – you don't care about me, or my being in love with somebody else, or my betraying you, good God! Least of all that! But you do wish I hadn't actually *mentioned* it, because then we could have gone on, at least *you* could, pretending that everything was all right, no, not even pretending, as far as *you* were concerned, everything was all right, you probably still think it is all right – and – and – you've – you've – all those times we've made love, sometimes the very same evening as Ned and I – and yet you took me – in your usual considerate fashion, just as you take your third of a bottle of wine with dinner or your carefully measured brandy and your cigar after it, *and* enjoyed it all the more because I felt guilty, God help me, *guilty*, and so tried harder for your sake – and you *admit* that, no, not admit it, simply state it as if on the difference made by an extra voice or something in your bloody Wagner – don't you see, don't you see that that makes you a freak! You're – you're – oh, damn! Damn. Damn you. (*Pause.*) Oh, damn. (*There is a silence.*) So you might as well listen to your Wagner.

Simon I must say you've quite warmed me up for it. And what are *you* going to do, have your cleansing bath?

Beth No, go to Ned for a couple of hours.

Simon Oh dear, more agonising in his poky little office. Or is that a euphemism for Ned's brand of love-play? Excuse me, but what precisely has all this been about? You complain of my reticence over the last ten months, but what good has all this exposition served, what's it been for, Beth? Ned's not going to leave his wife, I don't want you to leave me, you don't even think you're going to leave me – we have a perfectly sensible arrangement, we are happy enough together, you and I, insultingly so, if you like, but still happy. We could go on and on, with Ned, until you've gone off him. Why, why did you have to muck it up between you with your infantile agonizings?

Beth Because there's a problem.

Simon What problem?

Beth I'm going to have a baby.

Simon (*stares at her for a long moment*) What? (*another moment*) Whose?

Beth *That* is the problem.

> *She goes out. Simon sits in a state of shock. Dave enters left.*

Dave (*stands grinning at Simon*) Well, I worked it out, you'll be unhappy to hear. Suzy put me on to you. She just laughed when I told her the stuff you'd said, she and her bloke had dealings with your type in their last place. You were trying to get me out, that's all. Well, it hasn't worked, see. I'm staying. See. And another thing, Suzy and her bloke are looking for a new place. I said they could move in upstairs with me. Got that? Got that? You won't like tangling with them either. (*Stares at Simon.*) Having a bit of trouble sinking in, is it?

> *Turns, goes out, leaving the door open. Simon remains sitting, dazed. Then he goes to the drinks table, pours himself a small Scotch. Looks at it. Frowns. Adds some more. Stands uncertainly, looks at the telephone, goes over to it. Remembers something vaguely, presses the play-back machine.*

Wood (*his voice*) Hello, Hench, Bernard Wood, *né* Strapley here. I expect by now my little visit has passed entirely out of your consciousness, it was all of an hour ago that I left, and you've no doubt had any number of amusing little things to engage your attention. Your life goes on its self-appointed way, as I sit in my empty flat, my home. I've taken off my jacket, and I've lowered my braces so that they dangle around me – a picture, you

might say, of old Wood, *né* Strapley, quite abandoned
at the last. Imagine it, the jacket off, the braces down,
thinking of you as I speak into the telephone, clasped
tightly in my left hand as my right brings up, not
trembling too much – Hench – sweet little Hench – and
point the gun at my forehead – no, through the – no,
I can't do the mouth, the metal tastes too intimate – it'll
have to be – picture it – picture it – and as I – as I –
Hench, as I squeeze – squee –

> *Simon switches off the machine, interrupting the*
> *message. He sits motionless. Jeff appears in the*
> *doorway, left.*

Simon (*sees him, gets up slowly*) Ah yes. Jeff. All right,
are we then? Get back to – (*Thinks.*) – Oxford, did you?

Jeff I didn't get to the bloody corner.

Simon Oh really. Why not?

Jeff There was a police car, Simon, right behind me, then
right beside me, then right on bloody top of me with the
cops all bloody over me, breathalysing me, shaking me
about, and then down at the station for the rest of it.
That's why bloody not. And you tipped the buggers off,
friend, Christ!

Simon What? (*vaguely*) What?

Jeff No, don't deny it, don't deny it, please Christ don't
deny it. Davina told me when I phoned her. She told me –
you tipped them off. Christ!

Simon Oh. (*Thinks.*) That's what you believe, is it?

Jeff That's what I bloody know, Simon.

Simon (*calmly*) What sort of man do you think I am?
(*He throws his Scotch in Jeff's face.*) What sort of man
do you think I am?

Jeff (*sputtering, gasping*) Christ, Christ! My eyes! My eyes!

Simon watches him a moment, then takes out his handkerchief, gives it to Jeff.

Christ – (*Takes the handkerchief.*) Thanks. (*Little pause.*) Thanks. (*Little pause.*) Sorry. Sorry, Simon. (*Pause, goes and sits down.*) Can I have a drink? (*Pause.*) The bitch.

Simon hesitates, then goes and gets him a Scotch, brings it to him.

Thanks.

There is a pause.

Don't throw me out, eh? I've got nowhere to bloody go, and I don't want to go there yet.

Simon I'm going to play *Parsifal*. Do you mind?

Jeff No, lovely. Lovely.

Simon You sure?

Jeff Christ, yes. You know I adore Wagner.

Simon No, I didn't know that.

Jeff Christ, I introduced you. At Oxford. I bloody introduced you.

Simon Did you really? (*Looks at him.*) Such a long time ago. Then I owe you more than I can say. Thank you, Jeff.

Goes over to the hi-fi, puts on the record. The opening bars of Parsifal *fill the theatre. They sit listening as the music swells.*

The light fades. Curtain.

CLOSE OF PLAY

For Piers

Close of Play was first performed in the Lyttelton auditorium of the National Theatre, London, on 24 May 1979. The cast was as follows:

Jasper Sir Michael Redgrave
Daisy Annie Leon
Henry Michael Gambon
Marianne Anna Massey
Benedict John Standing
Margaret Lynn Farleigh
Jenny Zena Walker
Matthew Adam Godley or Matthew Ryan

Directed by Harold Pinter
Designed by Eileen Diss
Lighting by Leonard Tucker

Characters

Jasper
Daisy
Henry
Marianne
Benedict
Margaret
Jenny
Matthew

Act One

The curtain rises on the stage in darkness. There is the sound of organ music, at first faint, then swelling until it fills the theatre. As it does so, a faint pool of light spreads over Jasper in his armchair. He appears to be asleep. The music stops mid-chord. Jasper opens his eyes as the rest of the lights come up steadily, until the room is filled with bright summer sunshine.

Off, left, from beyond the French windows in the garden, the sound of children playing football. Henry's voice sounds among theirs.

Daisy (*comes through, on the run, goes to the French windows, calls out*) Henry – Henry, dear – will you ask them to keep it right down – right down, dear – because of the windows – oh, they can't hear – and as they're going to the Piece later on, surely they can wait – and Marianne's forgotten Nindy's potty again, can you believe. I know what she says about wee-wee being perfectly hygienic and Romans brushing their teeth in it but I don't like her putting her on our soup tureen, do you? But oh, good heavens, Jasper, you've got the lights on, didn't you realise dear, you don't need the lights now it's so light – it's not going to rain for a bit yet, you know – (*turning them off*) – there – there, that's better, isn't it? Now then, tell me, what did you think of the dumplings, nobody's mentioned them, I was afraid they hadn't thawed right through and I saw your face when you bit into one, you didn't bite into ice, did you, dear? I know how you hate cold in your mouth – it goes right through your system I know. Is that what happened, did you bite on ice?

Jenny enters, left, carrying a shopping bag.

Oh there you are, dear, back already, that was quick.

Jenny Is Matthew here?

Daisy What, Matthew? No dear, isn't he with you? He ran after you to catch you up, didn't he, Jasper?

Jenny Oh, what a nuisance. Why on earth didn't he stay here, as I told him?

Daisy What, dear? Well, never mind, you got the muffins did you – that's the main thing. (*Going to take them.*)

Jenny Oh yes, well, I'm afraid I could only get a dozen, Nanty, so I got half-a-dozen rock cakes as well, I hope that's all right.

Daisy What, what do you mean, but I ordered a dozen and a half muffins specially, didn't I, Jasper? They promised to keep them, they swore they would. Did you say who they were for, did you say they were for Professor Jasper Spencer?

Jenny Well no, I think I said they were for you, Miss Blightforth –

Daisy Oh, well, that explains it, you should have said Professor Jasper Spencer – they know his name in all the shops, don't they, Jasper, particularly the baker's. Well, never mind, dear, but rock cakes you say, I don't know who's going to eat rock cakes –

Jenny Matthew loves them, I know.

Daisy What, Matthew? Well of course if Matthew – anyway, how much is that I owe you, dear? The muffins are three and a half p. each, I know, at least they were last week and they can't have gone up again in spite of the Common Market, can they, Jasper?

Jenny Oh please, let them be my contribution – as a matter of fact I –

Daisy What, certainly not. Good heavens, we wouldn't dream, would we, Jasper, you're our guests, you know – so say three and a half p. the muffins – now Matthew's rock cakes dear, how much were they?

Jenny Oh four p. I think, but really Nanty –

Daisy What, four p. Did you hear that, Jasper, four p.? Matthew's rock cakes! So that's three and a half times twelve equals forty-two – now, where's my handbag – the muffins plus six times four equals twenty-four, the rock cakes – it was on the table, I know! Plus forty-two the muffins comes to sixty-six p. Ah here it is: sixty-six p. I owe altogether, dear. (*Rooting around in her handbag.*) Oh, but it's not here, but I'm sure I put it back after the milkman. Jasper, do you know what I did with it?

Jenny Actually, Nanty, I do think I'd better get back to the High, you see Matthew's only got today off from school, I have to take him back first thing tomorrow. (*Moving off left.*) So I'll see you later.

Daisy What? But it was here, you know, you know the one Jasper, small, green, in velours, you gave it to me yourself, you know how careful I am –

Margaret enters through the arch.

Oh hello, dear, we're just looking for my purse, my small green one in velours, you haven't seen it, have you?

Margaret No, I'm sorry, I haven't.

Daisy That's strange, where on earth . . . thank you so much for the dishes.

Margaret The dishes?

Daisy Helping Marianne with them, so sweet of you.

Margaret Actually Nanty, I'm afraid I didn't.

Daisy What? Oh, then she's had to do them all by herself, oh dear, well – well, never mind, she'll have finished them by now almost won't she, Jasper? So you come and tell us all your news, dear, it's so difficult at lunch, isn't it, with all Henry's and Marianne's little ones, and it's such a long time since we've seen you and Benedict, we're dying to hear all about your adventures on that TV programme. We saw you, you know, did Jasper tell you? Sitting there as cool as a cucumber with a beret on, wasn't it, and the way you talked to that little man with the working-class accent – where was he from, anyway?

Margaret Oxford.

Daisy What, not the University, you don't mean?

Margaret Yes. All Souls –

Daisy Good heavens, Jasper, did you hear that – the little working-class man who interviewed Margaret was from Oxford. Aren't you glad you didn't take that Chair after all? Well, you certainly put him in his place, dear, asking you all those questions and paying you those ridiculous compliments, and you just saying yes and no as if you couldn't be bothered with him to the manner born, I always say Jasper should have been on TV, don't I, Jasper, especially now they've got colour, because of his white mane, you know, so distinguished, but I suppose they're not interested in Latin translations and mediaeval what-nots, dear, you should have been a novelist like Margaret, dear, and you could too, couldn't he, Margaret, with his imagination, not that yours isn't very interesting too, dear, oh yes, I've read your novel, you know, as soon as I heard you and Benedict were really coming

down at last I went straight out and borrowed a copy
from the library, didn't I, Jasper?

Benedict enters through the French windows.

Benedict Oh, you're in here, are you darling? I've been
waiting for you in the garden for our little walk.

Daisy Oh well, she's been talking to your father, dear,
telling us all about her success and fame and what have
you, you must be so proud of her, dear.

Benedict What, Nanty?

Daisy What, dear?

There is a pause.

Proud of her, I mean.

Benedict Oh. Maggie, you mean?

Daisy Yes, dear.

Benedict Yes. Yes I am, Nanty. Very proud. (*Little
pause.*) Very proud. Very very proud. Aren't I, darling?
Um – um – (*Sits down.*)

Daisy Are you all right, dear? Is he all right?

Benedict What, Nanty?

Daisy Are you all right, dear? You've been very quiet
and grave, you know, all through lunch, and he hardly
ate a thing, Jasper, did he Margaret? You didn't touch
the dumplings didn't you like them?

Benedict Oh. Oh well, I'm not very – very keen on food
at the moment, am I, darling?

Daisy But you didn't speak either, hardly a word, and
look at you now, not at all your usual self, is he, Jasper –
but I know – I know what you want to cheer you up,

oh, how silly of me to have forgotten when I went to all
the trouble of remembering to get it in specially, but then
it's your fault, it's been such a long time since you came
to see us, now where did I put it? – Oh in the hall – or –
anyway, Jasper, you tell him all our news while I go and
find it – I'll be right back, dear. (*Going off left.*)

There is a pause.

Margaret (*goes to Benedict, sits down beside him*)
You're doing marvellously, darling.

Benedict What, darling?

Margaret Marvellously.

Benedict I feel – I feel –

Margaret I can imagine, darling. I can.

Benedict (*emotionally*) I know. I know you can. Thank
you, darling. (*Looks towards Jasper.*) Daddy – I – um –
I know I owe you an explanation for not being in touch
for such a long time. The truth is, I've been going –
going through rather a bad time, haven't I, darling? And
– and I didn't want to worry you. I expect you can guess
what it was. My drinking. Well, not to put too fine a
point on it, I wasn't just getting drunk now and then,
which is what you must have thought, Daddy, I was
actually on my way to becoming an alcoholic, wasn't I,
darling? So Maggie finally – bless her – put it to me that
I had to choose. Between her and my Scotch. And she
meant it. Didn't you, darling? She really meant it. So I –
I put myself in the hands of a psychiatrist who had a
very good reputation – at least some friends of Maggie's
thought very highly of him, didn't they, darling – Roger
and Liza – but he turned out to be an old-fashioned,
rather hard-line Freudian. So as far he was concerned,
I was classic text-book stuff. Went into all my relation-

ships – sibling rivalry, of course – you know, that I'd
always been jealous of Henry and Dick – Dick particularly,
of course, said one of the reasons I drank was because
I was guilty because I was glad that Dick was dead and –
well, you can imagine – and you, of course, Daddy,
which he got down to the old penis envy, naturally, and
when I told him I'd never actually seen your penis so
how could I envy it, it might be smaller than mine, after
all – (*Laughs.*) Well, that was in our first session, believe
it or not – eventually he got on to Maggie, of course,
said I envied *her* penis, didn't he, darling – in the form of
her talent, you see – and on top of all his – his clap-trap,
he was a pretty heavy drinker himself, I could smell
alcohol on his breath and – well, by and large he was
making things worse not better but of course the trouble
was – I did develop a degree of dependence on him and –
well, God knows what would have happened to me if
I hadn't finally broken free – with the help of, well,
Maggie, of course, I can't tell you how wonderful –
wonderful! she's been – but also of a new chap I
happened to hear about at the BBC – Vintross. Norman
Vintross. It's because of him that I haven't touched a
drop of Scotch for – what is it, darling – six, no, no,
he insists on an absolutely ruthless accounting – it's part
of his therapy, five, five weeks, Daddy, isn't it, darling?

Margaret Days, isn't it, darling?

Benedict What?

Margaret Days, I think, darling.

Benedict Yes, darling?

Margaret Didn't you say weeks?

Benedict Oh, good God, did I really? (*Laughs.*) Days
I meant, of course, Daddy, six days. But when you think
what I was up to – four bottles a day, Daddy.

Margaret More like three really, wasn't it, darling?

Benedict Oh now, darling – well, between three and four – three and a half on a good day, bad day, that's what Vintross has to contend with, Daddy, so in my view he's a bit of a genius, quite simply. But absolutely practical, that's his great – his great, isn't it, darling?

Margaret But he does fairly sophisticated things too, doesn't he darling? Hypnosis for example.

Benedict God yes, and you should see his eyes when he's putting me under, Daddy – brrr – like chips of blue ice, little chips of blue ice, aren't they, darling?

Margaret Well, I've never met him, don't forget, darling.

Benedict Oh. No, of course you haven't – but what he goes for above all is character, Daddy. In the traditional sense, rather like a Scots schoolteacher, eh Maggie? Says I've only one basic problem: I'm weak. Feeble. Gutless. A moral no-hoper. So the only possible solution for types like me is to avoid drink altogether. To stay out of pubs and licensed restaurants – I virtually move with the luncheon voucher set now, Daddy, and he's even shown me a trick for dealing with the BBC parties I can't get out of – he says most of the newsreaders have had to come to him at one time or another – anyway, how to stand – look, legs splayed and hands locked behind my back – (*Does it.*) to make it difficult to whip a glass from a passing tray or otherwise receive one –

Margaret Darling, I think I'll go for a little walk.

Benedict What, on your own, you mean?

Margaret Well, I think you and your father should have some time together –

Benedict Oh, well, that's all right, isn't it, Daddy? Don't go on our account – unless you want to do a bit of

creative mulling, of course – did you know Maggie's just
begun a new novel, Daddy – last week – isn't that
marvellous! and I expect she's frightened that I'm going
to launch into one of my panegyrics about what she's
meant to me – her support and – (*Takes her hand, kisses
it.*) – and in fact you can thank her for our getting down
to see you at last, Daddy, she absolutely insisted we
come, didn't you, darling, – well then, don't be too long –
I'll miss you –

Margaret exits through door left.

Benedict Isn't she remarkable, Daddy? Oh, I don't just
mean in her talent, although that's remarkable enough,
God knows, when you think what the odds were against
her finishing it. I mean me, of course, I was the odds.
Because you see, Daddy – oh, it sounds so bizarre now,
but in my worst phase – when I was adding Scotch to my
breakfast coffee, you know *that* stage – I got it into my
head that – well, that she was having an affair. A real
love affair, you see – and what made it more dreadful,
more nightmarish, was that I thought it was with
someone I knew but I didn't know who, if you follow –
I knew I knew the chap, even though there wasn't a chap
at all – not even evidence, Daddy, which of course simply
made me more insane. It got so I started to pick quarrels
with friends, people I work with at the Beeb, interpreting
their remarks, their looks, even – eventually even their
smells – tried to sniff them, if they'd been out of their
offices a suspiciously long time – and of course trying to
catch poor Maggie in the act, taxi-ing home at any hour,
climbing in through the lavatory window so they
wouldn't hear me in the hall, then up the stairs in my
socks, flinging her study door open after crouching
outside it for hours – and there she'd be, typing calmly
away, with her glasses on – you know she wears glasses
for her writing – and of course the inevitable cigarette

hanging from her lips, and she'd give me such a distracted,
absent-minded look, as if for a second she didn't know
who I was, let alone why I was there – and so – more
and more often I'd go, well, berserk – quite berserk – and
oh God – well, the drink, you see, and knowing she was
being unfaithful and not knowing who with but knowing
I knew him and then realising it was all a delusion – but
now when I think, think of the hell I put her through,
what she's suffered – endured because of me – well, even
Vintross, who's pretty tough about these things, was
appalled when I told him – he said – he said that I – I –
was a lucky man to have such an unlucky wife – (*Puts
his hand to his eyes, in tears.*) Sorry. Sorry, Daddy – but
I – I've always loved her, you know, but now – now –
sorry – I'll be – I'll be all right – (*Sits, overcome.*)

Daisy (*enters from left, carrying a Scotch bottle*) Upstairs
– it was upstairs in my bedroom, in the carrier bag, you
see, the one with the pink wool and the doorknob,
anyway, I've found it, that's the thing. (*pouring some into
a glass*) I got it in specially for you, because I remembered
how you like to settle down with a nice large one after
lunch – there, dear, you keep it beside you so you know
where it is – what, dear?

Benedict (*is staring appalled from the Scotch to Daisy*)
Nothing. (*Laughs.*) Nothing, Nanty that a – a Vintrossian
gesture . . . (*Gets up.*)

Daisy What, dear?

Benedict I've just realised that I haven't – haven't given
you a proper cuddle yet, Nanty – (*Goes over, puts his
arms around her.*) There, now I feel safe, eh, Daddy?
From temptation and harm.

Daisy Aaaah – aaaah – I always say you're the feeling
one, don't I, Jasper, feel things so quickly – anyway,

that's cheered you up, has it? I knew it would, didn't
I, Jasper, and it's a malt, you know – I asked for a malt –
and now you can relax and tell us some of your funny
stories about your life at the BBC – I was just thinking
the other day about my favourite, wasn't I, Jasper, that
Hugh Rhys-what's-it on the religious talks programme of
yours, the one who does the interviewing sometimes, you
used to keep us in stitches about, every time I hear him
talking things over with bishops and atheists and such
I laugh out loud, I do, don't I Jasper, he sounds so solemn
and Welsh, but there he was getting himself locked in his
office cupboard with his secretary and she thought – oh
dear, all those scratches, poor man! (*laughing*) And that
quarrel with his wife over the dish-washer he insisted
took saucepans and suds all over the kitchen floor short-
whatnotting the fridge and the ice-cream gateau for his
daughter's birthday melting into the fish for the cat – oh
dear, oh dear – (*laughing*) what's he been up to recently,
your Hugh Rhys-what's-it, something hilarious, do tell
us?

Benedict (*who has moved away from Daisy, grinning
fixedly, his hands locked behind his back*) He's – um –
actually he's dead, Nanty.

Daisy What, dear?

Benedict Dead.

Daisy Good heavens, do you hear that, Jasper? Hugh
Rhys-thing – but how, how, dear?

Benedict Oh, it was a – well, as a – what happened
apparently – (*Stops.*)

Daisy What, dear?

Benedict (*looks yearningly towards the Scotch*) Well –
well actually, Nanty, do you mind – (*Goes and sits down*

some distance from the Scotch.) – if we – I – I don't go
into it at the moment, I'm – you see it – it upsets me to
think about it because in a way, well, in as much as
I used to – to make him a bit of a butt and forgot how
fond – how fond – you know what I mean, don't you,
Daddy, perhaps you could explain – explain to Nanty?

> *Sits, head lowered. There is a slight pause. Off, the
> sound of boys' voices, and Henry's getting louder as
> they advance in a rush. A ball bounces into the room
> and towards Jasper.*

Daisy Of all the – of all the –

Henry (*bounds in through the French windows, breathing
hard and sweating*) Oh golly – everyone all right?

Daisy Well, dear, it nearly bounced into your father's
face, didn't it, Jasper?

Henry Oh, sorry, Daddy – (*Takes the ball from Daisy.*)
All right, boys – (*going to the French windows*) – now
keep it down at the bottom – right to the bottom –
(*Throws the ball out.*)

Daisy Yes, dear, but you see I can't help worrying about
the windows –

Henry No, further down, Tom – right down – (*Turns.*)
We're going to the Piece soon, Nanty, so don't worry –

Daisy I know, dear, so couldn't they wait until then –
because even at the bottom there are the outhouse
windows –

Henry (*has gone to the drinks table, squirted himself
some soda water*) Whew! (*draining it off*) You were wise
to stay out of that, Ben, I remind me of that chap, I told
you about him, didn't I, Daddy? (*Squirts some more.*)

Daisy You do see what I mean, don't you, dear?

Henry – did a dozen laps around the park in the sun, gulped down a jug of lemonade, dropped dead.

Daisy I don't want to spoil their fun, you know that, dear, but – what, good heavens, why?

Henry Bad heart, Nanty.

Daisy Well then, why did he do it, run a dozen times around in the heat – any fool knows that's madness, don't they, Jasper, why did he, dear?

Henry Well, actually, now I come to think of it, because I told him to, Nanty.

Daisy What, oh well, of course that's different, dear – but why did you?

Henry I must have thought he needed the exercise, I suppose. Perhaps if he'd taken enough of it earlier, he wouldn't have killed himself taking it later.

Daisy So really he only had himself to blame, you mean, dear.

Henry Well, no. Really he had me to blame, didn't he? Or would have, if he'd survived. But to be fair to myself, I didn't tell him to do his running in the midday sun, nor to gulp down ice-cold lemonade afterwards. At least I hope I didn't. But on the other hand I certainly didn't warn him not to, either. But then I didn't know at the time he had a bad heart. And nor did he, come to that. Still, we got to the right diagnosis between us at the end, didn't we? Poor chap. I liked him rather a lot, he played the clarinet for the LSO, I always try not to think of him every time I hear that Mozart piece you're so fond of, Daddy, how does it go – you remember it, Ben? (*Tries to hum a few bars.*)

Daisy Oh, I know – (*Hums it very pleasantly.*)

*Henry joins in. Daisy and Henry hum the opening
section.*

Henry (*squirts more soda water*) And here I am myself,
my stomach packed with casserole, golly, it was good,
Nanty, wasn't it, Ben – *and* jacket potatoes and those
doughy things –

Daisy Dumplings, dear, did you like them?

Henry Oh damn!

Daisy What, dear?

Henry I'm on call today and I think I forgot to leave
your number, Daddy – well, I expect they'll know where
I am. And anyway, the call I don't make may save a life,
eh? (*Laughs.*)

Daisy Oh, don't be silly, Henry, you're a very good
doctor, isn't he, Jasper, isn't he, Ben, a very good doctor,
Henry –?

Marianne (*enters from left flourishing a child's potty*)
Dumdee-dee-dum-dum-dee-dee-dum – it was under my
seat all the time, Nanty. In the van.

Daisy What? Oh good, dear, I'm so glad – but isn't he a
very good doctor, Henry?

Marianne I should jolly well say he is, who says he isn't?

Daisy Henry, dear.

Marianne Oh ho, at it again, are we, hubby mine? I don't
know what's been getting into him recently apart from
the usual overwork, but the only thing wrong with him
is that he's too jolly good a doctor, isn't he, Gramps, and
cares far too much and won't let himself let up for a
minute. Have you heard about his latest acquisition,
I bet he hasn't even mentioned her, has he?

Daisy Who, dear?

Marianne Mrs O'Killiam, Nanty.

Daisy Oh, is that the lady whose hair has been falling out, and wants a golden wig on the National Health –?

Marianne No, no, Nanty, that's poor old ga-ga Mrs MacDougall, no, Mrs O'Killiam's a real case, in fact she's simply the most desperate case in the whole practice, Gramps, none of the others will touch her with a bargepole.

Henry Now, darling, that isn't quite true –

Marianne Oh yes it is, darling, you know perfectly well her husband's in jail for some quite unspeakable offence against an eighty-year-old woman, Gramps –

Daisy Why, what did he do to her?

Marianne Well, for one thing he –

Henry Darling, I don't think – um, you know –

Marianne All right, darling, for Nanty's sake –

Daisy No no, I like hearing about things like that, don't I, Jasper?

Marianne Anyway, Gramps, as if that wasn't bad enough she's got two brutes of sons of about twelve and fourteen who are always in trouble with the police themselves –

Henry Well, of course, with their background –

Marianne Oh I know, darling, absolutely no chance, and a little girl called Carla –

Henry Wanda, darling.

Marianne – who's hydrocephalic, Gramps.

Daisy What, dear?

Marianne Water on the brain, Nanty. (*holding her hands away from her head*)

Daisy Oh, we've got one of those, haven't we, Jasper, he rides past here on his bicycle looking like Humpty Dumpty, poor thing –

Marianne But the worst of it is she's in a hideous way herself, I shall never forget Henry's description of her the first time he saw her, Gramps. He said, he said to himself as soon as he clapped eyes on her, 'Hello! Carcinoma!' didn't you, darling?

Daisy Hello who, dear?

Henry Although actually I was wrong, it's almost certainly a form of anorexia nervosa –

Marianne Well, anyway, she's called him around every night this week, and after surgery too, he comes back looking grey with fatigue, Nanty – and this morning, Gramps, just as we were leaving one of her boys turned up and told Henry his mum wanted him straight away –

Henry But I really don't mind, darling –

Marianne Oh, I saw that look on your face before, of course, he said, of course, Gramps, and you would have gone too, wouldn't you, if I hadn't asked him if it couldn't wait until this evening? And do you know what he said, you didn't hear, did you darling, the little squat one with the dribble and the funny lip, he said – well, he'd fucking well better come then.

Daisy What, dear?

Marianne Sorry everybody, but that's what he said.

Henry Oh, it's his normal vocabulary, he talks to everybody like that, and I *am* on call, darling.

Marianne Yes, darling, when aren't you on call? I'd better get this to Nindy before it's too late, if it isn't already.

Daisy Oh, and thank you for doing the dishes, dear!

Marianne What, oh golly, Nanty, did you mean for me to do them?

Daisy What, you mean you haven't, you mean!

Marianne No, Nanty, I'm sorry, I haven't.

Daisy But I saw you at the sink, you see, so I assumed – I wish I'd known you weren't going to do them, dear, because then I could have got them over and done with by now myself, you see.

Marianne Well, honestly, Nanty, one moment we were all in the kitchen, and then Jenny'd gone –

Daisy To get the muffins, dear.

Marianne And then old Margaret had sloped off somewhere – and then you'd vanished –

Daisy Only because I was worried about the ball and the windows –

Marianne Oh golly, well let me deal with Nindy and I'll come back and do your dishes for you, all right? (*Goes out through the French windows.*)

Daisy No no, dear, I'll do them, I don't mind doing them, oh, I do hope she didn't think I meant – Henry, you don't think she thought I meant –

Henry No no, Nanty, of course she didn't – but hey, I haven't asked after your headaches – Nanty's been getting some very bad headaches, Ben, hasn't she, Daddy? (*Putting his arm around Daisy.*)

Daisy Oh, they've been terrible recently, haven't they Jasper? I've tried doing what you said, lying on a hard surface in a dark room with moist pads over my eyes, but it doesn't stop the throbbing or the nosebleeds, does it, Jasper?

Henry Nosebleeds?

Daisy Oh yes, terrible nosebleeds and a humming in my ears and seeing things double –

Henry I see. Well, Nanty, I think we ought to have someone take a proper look at you. I can't promise he'll cure them but I won't let him make them any worse.

Daisy Oh, Henry – aaah – so kind, so thoughtful – oh, and look, dear, tell Marianne she's not to touch the dishes, I never meant her to, you know – they won't take a minute, tell her – (*going out through the arch*)

Henry Actually, Daddy, I think I'd better try and fix up an appointment for Nanty as soon as possible – nothing to worry about, just a few tests, X-rays, that sort of thing – all quite routine, but to put our minds at rest, we don't want anything happening to our Nanty, do we, Ben?

Benedict (*who has been gazing at floor, hands locked*) Mmmm?

Henry You all right?

Benedict Oh. Oh well, um – yes, yes. Thanks.

Henry I must say it's terrific to have you here again after all this time.

Benedict Oh. Yes. Thanks. Thanks, Henry.

Henry And Maggie, too.

Benedict Oh, she was very keen to come. Very keen.
Very very keen.

Henry Oh. Well, that's flattering, eh, Daddy? Where is
she, by the way? I've hardly had a chance to speak to
her.

Benedict No.

Henry What?

Benedict What?

Henry Maggie?

Benedict Oh. Oh yes.

Henry Has she gone out?

Benedict Yes. Yes, I think so, yes. For a walk, hasn't she,
Daddy – something to do with her novel, you see. She
gets these fits. Inspiration, I suppose. Yes.

Henry Are you sure you're all right, Ben?

Benedict No. No, I seem – something slightly wrong
with my – my stomach – perhaps those doughnuts in the
casserole – but very queasy.

Henry I'll get you some Alka Seltzer, where is it, Daddy?

Benedict What – oh no, no, not Alka Seltzer, never works
for me – besides I don't want to make a fuss – I'll tell you
– I'll tell you what, (*getting up*) perhaps a drop – just a
little drop of this might do something for me. (*Picks up
the glass with a trembling hand, takes an enormous
gulp.*) Have to be careful though, eh, Daddy, no back-
sliding, eh? You see, Henry, I was telling Daddy, I've
given this stuff up virtually at last, haven't I, Daddy? I go
to a chap, you see.

Henry A chap?

Benedict Yes. His name's Vintross. A bit of a genius in my view. He's been treating me for – things.

Henry Oh. A psychiatrist.

Benedict No. A pediatrician, actually. But he does things like me on the side. Privately. God you should see his eyes when he's doing hypnosis, I was telling Daddy about them, wasn't I, Daddy? (*pouring himself more Scotch*) They're the deepest-brown eyes I've ever seen, and they burn, burn, down – he's bloody expensive, you can imagine.

Henry Yes. Yes. I can.

Benedict But then that's part of his treatment, you see. Charges the equivalent of a double Scotch for every three minutes of his time, he worked it out at. You're not cured, he said, until you get my bill. If you can look at it without taking a drink, there's hope, and if you pay it you won't be able to afford a drink, apart from meths, of course, and if you don't pay it, I sue. (*Laughs.*) Vintage Vintross, that is. Jokes are a part of his style.

Henry Oh – oh well, he sounds just the job, doesn't he, Daddy?

   Matthew enters through left door, stands uncertainly.

Oh hello, Mat, and what have you been up to?

Matthew Oh – um – well, um – nothing, um – (*Laughs.*)

Henry How's the soccer coming?

Matthew Oh – well, I mean, um – you know.

Henry Made a team yet?

Matthew Well – just the house team.

Henry Oh, well that's jolly good – isn't it Ben? Congratters, Mat.

Matthew Oh – well, um, thanks. (*Laughs.*)

Henry Oh and hey, I don't know if Marianne mentioned to you – we're taking the boys to the Piece soon for a footer around – why don't you come along and show them what you can do, and then show me how to do it, eh?

Matthew Oh – well – I – Mummy asked me to go for a walk with her, you see – I – I – was meant to meet her at the baker's but well, you haven't seen her?

Henry She hasn't been through here.

Matthew Oh well, she's probably gone looking for – I'd better – better go and see if – um – (*Makes towards the exit, left.*)

Henry Anyway, we'll be on the Piece later if you do want a game –

Matthew Right – right – (*He goes out.*)

Benedict (*who has poured himself more Scotch*) God, he's getting like Dick, isn't he – it makes the brain to reel and the heart to lurch how like Dick he's getting, doesn't it? Is he top dog at school, the way Dick used to be?

Henry Well, actually that reminds me – I was going to mention it, Daddy – and I'm glad you're here, Ben, you can tell me what you think – you see I had a letter from his housemaster the other day, he seems to think of me as in sort of loco parentis and he didn't want to worry Jenny with it – but he's a little concerned about our Mat. Says he's been rather withdrawn this term – well, since Dick's death – well, I suppose that's hardly surprising, but apparently, although he's dropped every one of his old chums, he's taken up with a boy – well, quite a bit younger than himself and – in a nutshell, the housemaster isn't too keen on it. Thinks it's all a bit too hot-housey.

That's why he's wangled Mat into the football team, to make him mix more, you see, although actually Mat's not too good at football, but then this friend of his doesn't play at all. He's an asthmatic.

Benedict Ah-hah! One of those, eh?

Henry What? Well, you see, what troubles me is, I'm not sure he should interfere at all – I mean, the football's all right, if Mat comes to enjoy it – but otherwise, well, this relationship may be filling an important need, mayn't it, and then given how delicate – delicate these matters are, especially at that age – well, what do you think, Daddy?

Benedict (*laughs*) God, doesn't it bring it back, though?

Henry What?

Benedict All of it – the sodomy, buggery, public-school duggery – much more fun than state schools. In state schools you give them ten quid a week, kit them up with contraceptives, hand them a list of VD clinics, pack pot into their lunch boxes, nothing furtive, nothing passionate, nothing to prepare them for life – hey, remember old Prothero, Hen, old Prothero – did we ever tell you about old Prothero, Daddy – used to come and sit on the edge of the bed after lights, tucking in the middle-school chappies, and if there'd been a caning he'd want to inspect the stripes, put on ointment –

Henry Golly yes, old Cheeks! (*Laughs.*)

Benedict That's it! Cheeks – Cheeks Prothero! Had a crush on Dick, didn't he, Hen – and old Coote – Coote Wilson – and – all of them, come to think of it, didn't they, Hen? Had crushes on Dick, fighting over him they were! Like bloody monkeys! God, I'm glad you sent us to one of the best schools in the country, Daddy, aren't you, Hen?

Henry I certainly don't think it did us any harm.

Benedict (*pouring himself another drink*) Vintross is queer. Gay, I mean. Did I tell you?

Henry Is he? No, you didn't.

Benedict He's got this Filipino houseboy. Opens the door, takes your coat. Got a pretty beaten look to him, so I expect there's a cupboard full of things, eh, handcuffs, leg-irons, whips, masks, SS uniforms, that sort of gay, you see. Ballsy-gay. Sometimes his eyes go just like a cat's – a vicious green. You know?

Henry The house-boy's?

Benedict Vintross's. Vintross's eyes.

Henry I thought you said they were brown –

Benedict No, no. Green, eh, Daddy? Vicious green. Like a cat's.

Henry How's the stomach?

Benedict Flat as a board. Keeps himself in top nick, you see. Probably with the Filipino, eh? (*Laughs.*)

Henry No, I meant yours. Is it settling down?

Benedict Oh. Well, still a bit – hey, Hen, I must show Hen, eh Daddy – Vintross's party posture – look – hands so – feet thus – (*Tries to adopt it, still holding his glass, stumbles backwards.*) Oooooooops!

    Henry catches him.

Thanks. See what I mean, bloody difficult.

Henry Yes. (*Watches him, looks anxiously towards Jasper.*) Oh – that reminds me – that little Welsh friend of yours, the one that got his finger stuck in his flies at the Israeli Embassy – we were having a good laugh about him just the other week, weren't we, Daddy? What's he been –? (*laughing*)

Benedict (*laughing*) Old Hugh Rhys – um –

Henry Yes –

Benedict (*stops laughing*) Oh. Dead, Henry.

Henry What?

Benedict Dead. Yes. Dead.

Henry That little Welsh – good God, good God, but – but well how, Ben, what happened?

Benedict Killed himself. Didn't he, Daddy? Telling Daddy and Nanty earlier –

Henry But why?

Benedict Don't know, Henry. Don't know. All I know is that one night last week he got out of bed, told his wife he wanted some air, walked up to Hampstead Heath, took off his trousers, hanged himself.

Henry With his own trousers?

Benedict They found a washing line too, but it had got tangled in the tree.

Henry And he didn't leave a note – nothing to explain –

Benedict Oh yes. He left a note. Pages and pages, in fact. Must have spent the day writing it – alone in his office – pages and pages – pinned them to his shirt.

Henry Well, what did it say?

Benedict Don't know. It rained during the night. Illegible. Every word. Pathetic, eh, Daddy? Poor little Hugh Rhys – um –

There is a pause. Henry releases a sudden wild laugh.

Benedict What?

Henry Oh, I'm sorry – so sorry – don't know where that came from – I certainly didn't mean any disrespect to Hugh – Hugh Rhys, um –

Benedict That's all right, Hen, we know why you laughed, don't we, Daddy? Matter of fact I laughed myself when I heard – I mean trousers, tangled washing line, unreadable suicide note – like all the other stories I used to tell about him. Right?

Henry Well yes, I suppose –

Benedict Except this time he's dead, of course. That's the difference. But a big one. Crucial, in fact.

Henry Yes. Yes, indeed.

Benedict Isn't that right, Daddy? (*Pours himself more Scotch.*) And of course appropriate. Hugh Rhys – um's death. An appropriate death. Like Dick's, in a sense. Eh? (*There is a pause.*) I mean, you think of Dick, the brightest and the best of us, eh, we know that, Daddy, don't we, Henry – well of course he was, because he was just like you, Daddy, wasn't he – fellowships just like you, lectureships just like you, a readership just like you, would have ended up with a professorship just like you. Maybe even an OBE, Daddy, just like you, and then a wife he loved, just like you, Daddy, I mean you loved Mummy, didn't you? The tragedy of your life her death, wasn't it, if you see, and a son he adored, just as you adored him, and is turning out just like him as he went on turning out just like you. Apart from being dead. Just like Mummy. See, Daddy?

Henry No. No. I don't think we do see, quite, Ben. But perhaps we shouldn't discuss –

Benedict No, no, look at it this way. Where was Dick different from Daddy? Where? A bit raffish, right? Bit of an adventurer, right? (*Laughs.*) Reckless. Reckless and raffish – not like Daddy, eh, nobody's ever called you reckless and raffish, have they, Daddy? And so his motorbike. See. See how it fits?

Henry looks towards Jasper.

Roars over here, has one of his intimate chats with Daddy, and then later, far too late, when he was tired, his head spinning with Daddy's ideas and jokes and anecdotes and gossip, eh, Daddy? What does he do? Does he stay the night? Upstairs in bed in his old room? Does he stay the night? No. Not old Dick. Back, back on his motorbike, roaring off again – past Newmarket, past Baldock, Royston, Hitchin – faster and faster, and then off – off the road – hurtling right off the road and over the bank and into the tree into the dark! And we say – we say – if it hadn't been for his motorbike Dick'd still be alive. True. But – but if it hadn't been for Daddy, then he wouldn't be dead. Vintross says. (*Pours himself more Scotch.*) Now do you see?

Henry Well – um, Ben – look, what would Vintross say if he could see the amount of Scotch you're knocking back, old chap?

Benedict Say it was quite all right. As long as I can cope with it in a situation I can't cope with without it. That's what he'd say.

Jenny (*enters left*) Oh, sorry – but has he come back, Matthew?

Henry Yes. But he went out again – I think he was looking for you –

Benedict Hey, Jen, we were just saying about Matthew – so like Dick, isn't he? So like him?

Jenny Yes – yes, I suppose he is –

Benedict Henry was telling us about that letter he got from his housemaster – on his little sexual problems – don't you pay any attention, Jen? Dick had the same, used to steal too, didn't he, Hen? Has Matthew started stealing yet? Well, don't worry, if he turns out like Dick he'll be all right, eh? Apart from being dead, I mean.

Jenny Matthew's housemaster wrote to you?

Henry Yes, well it was just a – nothing to – didn't want to bother you –

Jenny I see. Which way did he go, Matthew?

Henry Out the front way, I think – but Jenny, really –

Jenny goes out left.

Golly, Ben, I do wish you hadn't mentioned that to Jenny.

Benedict What? (*Pouring himself more Scotch.*)

Henry About Matthew. I did say it was confidential, didn't I, Daddy?

Benedict Oh. Right. But there's another thing. The funeral. We've never talked about the funeral, have we, remember it, Daddy? Our standing there in the chapel and they brought him in and put him down on that conveyor belt and that lady started on her organ, that old lady with the deaf-aid. And then the door in the wall, the trapdoor in the wall slid open, and he began to slide towards it and then through it, remember, Hen? You don't do you?

Henry Of course I do, it's just that – well I don't think we should –

Benedict Well, what happened? What happened as he slid through?

There is a pause.

You don't want to say, do you? Well, I don't mind saying. I'll say it, Daddy. What happened as he slid through is – I threw up. That's what happened. Isn't it? Because I was drunk. (*Pause.*) You know, I used to be pretty ashamed about that. Thought I'd disgraced the whole proceedings. That's what I thought. (*Drinks.*) Until Vintross put me right. Know what he said, Vintross? He said it doesn't matter whether you're drunk or sober, sober or drunk, the coffin slides through just the same, the door in the wall slides open just the same, same old lady plays an organ just the same – and then, next please! Next please! You can't disgrace it because you can't even interrupt it. Unless there's a resurrection, of course! (*Laughs.*) Just a business, disposing of the dead. That's how he cuts through things, old Vintross. Right to the heart. (*Pours himself more Scotch.*)

Henry (*goes to him*) Ben, that's enough. Quite enough. (*Tries to take the bottle away.*) Think of Daddy –

Benedict What?

Henry Think of Daddy! (*low and intense*)

Benedict Think of – oh, oh, shit-eating time come round again, eh, Henry? Shit-eating time. Well, let me tell you something else Vintross says.

Henry I don't think we want to hear anything else Vintross –

Benedict He says – he says the trouble with me – he says the reason I was nearly an alcoholic virtually until he got his hands on me – was that all my life I've been made to eat shit, I've been the family shit-eater – apologise, explain, grovel – and he said – when I told him Maggie wanted me to come up, he said – go – he said go – but

on no account – never – never – again – for any reason –
was I to eat shit. Never again, not for you, not for Daddy
even. No more shit-eating. See! Never!

There is a pause.

Marianne (*enters through the French windows laughing*)
Darling, I must show you – (*Shows Henry contents of
pot.*)

Henry Golly, yes!

Marianne It was Gramps' magic, honestly, Gramps! She
sat there straining and straining until I said do it for
Gramps! And out it came. Gushing!

Henry Golly!

Marianne What she must have gone through holding it
back, poor darling – anyway, thank you, Gramps – and
darling, they really are a bit desperate about going to the
Piece, they're loading themselves into the van, so if you'd
just give this a sluice – (*Hands Henry the pot.*)

There is a long honk from off, left.

Oh oh – I told Tom not to – anyway I'll see you out
there – (*Sees Benedict.*) Is everything all right?

Henry Oh yes, fine, fine, just having a jaw!

Marianne The three chaps together, eh? Jolly good for
Gramps.

*Goes out left to another long honk. There is a pause.
Henry looks at Benedict, looks at Jasper, looks at
Benedict again, puts down the pot, goes over. Puts
a hand on Benedict's shoulder.*

Henry We never knew you felt like that, did we, Daddy?
But Ben, I promise you I've never wanted you to eat – and
nor has Daddy, I know – but perhaps it was important

for you to say it, eh, Daddy – and get it out of your system once and for all.

Benedict Old Hen. (*Puts a hand on Henry's hand on his shoulder.*)

Henry Old Ben.

Benedict Old Hen.

Henry You don't think you ought to lie down now? You look – um –

Benedict No – no – I'm all right now. Purged, you see. Purged. Just as Vintross said.

Henry Well that's – that's –

Low honk, off.

Henry Oh I'd better – (*Looks towards Jasper, smiles reassuringly.*) You um – well, you won't have any more of that, though, will you?

Benedict What? Oh no – no – don't need it now – just want a nice calm chat with Daddy now. That's all. Eh, Daddy? Talk over old times. Without – without any – eh, Daddy?

Henry Good. That's the job, eh, Daddy? Well then, see you both later. (*Goes out left.*)

Benedict God, I love Henry, don't you, Daddy? Oh I know Dick was always his favourite brother and he was always Dick's favourite brother and I was the one left out from their favouritism, but God how I loved them both. I suppose that's what I was, am, Daddy, when you think about it, a – a sort of only son with two favourite brothers and a dead mother and a – a father who – who – well, why should you? Nobody has to. (*Gets up, pours himself more Scotch.*) Nobody. Vintross says – (*Gulps*

down Scotch.) My Maggie's frightened of the dark. Did
you know that? My Maggie? I hold her against it very
tight, tight against it, and I say don't be afraid, Maggie,
don't be afraid, my Maggie, I'm here – Ben's here, Ben's
here – and when I painted her study up for her I did it
in light colours, pastel colours, Daddy, and I bought her
a typewriter, and I change her ribbons, you know, all
she has to do is the writing, you see, clackety-clackety,
clackety-clackety – pages on pages, chapters on chapters,
clackety-clackety-clackety, and then when I come back,
grey with fatigue, back from the BBC, and loving her
and holding her and changing her ribbons – up I go to
see her, longing to see her – and she looks at me – she
looks at me as if I wasn't there, Daddy, and never had
been. Never had been. But *he'd* been all right, *he'd* been
– I catch the whiff of him now and then, smell the smell
of his spoor on her, smell it all over her, on my Maggie,
and I know who it is, I know who it is, and one day I'll
get him by his whiff, the whiff of his spoor, or catch
them at it, the two of them. Whoever he is. At their
fuckity-fuckity, clackity-fuckity, fuckity-clackity!
(*Lurches sideways.*)

Daisy (*enters through the arch*) What, dear? Having a
nice chat, the two of you, that's nice, dears. I've done the
dishes, just as well, as Marianne's gone off to the Piece,
I heard the honking. I do wish he wouldn't, Jasper, it's
little Tom, you know, sets my head off, and now the mat –
the mat's gone from the back kitchen, would you believe,
Jasper, after I put it down specially? So I've got to get the
one from the front – and how are you feeling now, dear?
You look much more relaxed, doesn't he, Jasper, much
more yourself, dear, that's good – (*Goes out left.*)

Benedict What? (*Stumbles after her. Stops.*) And do you
know what Vintross says about her, Daddy, says she made
me eat shit too, when I was little, because she wanted to

be our mummy, and when she couldn't be our mummy, made me eat shit to make up –

Daisy (*returns carrying a large doormat*) For the mud, you see.

Benedict – when I was little –

Daisy What, dear?

Benedict Saying Vintross says – Vintross –

Daisy Who, dear? Oh, that little Welsh friend of yours, so sad, so sad –

Benedict When I was little, Nanty, you made me eat and eat and eat.

Daisy What? Oh well, dear, I did my best to keep your tummy full, of course I did, didn't I, Jasper, but then you were such a greedy mite, you know, wasn't he, Jasper, like Oliver Twist dear, always asking for more. (*Laughs.*)

Benedict Wanted to be our mummy, didn't you, Nanty? Take the place of my mummy?

Daisy What? Oh oh – oh no – I knew I could never take her place, didn't I, Jasper, even though people said we were almost look-alikes – didn't they, Jasper – not usual, you know, in second cousins once removed except she had golden hair that came right down her back to sit on, sit on her own hair, she could, couldn't she Jasper, oh, really very glamorous, your mother, dear, aaaah, such a pity she didn't live to see what you've become! – Isn't it, Jasper?

Benedict What?

Daisy She adored you all, didn't she, Jasper?

Benedict Me? Adored me? Me too?

Daisy Well, dear, it was different with you, you were just an insignificant scrap at the time, and always crying for a feed, you know, while Henry was bigger and she could talk to him and Dick – well Dick, she idolised, Dick – but then we all did, didn't we Jasper? Because he was so pretty and clever.

Benedict laughs.

What, dear?

Benedict Dead, Nanty. Gone. Pretty Dick. Clever Dick. Through the door in the wall. On his motor-bike.

Daisy Yes, dear, I know, dear. So sad.

Benedict Why didn't you stop him?

Daisy What, dear?

Benedict Why didn't you stop him, Nanty. Killing himself. Why?

Daisy Oh really, Benedict, oh really, dear, I've told you before, haven't I, Jasper, every time you come down, dear, I've told you, you can't have forgotten, can he Jasper? I've told you and – told you, dear, I told him not to, didn't I, Jasper, and if he'd listened to me it wouldn't have happened, would it, Jasper? It's late, I said, you're tired, I said, stay the night, make him stay the night, Jasper, didn't I Jasper, and he said – what was it he said, or was it you Jasper, one of you said – oh nobody can stay the night, Daisy or Nanty, whichever of you it was said it, and they both laughed, the pair of them, and off he roared, off he roared, poor silly boy, in that helmet pulled down and those great gauntlets, and his head so low over the handlebars, roaring off, and I knew, I knew, if he'd listened to me it wouldn't have happened, would it, Jasper, but then nobody listens to me, it was just the same with your mother, you know, when I told her to go straight to the doctor with that lump, I knew that lump as soon as I saw it, didn't I Jasper? Rose, I said, Rose, Rose –

Benedict stumbles towards the door, left.

What, where are you going, dear?

Benedict (*in a child's voice*) Old room, Nanty, lie down in my old room when I was little, Nanty –

Daisy There's a good boy, aaaah, but oh, not your old room, dear, Matthew's in there, and all his things and Jenny's using Dick's, of course, they're staying the night, you see, so you use Henry's, dear – Henry's old room –

Benedict goes out. As she speaks, the stage begins to darken.

Did he hear, oh, I hope he heard, he always makes such a mess when he comes down, not that it isn't lovely to see him, for your sake, I know, dear, but sometimes I think he tipples – (*Lifts her hand to her mouth in a drinking movement.*) – a little too much, it's all very well to say he needs relaxing but not when he turns things upside down, and he takes after Rose that way – she liked her glass too, but of course she didn't let it go to her head like that, and oh, why did he have to upset me with remembering Rose and Dick, poor dears, and now my head, pounding because of the honking, pounding you know – and all the times I've asked them not to let Tom – but then it's true, true nobody listens to me, they go in and out and don't do the dishes and make fusses but not one of them says about tea, what am I meant to do about tea, Jasper? Do I lay for everybody on the assumption or what, do I, do I lay on the assumption, that's what I want to know, Jasper, well, that's what comes of letting them treat me as housekeeper, that's what they think I am, well it won't do, it's not good

enough, it's time they were told what I really am, and you
should tell them, dear, yes, it's up to you to tell them,
Jasper, now we've got them all together and – oh, good
heavens, oh no – (*seeing the pot*) – what's this doing –
but it's half full, you see, you see what I mean – left for
me to – sometimes I think Marianne – no wonder my
head – my poor head – (*Begins to go out under the
arch.*) – and oh, the windows, I'm locking the windows
so they can't come in this way (*Shuts them.*) and
tramping mud. (*Locks them.*) There, there, at least I
won't have mud this time – (*going out through arch*)

> The stage continues to darken to half-light. Jasper lets
> out a sudden, terrible groan. Puts his head back.

> *Curtain.*

Act Two

The same. About an hour later. Jasper as before. The stage is in semi-darkness. It is raining heavily. There is a sudden rattling at the windows. Marianne's voice, Henry's urgently, with the cries of children.

Marianne (*off*) Gramps – Gramps –

Henry (*off*) Daddy – Daddy – can you hear me!

Daisy (*enters on the run through the arch*) No, no, not there – not that way – oh it's so dark – (*Turns on the lights.*) I've opened the back-kitchen door – I've put a mat down in the back kitchen – the back kitchen, dears, please –

Henry For heaven's sakes, Nanty, we're getting – all right, but you go in that way, darling. I'm not having you get any wetter – Nanty – Nanty – open the door for Marianne!

Daisy What, oh – (*Opens the French windows.*) Oh, there you are, dear, are you all right? I didn't mean you of course, just the children – I wanted to make sure they'd go around by the back kitchen where I've put another mat especially, you see –

Marianne (*during this enters, with a man's raincoat over her head, in wellington boots*) I must say, Nanty, I didn't expect you'd actually lock the door on us – but golly, what a business – (*taking off her raincoat*)

Daisy Here, dear – let me – (*taking the coat*)

Marianne One minute thumping the ball about, the next absolute buckets, like the Old Testament, Gramps – (*Lifts a leg.*) I say, Nanty, do you mind –

Daisy What? Oh. (*Pulls at the boot.*) And the one in the back-kitchen had gone, I think the boys must have – (*Pulls the boot off.*)

Marianne (*staggering back*) Whoops!

Daisy All right, dear? You know, for football posts, I know they do sometimes.

   Marianne lifts the other leg.

(*Pulls it off.*) So I had to put the one from the front door down – there, there we are –

Marianne Thank goodness we had our bad-weather gear in the van – we had to sprint like billy-o to get it and then we thought Nindy had dropped her pot –

Daisy What, oh no, dear, her pot was here, where you left it. Half full and more.

Marianne (*laughing*) Yes, Henry remembered after we'd sent poor old Nigel haring back for it with my plastic bonnet over his head –

Daisy I suppose I'd better go and put these –

Henry (*enters under the arch, towelling his head*) Phew, what a soaking –

Daisy Oh Henry, you saw the mat, did you?

Henry What, Nanty?

Daisy The mat. I put down the mat.

Henry Oh.

Daisy Well, they did use it, dear, didn't they? I had to get it round from the front, you know, because the one at the back – I think the boys – must have taken it for their football –

Marianne No, they didn't, Nanty. They haven't touched it, not after all the business last time when they were using it as a sleigh and you were jolly sharp with them.

Daisy Oh, well, as long as they've used the one I've just put down – they did, didn't they, Henry?

Henry Well, actually, Nanty, there wasn't a mat there.

Daisy What, what do you mean? I've only just put it there, haven't I, Jasper? It can't have gone too.

Henry Well, Nanty, I can assure you, there's no mat there.

Daisy Where?

Henry The kitchen.

Daisy The kitchen! But I told you to go by the back kitchen – I opened the back-kitchen door especially – I told you –

Henry Oh sorry, I just heard kitchen –

Daisy Oh, good heavens – and after all the trouble I went to – well, where are they now, what are they doing? And there'll be mud on their boots – where are they?

Henry Now now, Nanty, don't panic, I've told them to take off their shoes and dry and wash themselves and to sit quietly down at the table.

Daisy The table, which table?

Henry Well, the kitchen table.

Daisy Why?

Henry Well, for their tea.

Daisy Their tea! But they can't have digested their lunches yet!

Marianne Well, you know the boys, they can be digesting their lunches while they're eating their tea – (*Laughs.*)

Daisy But I've laid for everybody, haven't I, Jasper? I've laid for everybody, a proper family tea – muffins and – rock cakes even –

Marianne Oh, they don't need muffins and rock cakes, just some bread and butter and Marmite and milk –

Henry We'll do it, Nanty, no need for you to bother yourself.

Daisy Oh, it's not bothering myself I mind, I'm used to that, aren't I, Jasper? The point is I laid tea for everybody, as nobody told me any differently, can't they wait?

Henry They can't really, Nanty, no. I know it's unreasonable of them, to be at the age when they're permanently hungry –

Marianne And anyway, Nanty, as you won't allow them anywhere but the kitchen – and what can they do there but eat – at least that's the way they see it –

Daisy I've never said they can't go into the spare rooms upstairs, I've never said that, although now you mention it they couldn't. because of course Jenny's in Dick's and now Matthew wants one to himself, he's in Benedict's and Benedict's lying down in Henry's, and they'd wake him, wouldn't they, Jasper?

Marianne Well, of course, if Benedict needs to lie down – Anyway, they've got to have it now because poor old Henry's got to go and see Mrs O'Killiam –

Daisy Who?

Marianne – and it's all getting a bit – so, for goodness' sake, darling, let's give them their tea at home –

Daisy What, take them home? You can't take them home, I've sliced three loaves and buttered the slices, no no, you can't take them home you know, not without their tea, can they, Jasper?

Henry But Nanty, if it's asking too much of you –

Daisy If they need their tea now, let them have it now, by all means, I'll go and see to it straight away – here, Henry, you'd better give me that – (*Takes the towel away from him.*) and I'll put these in the back kitchen – (*as she goes*) and oh, by the way, if Nindy wants her pot you'll find it sluiced in the down lavatory.

There is a pause.

Marianne Golly, well we seem to have put our foot in it again, don't we, darling?

Henry I think she's got one of her headaches, darling, and a bit tired with it. You know.

Marianne Oh. Oh well, poor old Nanty – I'd better go and keep the peace.

Henry No, I'll go, darling, you relax and have a jaw with Daddy, you haven't had a proper one yet.

Marianne Well, you are marvellous at dealing with her, I'll take over later, when you've got her back under your thumb.

Henry Righto, darling. (*Goes out through the arch.*)

Marianne I don't know what it is about Nindy's potty that brings out the worst in Nanty, do you, Gramps? All that fuss over the soup tureen last week and then hiding it in the kitchen cupboard, did Henry tell you about that, Gramps, before lunch when she thought I'd forgotten it again, not that I hadn't learnt my lesson, though what could be less offensive than a toddler's wee? I mean I wasn't going to dish it out as soup or anything – Oh I'm not getting at Nanty, Gramps – Gosh I'm just as bad as she is sometimes. I know I am, why just the other afternoon I had quite a funny moment, well it wasn't funny at the time, oh it was the usual sort of thing, Gramps, Nigel and Simon were quarrelling in the cubby-room over whose turn on the skateboard I think it was while I was dishing up their six o'clocks, Horlicks for Nigel and Tom and Piers, Ovaltine for Simon and Nindy and me, and I was stirring away as usual, out of the corner of my eye I caught myself watching them at it, Simon had the skateboard hugged to his chest and Nigel trying to struggle it out of his arms, and on their faces there were such expressions, but oh, perfectly normal, Gramps, golly! (*Laughs.*) They were just being children, humans, that's all, but still I caught myself, I was the horrible one, caught myself wishing they were, all of them, Tom and Piers and Nindy too, though Piers and Tom were upstairs quite innocent in front of children's television for all I knew and Nindy was sitting in her high chair humming bubbles out quite nicely and for all I knew feeling quite nice, but all of them, I wished all of them, this one too, isn't it a horrible Mums? (*to her belly*) Oh, it was just a flash, Gramps, just an out-of-the-corner-of-my-eye thing, deep and midnight stuff, but it had never happened before, you see, Gramps, so of course now I keep remembering it, it pops in and out when I least expect it, that I actually wished – oh, I know I'm not like that really, or the house would be full of corpses – (*Laughs.*) All I mean is that it's a jolly funny business, life and parenthood and all that – and if my Henry weren't around now that this thought's taken to popping in and out more and more and sometimes all the time even – I might be in danger of going – well, a bit potty. (*Laughs.*) What do you think, Gramps?

Margaret enters. She is smoking.

Oh, hello, Maggie!

Margaret smiles.

But I say, you haven't been out in this, have you?

Margaret Yes.

Marianne Golly, why?

Margaret Oh – for a walk.

Marianne Gosh, didn't you get wet?

Margaret I took shelter in a phone box.

Marianne Oh. How did you get back?

Margaret In a taxi.

Marianne Gosh, that was lucky, how did you get hold of one?

Margaret I telephoned for it.

Marianne Oh, of course. Not lucky then, just jolly sensible. (*Laughs.*)

Margaret Do you know where Ben is?

Marianne No – oh, yes – upstairs, didn't Nanty say, Gramps, having a snooze.

Margaret Oh. (*Makes to go off.*)

Marianne Why don't you let him get on with it, as he probably needs it from what Henry says – I mean, it's such a long time since we've seen each other and I'm longing to hear all about your success, aren't we, Gramps?

Margaret hesitates.

Come on then!

Margaret sits down.

Jolly good! Now – now then, tell us all about your –
whoops! (*Little pause.*) Whoops! (*Little pause.*) And
again! He still thinks we're footering about on the Piece
with Henry and the boys – and a hefty kick – and a
hefty kick – he's developing too, aren't you? (*Looks
down, pats her stomach.*) I just realised the other day
that that's why I always assume my babies are he's, even
Nindy, they've all had such hefty kicks, even Nindy –
(*Laughs.*) – although Tom was the worst, I honestly
think he decided to boot his way out, while Nigel was a
bit more like a clog-dancer, Henry used to say. (*Laughs.*)

There is a pause.

Margaret (*as if making an effort*) And which would you
prefer this time?

Marianne What?

Margaret Boy or girl?

Marianne Do you know, I really don't mind, Maggie. I
mean, I suppose a sister for Nindy would be convenient.
At least for Nindy. But then so would another brother
for Nigel, Simon, Tom and Piers. Or a sister for Nigel,
Simon, Tom and Piers, come to think of it. Or a brother
for Nindy. Not that they've given it a thought one way
or another, and Henry says he'll take what comes as
usual, and Gramps hasn't expressed any views either
way, have you, Gramps, so I'll settle for my routine, run-
of-the-mill eight-pounder thank you very much, God, if
you know what I mean. (*Laughs.*)

Margaret I think so. You incline towards a baby, and
you have a strong preference for either sex.

Marianne Yes. (*Little pause.*) I really shouldn't make such a display, should I?

Margaret I don't see how you could help it.

Marianne (*laughs*) No, that's true enough. Anyway, enough of babies! I was saying to Henry on our way here this morning that the few times you and I have had a proper natter it's really only me nattering away about the one I'm in the process of having or the ones I've already had and you have to go through the same old motions and ask the same old boring questions, and this time I wasn't going to let you, especially with so much to talk about yourself, I mean blossoming virtually overnight into a famous writer and tele-person even, golly, you must be jolly chuffed!

Margaret Well, um –

Marianne No, honestly, I'd be swollen with pride, wouldn't I, Gramps! And what have the reviews been like? I've scarcely seen any.

Margaret Oh. What are called mixed.

Marianne Jolly good, eh, Gramps? One of the ones I read was very nice. It said you were like a scalpel, gosh. (*Laughs.*) I think it was meant to be nice, anyway.

Margaret That was *The Times*.

Marianne Was it? You read them all then, do you? I don't know how you could bear to. I mean the bad ones. If there were any.

Margaret I'd rather read them myself than have them read out to me by friends.

Marianne You're absolutely right, anyway what does it matter what they say, it's been a great success, hasn't it, and I'll bet that infuriates them.

Margaret Who?

Marianne The ones who were snide and snarky, there was one I came across made me absolutely livid!

Margaret Oh. *The Guardian.*

Marianne No, it wasn't *The Guardian.* Could it have been the *Telegraph*?

Margaret No.

Marianne Oh, that was a good one, then?

Margaret They didn't review it.

There is a pause.

Marianne Anyway, as long as you think it's good, that's what counts, isn't it, Gramps?

Margaret Thank you. (*Lights another cigarette.*) And have you read it yet?

Marianne Oh gosh, yes, haven't I said?

Margaret I had the impression you called out something at lunch. As you passed the dumplings.

Marianne I know, it's such a shambles, isn't it? I was just saying to Henry that our lot must do a marvellous job of putting you and Ben off family life. (*Laughs.*)

There is a pause.

Margaret And what did you say?

Marianne What?

Margaret As you passed the dumplings.

Marianne Oh – oh golly, nothing profound, knowing me. Just the usual congratters, I expect.

There is a pause.

Margaret Did you enjoy it?

Marianne Oh – oh, now I've got to be careful not to plonk my great foot in it, but to be honest I can't say I actually *enjoyed* it, Maggie, I didn't know you wanted me to, I mean let's face it, it isn't just a jolly good snorter of a read, like the usual stuff I get my nose into, for one thing you have to be on your toes all the time, but I admit I've done my share of boasting about our being fellow sisters-in-law, especially after that TV thing.

Margaret I'm glad you got something out of it.

Marianne Of course we always knew you were brainy, but not so devastatingly brainy, eh, Gramps? The way you conjured up all those weird people and being so – so ruthless and – and devastating about the whole bunch of them. Am I being very feeble?

Margaret You found them weird, did you?

Marianne You and old Ben don't actually know types like that, do you?

Margaret Yes, actually.

Marianne Then no wonder you put them in a book, that's where they belong, isn't it, Gramps? Whoops – he's at it again! (*Laughs.*)

   There is a pause.

But tell me, how long did it take you to write? I can never remember when you started, but you seem to have been at it for years.

Margaret Two.

Marianne Years?

Margaret Yes.

Marianne Golly!

Margaret From conception to delivery.

Marianne Gosh!

Margaret I know. Especially when you think what can be turned out in nine months.

Marianne What do you – oh, I see! (*Laughs.*) Oh, but anyone can produce one of these, can't they – or is that what you meant?

Margaret No, I think I meant – (*Stops.*)

Marianne What, Maggie?

Margaret Oh – merely that we're very different people.

Marianne Who, you and I, you mean? Well, I'll say we are! (*Little pause.*) Although when you think about it we're only different because you're brainy and I'm not, otherwise we're at least women, after all, aren't we?

Margaret Which amounts to what? That we've both got wombs for breeding and breasts for feeding but we're under no obligation to use what brains we've got for thinking.

Marianne Yes, I know, but isn't it awful how they rust over if we don't?

Margaret Which?

Marianne What?

Margaret Which rust over, our wombs, our tits or our brains?

Marianne Oh, I was thinking of myself, so I meant brains of course. But perhaps all three when you put it like that.

There is a pause.

Margaret (*lights another cigarette, puffs at it, looks at Marianne*) Actually, my reproductive organs work with regulation efficiency.

Marianne Oh. Oh, well, jolly good, eh, Gramps?

Margaret Otherwise I wouldn't have needed two abortions.

Marianne Oh. Oh, I didn't know.

Margaret I know.

Marianne I'm sorry.

Margaret What for?

Marianne Well, if I've been clumsy.

Margaret I don't think you've been at all clumsy. I had the first when I was nineteen, to prevent an unwanted baby – by an unwanted middle-aged schoolteacher.

Marianne I suppose somebody might have wanted him, though, mightn't they?

Margaret His wife didn't, when he tried to go back to her.

Marianne I meant the baby. Because of all the people desperate to adopt, you know.

Margaret Yes, I do know. But I wasn't prepared to be their beast of burden. The second was Benedict's, two years ago.

Marianne You really don't have to tell us about it, does she, Gramps?

Margaret Oh, I don't mind.

Marianne But I do rather, I'm afraid.

Margaret Really, what of? You've always been so open and free about that aspect of your life. Not that the Ben abortion's particularly interesting, I admit. But it happened to coincide with my beginning my novel, and as I didn't want a baby anyway, I wasn't going to let it muck up my creative processes, if you follow. Fortunately there's a bright lady gynaecologist in Hampstead –

Marianne (*rising, takes a few steps*) Oooh-oooh –

Margaret What, what is it? (*going to her*)

Marianne Sofa – sofa – Henry – quickly – ooooh – (*Collapses awkwardly on it.*)

Margaret Oh my God, oh my God, I'll get him – (*Goes towards the arch.*)

Matthew has appeared at the French windows. He stands uncertainly, watching. He enters, hesitant.

Marianne (*holding Margaret's arm*) No no – my leg – please rub it – quickly.

Margaret seizes her leg, begins to rub.

Matthew Um, if – if you see Mummy – um –

Marianne No, no, the other one, the other one – (*irritably*) – quick – quick – rub!

Matthew I'll be – um – I'll be up in my room –

Goes out left quickly.

Marianne Oh God! God! Rub – rub!

Henry (*runs easily through the arch*) Ah, the old crampers, eh, darling – here, let me, Maggie, I've got the trick of it – (*Takes Marianne's leg, begins to massage it expertly.*)

Marianne Aaaah, aaah – (*with increasing relief*) – that's it, aaah, clever old stick – there now – Golly, poor old Maggie, she thought I was going to litter right at her feet, didn't you, Maggie?

Henry (*laughs, turns, sees Margaret's face*) Are you all right?

Margaret Yes, thank you. As everything seems to be under control I think I'll go and look at my husband.

Marianne Jolly good! (*and as Margaret goes out*) Not that I'd have dared, would I, Gramps? Litter, I mean, she'd probably have trampled on him, well, at least now we know, don't we, Gramps? She's not infertile or frigid, darling, she has them killed, she sat there boasting about it, didn't she, Gramps? She was horrible, quite horrible, wasn't she, Gramps? So you come here for a minute, come on.

Henry hesitates, sits beside her. Marianne takes his arm, wraps it around her, leans into him.

There, now I feel safe, no one can harm us now, can they? We won't let her get you – aah – squeeze me, a little pressure, you know – that's right – aaah – aaah –

Henry Well, don't get too comfy, darling, or you'll go into one of your snoozes.

Marianne No, no, course I won't – course I won't – (*in a little girl's voice*)

Henry strokes Marianne's hair, pushes a lock back, looks into her face. After a moment an expression of enormous sadness comes over his face. Then he looks at Jasper, smiles. Daisy enters under the arch.

Daisy Oh, oh, you're both in here now are you? No, no, it's all right, it's just that Henry suddenly vanished and there's a terrible squabble over those blasted rock cakes.

Henry makes to get up.

Marianne No, you don't, you've done your stint with Nanty and you've still got Mrs O'Killiam to come –

Daisy goes out under the arch.

Henry (*lets out his sudden strange laugh*) Golly, sorry, sorry, Daddy. (*Does it again.*) – Must be – must be what they mean by *fou rire* – because actually she's not really quite as – as grotesque – Mrs O'Killiam – as somehow I'd led Marianne to believe, I mean it's true that she's thin, she was certainly off her food, from depression, really terrible depression, but her face – her face is – rather touching, delicate, and there's something in her eyes, behind the fatigue and giving up – rather – well, rather lovely, haunting – she touches one, you see, in her despair. I don't know why I led Marianne to believe, even right at the beginning that she was – of course it's true her boys are brutes, that's certainly true and – and they like to catch cats, you know, and tie plastic bags around their heads – and the little girl, well she's not a hydrocephalic but she does have adenoids that give her face a swollen – from time to time – and her husband, well, it's nothing to do with an eighty-year-old woman, I don't know why I – I – you know how truthful I've always been, perhaps it was simply lack of practice that led me to – to – (*laughs*) – he's certainly been in trouble with the police, of course, for something to do with cars, I think it was, and he's abandoned her and as I say she is – quite naturally – given the way life's treated her – and – and – but please don't believe I ever, I ever intended, planned, or wanted to – actively wanted to – make love to her. I didn't, Daddy, I didn't. Even though she is now my mistress. (*Pause.*) You see, what happened was, well, about a month ago I went around to see her, and the door was open, on the latch, so I knew she was expecting

225

me, and so I went in. And there she was. On the sofa.
And a strange noise coming from upstairs. Rather
alarming, actually, until I realised it was just the little girl
asleep, snoring – and the boys were out, doing something
hideous, I suppose, anyway they weren't doing it inside –
So. So it was just her. On the sofa. Looking so defeated
and – and hopeless – and the snoring from above. And
me. And she said, oh doctor, oh doctor. She's – she's Irish
you know. And started to cry. So I went over to her
and put my arms around her, to comfort her. And she
seemed to want, to expect – to *need* me to – and – well –
anyway – I did. You see, it was something I could do,
something I could give her, there being so little one can
give even those who love one, isn't that true, Daddy, and
here was something so simple, I've always found it easy
to, well – and there's always been something about her
that touched me, you see – and – and afterwards she
clung to me as if – and I cuddled her and everything was –
I like to think it was peaceful for a little time, it wasn't
sex, you see, not for her either. (*Pause.*) I prescribed
myself, if you like. On the National Health. Anyhow,
that's how I tried to look at it. (*Laughs.*) As I say, holding
her. (*Little pause.*) I didn't feel guilty or ashamed, or
embarrassed. Not at all. And I massaged the back of her
neck, where she gets pain, and looked in on Carla, and
discussed an operation on her adenoids and then went
home as if I – as if for once I'd been an effective doctor.
(*Smiles. Pause.*) But of course nothing ends – nothing
like that ends with the act, does it? Why should it? Give
someone Valium for much-needed calm and in no time
they're desperate for their calming Valium, and it's no
good explaining to them – Anyway. (*Laughs.*) Now she
looks upon me as her lover. Her man. She's as possessive
of me as – well, she feels she has a right to me, as she's
given me her body, as she puts it. She is Irish, after all.
And so in return she thinks she's entitled to something

from me – oh, not just money, other than the odd pound
here and there, and who can blame her for that? But
well, more of *me*. My time. My attention. My love. And
now she's taken, poor soul, to threatening me. (*Pause.*)
I have a feeling she's told her brutes of boys. Or perhaps
they've watched. Or she's allowed them to watch – no,
no, I'm sure that's unfair, unworthy – it's just that there's
a window and once I thought I – oh, I don't know. It
doesn't really matter, does it? But if I don't go around,
then they come around, to the surgery – and this
morning, of course, to the house – so – so – it'll get
worse. I've tried to think it through – right to the worst
end – the scandal, and I'll be struck off, I suppose, and
then what it'll mean for old Marianne and the children –
one day – and – and – then I've tried to put it in the
larger scheme, *sub specie aeternitas*, no *aeternitatis*, sorry
Daddy. (*A little laugh.*) And then it struck me, you see.
The real thing. That I didn't care. I'd even quite welcome
it. Because once you do begin to look at it *sub specie* it's
really all such a pitiful charade, isn't it, or perhaps not
even pitiful, merely a charade, with none of it mattering
at all in view of what happens all over the world, every
minute of the day, and when one thinks it through that
far – no, no, when *I'd* thought it through that far I felt a
tremendous relief, you see, because then I could face the
fact – the fact that I've never cared, never, I've always
really known that nothing matters, and I remembered
the night Dick was killed – when I left you that night
and went home and sat in the kitchen, the house was
breathing, you know, with life, Marianne upstairs
waiting for me, children in all the rooms, another in
Marianne's womb – and Mrs O'Killiam in her loneliness
also, as it's turned out, waiting for me – and some poor
devil who'd lost his eye and his daughter in a car crash
I'd been to see – and Dick dead, Dick, and I didn't care,
not about any of us, not about Marianne or Tom or

Piers or Nigel or Simon or Nindy or the unborn or any
of the Mrs O'Killiams anywhere, or you here mourning
the only one of us you loved – and so I gave myself a
couple of jolly hard punches, Daddy, right in the face,
to make myself care about something – and then old
Marianne came down, poor old Marianne, and I looked
at her and thought, no, no, I don't care about you either,
poor old girl, and now there's Nanty with a brain
tumour more than likely so you see, Daddy, so you see,
what is the point, the point of caring for each other and
loving each other when the end is always and always the
same, *sub specie* or any way you look at it, Daddy, do
you know by any chance, God-given chance? (*Pause.*)
Do you? And if you don't why did you bring us into the
world, how did you dare – how did you –? I'm sorry.
I'm sorry to be so childish. I should probably have asked
that years ago, but if you can answer now I'd be jolly
grateful. So I'll know what to say to my lot when the time
comes. Can you, Daddy? (*Laughs, stares desperately at
Jasper.*)

    Margaret enters from left. There is a pause.

Margaret Sorry. Am I interrupting?

Henry What? Oh, good heavens no, Daddy and I were
just having one of our jaws, weren't we, Daddy?

    Margaret lights a cigarette. Her hand is trembling.

I gather you and Marianne had a bit of a ding-dong, I
hope you didn't take it too – too – I know she didn't.

Margaret Look, the thing is, I've got to get back to
London soon.

Henry Oh. What a pity.

Margaret And I've just looked in on Ben.

Henry Ah. Yes. How is he? I'm afraid he might have had a spot too much, we were reminiscing, you know what it's like when we haven't seen each other for a bit, eh, Daddy? (*Laughs.*)

Margaret He's sprawled across the bed of his childhood, with his thumb in his mouth. He's making little mewling sounds at the back of his throat. He's dribbling. And he stinks of Scotch.

Henry Oh. Well, um –

Margaret So I gather he's been through his fit and frenzy stage, has he?

Henry Well. Well, perhaps he did become a little – I'm sorry, Maggie.

Margaret I'm not, I'm afraid. He was due for another bout, and I wanted him to have it here. I'm returning him, you see. Giving him back. Sorry. That's unnecessarily brutal. But I've had quite enough of him, and I need you to keep him here, please, until I've moved myself out of the flat and found a place where I'll be safe. Actually, my publishers have already set that side of things in motion. (*Pause.*) No doubt you think I'm being very hard. Yes. Besides, I'm not Ben's wife any more. Let alone his nurse, surrogate mother, victim and tart on demand. I'm a writer. My first book taught me that much. Whatever you think of it. And now that I've begun a new one, I'm going to need all my wits and as much peace as I can manage. Along with the usual ration of luck and inspiration. You see. I'm sorry. I *am* sorry to take advantage. But then Henry is a doctor, so he'll know what to do. And as you're also a decent man and a loving brother I'm fairly sure you'll do it. Oh, and there's something I should tell you. As far as I can establish, his Vintross doesn't exist. At least the only

Vintross I can trace is a car-park attendant at the BBC.
And I don't know if he got on to Hugh Rhys Jones, but
if he did, Hugh Rhys Jones didn't stab himself to death
in a Chinese restaurant or whatever. He's merely been
transferred to Cardiff. Which may amount to the same
thing, of course. (*Gets up.*) I've heard there's a good
clinic outside Staines. I'll get my publisher to send you its
address. And of course any committal papers you want
me to sign. Oh – and my apologies to Marianne –
explain that I was a trifle on edge. And now I'd better
get away before he makes one of his spectral recoveries.
They can be rather unnerving. (*Turns left to go out.*)

*Benedict enters from left. He is trembling. His colour
is ghastly. He walks slowly to Margaret. Stands in
front of her.*
Henry gets up.

Benedict It was Dick, of course. Wasn't it? Yes, it was
Dick. He's just come back, you see, and told me so.
Back, Henry, Daddy. Old Dick. Just as he used to be,
twenty-five years ago. And he was wearing that smile,
you know the smile, Henry, when we'd caught him out
in one of his little meannesses, his stealings, and he'd
decided to make it up. And then – then, Daddy – he put
his hand out towards me, as if he was going to touch
me. And I said, 'Dick, Dick –' and he turned and went.
Went away from me.

Henry Ben – old Ben – it wasn't Dick –

Benedict Yes, it was, Hen. It was, Daddy. And I
understood what it was old Dick, our old Dick, Henry,
had come back to tell me, Daddy. What was it like to
have Dick's willy inside you, darling? Did he hold you
against the dark, as I did? Did he? (*Smiles pathetically.*)

Jenny enters through the French windows.

Jenny I take it he's not come back, then?

Henry Oh. Well, actually I think Ben saw him a short while ago. Didn't you, Ben?

Benedict What?

Henry He came into your room for a moment, you were just telling us. Because that's where he's staying the night, you see. Matthew.

Benedict Matthew?

Henry Yes, Ben. Matthew, old chap. (*Goes to him gently, takes his arm.*) Matthew, you see.

Benedict Oh. Oh yes, Matthew – so alike, so alike it makes the heart – heart – sorry, Hen, sorry – sorry – darling. Sorry, Jen. Sorry, Daddy.

Jenny Did he say anything?

Henry No, apparently he came in and saw – well, old Ben was having a nap, weren't you, Ben, so he went away again, apparently, from what Ben was saying, didn't he, eh, Ben?

Jenny Well, that's our day together. He has to be back first thing tomorrow. Our only day together in a month and then another month until half-term, and I can't go on looking for him any more, I'm soaked through, my feet are wet and I'm worn out, he's quite worn me out with his – of course you realise it's deliberate, don't you? I expect you've all noticed how he avoids me, when I so much as put my hand on his arm he flinches, draws away from me – he loathes my touch, you see, his mother's touch. Oh yes – yes – I'm sure you've noticed – perhaps you want it even, do you? So that you can see he's still Dick's son, not mine, I expect that's why you wanted him to stay on at that school – isn't it – well, I'll tell you one thing, he's not going back, no, he's not going back there, with that housemaster – I hate that housemaster – writing to you, how dare he write to you! How dare you let him! (*to Henry*) Well he won't any more, you won't any more, he's coming back home with me, to live with me where I can watch him and guard him and look after him, I've a right to that, if I'm going to die for him a thousand times a day I've a right to that, I'm not going to let him end up like Dick, no I'm not, we're never going to set foot in this house again – neither of us! Neither of us! He's my son. Not yours! (*Looks around at them.*) Yes, this is Dick's frump speaking. Dick's frump! That's what you all thought of me, as you couldn't understand how your brilliant Dick could come to marry me, could you – but then you didn't know him, didn't see him as I saw him, night after night, crying, or curled up – so pathetic – but I knew it was hopeless, hopeless, nobody could have saved him, nobody, every time he went off on that motorbike I knew – knew what he wanted and at the end I almost wanted it too, yes I did, because if he couldn't find anything in me or our Matthew to keep him then he might as well – well, I'm not letting him go like that, not letting my Matthew go like that. I'm not. I'm not.

Margaret (*goes to her*) Jenny – Jenny – I know what you're feeling –

Jenny (*slaps her*) Do you? (*Laughs.*) Do you? With your nasty mean little novel, do you think – do you think he cared for you either? Why, why you were one of hundreds, hundreds, there was an Australian sociologist at the same time as you, the very same time, she was called Dick's kangaroo because she'd hop into bed with him anywhere, even places where there wasn't one, that was the joke about her, and his students, Dick's lucky dips, and that furry little woman in the bursar's office, all going on at the same time –

Matthew enters through the French windows. There is a pause.

Matthew Um – (*Clears his throat.*) – Hello, Mummy.

Marianne (*enters through the arch*) Ah, all here, jolly good – Nanty's seeing them around to the van, darling, and I've just potted Nindy but no luck this time, even Gramp's magic didn't work, you must have spent her last penny after lunch, eh, Gramps, anyway we're all set, darling, sorry we've got to leave so early, old Henry's fault for being needed as usual, but golly, it was lovely seeing us all together again, eh, Gramps?

Daisy (*enters from left*) I've got them all in, dears, now Nindy's got the potty and Nigel's looking after the boots and Simon and Nigel are in charge of the coats and Tom's promised not to toot the horn, but before you go, dears, there's something you want to tell them, isn't there, Jasper, I've been thinking, dear, and they have a right to know who I am, haven't they, dear? We're married, you see. Jasper and I. (*Pause.*) Aren't we, Jasper? There! (*Laughs.*) We knew that would surprise you. Didn't we, Jasper?

There is a pause.

Oh, it wasn't a proper ceremony, in church and in white, with bridesmaids and bouquets or anything like that, no no, it was just a thing in an office, the most ordinary thing in the world except for a sweet old lady who played the organ, didn't she Jasper, but it was all a bit of a rush, you know, people waiting in the waiting room, and leaving as we entered, weren't there Jasper, but they have to keep at it all the time, you know – quite a little business in its way, but Jasper was, well you know how he feels things, always so quick, isn't he, dear? His shoulders shook and his mouth trembled, it did, you know! And so distinguished with his white mane and a carnation in his button and he even cried, didn't you, Jasper, and he was so ashamed because he thought he was holding them up, you see – with so many to come, and probably queues forming – but I said, I told him, they're used to it, you know, people crying and overcome and behaving strangely, they allow for it, dear, they take it into account, they'll fit everybody in so don't you worry, and sure enough it just swung open, the door on the other side, you see, not where we'd come in, but on the other side – oh, so well organised – and out we went, didn't we, Jasper, out we went! And the people who'd been before us were still on the pavement, laughing and chattering, weren't they, dear, and clambering into their cars, and another car arrived, didn't it, Jasper, with a new lot, you see, just as I said, and then our car came up, we'd hired it especially, oh so grand it was, shiny and black to take us home, and home we came, didn't we, Jasper, and I said as we went, there there my love, my sweet, my darling – it's all over, it's finished, wasn't it easy and quick, all finished at last, and he said, 'Rose, Rose –' aaaah! – and I said, 'No no, Jasper, I'm not your Rose, my dear, I'm your Daisy, dear,' and 'Oh my dear Daisy,' he said, so sweet he was – 'Oh my dear Daisy, not over, my Daisy, but beginning my love', he was tired, you see, weren't you, Jasper, quite dead you were, weren't you, my dear, we'll have children, he said, to keep us going, send them forth in life, didn't you, Jasper, think of them waiting, waiting to enter, we'll bring them forth, for life awaits them, the door will open, we'll send them towards it – didn't you, love, aaah aaaah, my darling – the door will open, we'll send them towards it –

During this speech and the following speeches the room is brightening – through natural sunlight after the rain to an unnatural brightness.

The door will open, we'll send them towards it – the door is open –

The Rest (*except Jasper*) We'll send them towards it.

Jasper is struggling, as if to rise. His eyes fixed in wonder.

Henry The door will open –

Benedict We'll send them towards it.

Daisy The door is open –

All We'll send them towards it!

Jenny The door is open.

All We'll send them towards it, the door is open, the door is open, we'll send them towards it.

Jasper has almost made it to his feet.

All The door is open, the door is open, the door is open!

Stillness. A prolonged honking of the horn. Jasper subsides into his chair.

Daisy Oh, really – I did tell him not to!

Henry Sorry, Nanty, but it's hard to resist –

Marianne – Anyway, Nanty, we are just off, this second, don't worry – well, Jenny – (*Kissing her*) and Margaret (*coolly*) and Ben (*kissing them both*) I hope it won't be so long next time because Gramps does love it when you – and old Mat – see you next hols, eh –?

Henry (*meanwhile*) Ben, you um, well, we'll be in touch and – and Maggie – um, um, take care the two of you, um (*putting a hand on Benedict's shoulder, kissing Margaret*) and Jenny, my dear, now you're not to worry, everything'll be – and Mat – keep up the good work!

Daisy (*throughout this*) – aaah, what a shame you couldn't stay for tea, it was all laid, you know, especially, but everything's in, don't worry, Nindy, the potty, Nigel and Tom, the boots and coats – so that's all right – nothing forgotten this time –

Henry And Nanty – (*kissing her*) – I shan't forget about the headaches, I'll see to that straight away –

Daisy Oh, thank you, dear, so sweet, and I'll keep on with the moist pads, shan't I, Jasper?

Marianne (*kissing her*) I hope we weren't too much for you this time –

Daisy What, no no, of course not, dear – they were no trouble, the boys and little Nindy – aaah! – You're never any trouble, are they, Jasper?

Honking off.

Marianne Well, darling, mustn't keep Mrs O'Killiam waiting!

Henry Golly no, well, God bless, God bless – and see you, Daddy, as usual.

Marianne Yes, God bless, Gramps – see you as usual.

Henry and Marianne go out left to the accompaniment of honking. The honking stops.

Daisy Oooh – you see how it starts my head off – well, there we are, at least we can have a proper grown-up tea, we adore the little ones, don't we, Jasper – but I must say they make it difficult to have a proper grown-up – but I've kept most of the rock cakes for you, Matthew, I know Jenny got them for you specially so I only allowed them half each so you can have a good tuck-in dear, but oh, that reminds me I still haven't settled – now how much did we say it was, Jenny, sixty-six p., but of course

236

my purse, I still haven't found – did I ask you if you'd seen it, Matthew, have you seen it, dear, my purse, small, green, in velours –?

Matthew (*with sudden fluency*) Your purse, gosh, no, Nanty, I haven't seen any purse at all, a small green one, did you say, in – well I'll certainly keep an eye out for it, it's terrible when one loses things, I do it all the time, don't I, Mummy? I hope there wasn't any money or anything valuable in it.

Daisy Well about four pounds eighty-fivr p., but it must be here somewhere, you see it's the purse, that's what I care about, it was a present from Jasper, years ago, wasn't it, Jasper?

Jenny (*who was watching Matthew during his speech*) Ready for our walk, darling?

Matthew Oh, but –

Daisy What, walk, but what about your tea, aren't you going to have our tea first?

Jenny No, I'd like to go now. And straight away, darling, and together if you please – (*goes over, takes him by the hand, tightly*) – so that we can't lose each other.

Daisy Oh, well, I must say – you'd have thought they'd have waited, wouldn't you, Jasper, they could have had tea first as they're always so hungry –

Benedict (*during this, has gone over to Margaret, has stood staring directly into her eyes*) Ready, darling? I'm rather anxious to get back. To give Vintross a ring. He'll want to know how things are. And you must want to get back, too. I know what it's like now – when you start a new one. (*Little pause.*) Coming? (*Little pause.*) Coming, darling?

Daisy What, what do you mean – you're not going too – but the tea's out you, know – or Benedict, a drink, dear – you always like a drink before you go.

Benedict Oh no, Nanty – (*leading Margaret towards the French windows*) I've given that stuff up now virtually for good, haven't I, Daddy? But we'll be back soon – we won't leave it so long before the next time, Daddy, that's a promise. (*They go.*)

Daisy What, well that's all very well but after all the trouble I went to – and the muffins – all those muffins – and what for? What for? Lay it down on the assumption and then just clear it all away again – you see – like a housekeeper – but what about you, Jasper, how do you feel? Are you all right, dear, you've gone very quiet all of a sudden?

Jasper makes a slight noise.

Daisy What, dear?

Jasper The door is open!

Daisy Dear?

Jasper The door is open!

Daisy Oh, you're feeling the chill again, and such a warm sunny evening now that it's rained, but of course if you're feeling the chill, I know how it goes right through you, right through your whole system – (*going to the French windows, shutting them, locking them*) – there – is that better – and oh, the light – we don't need the light any more now that it's light (*turns off lights*) – and my headache, you know, much better now that everybody's – (*collecting the Scotch, bottle and glass*) – not that we don't like having them, of course – though they might have stayed for tea – (*as she goes out through the arch*) – don't we, dear?

Pause. The lights continue to go down steadily, until only Jasper in his chair is lit. That light remains for a few seconds and then, as it goes down, the sound of organ music, distantly, then swelling to fill the theatre as:

Curtain.

QUARTERMAINE'S TERMS

For Beryl

Quartermaine's Terms was first presented by Michael Codron on 28 July 1981 at the Queen's Theatre, London. The cast was as follows:

St John Quartermaine Edward Fox
Anita Manchip Jenny Quayle
Mark Sackling Peter Birch
Eddie Loomis Robin Bailey
Derek Meadle Glyn Grain
Henry Windscape James Grout
Melanie Garth Prunella Scales

Director Harold Pinter
Designer Eileen Diss
Lighting Leonard Tucker

Characters

St John Quartermaine
Anita Manchip
Mark Sackling
Eddie Loomis
Derek Meadle
Henry Windscape
Melanie Garth

The Set

The staff room of the Cull-Loomis School of English
for foreigners, Cambridge, or rather a section of
the staff room – the last quarter of it. On stage are
French windows, a long table, lockers for members
of the staff, pegs for coats etc., and a number
of armchairs; on the table a telephone, newspapers
and magazines. This is the basic set. to which, between
scenes and between the two acts, additions can be
made to suggest the varying fortunes of the school.
Offstage, left, a suggestion of hard-backed chairs,
and off left, a door to the main corridor of the school,
where the classrooms are.

The Period

Early 1960s.

Act One

Monday morning, spring term. The French windows are open. It is about nine-thirty. Sunny.

  Quartermaine is sitting with his feet up, hands folded on his lap, staring ahead. From off, outside the French windows, in the garden, the sound of foreign voices, excited, talking, laughing, etc., passing by. As these recede Anita comes through the French windows carrying a briefcase.

Anita 'Morning, St John.

Quartermaine Oh hello, Anita, but I say, you know – (*getting up*) you look – you look different, don't you?

Anita Do I? Oh – my hair probably. I've put it up.

Quartermaine Well, it looks – looks really terrific! Of course I liked it the other way too, tumbling down your shoulders.

Anita It hasn't tumbled down my shoulders for three years, St John.

Quartermaine Oh. How was it, then, before you changed it?

Anita Back in a ponytail. (*She indicates.*)

Quartermaine That's it. Yes. Well, I liked it like that, too.

Anita Thank you. Oh, by the way, Nigel asked me to apologise again for having to cancel dinner. He was afraid he was a little abrupt on the phone.

Quartermaine Oh Lord no, not at all – besides, it's lucky he was abrupt, you know how Mrs Harris hates me using the phone, she stands right beside me glowering, but I managed to understand exactly what he was getting at, something to do with – with a lecture he had to prepare, wasn't it?

Anita No, it was the new magazine they're starting. The first issue's coming out shortly and they still haven't got enough material so they had to call a panic editorial meeting – it went on until three in the morning –

Quartermaine Oh. Poor old Nigel. But it sounds tremendously – tremendously exciting –

Anita Oh, yes. Well, they're all very excited about it, anyway, they're determined it shouldn't just be another little Cambridge literary magazine, you know, but they want to preserve the Cambridge style and tone. Anyway, I'm sorry we couldn't have the dinner, and at such short notice. Did you find anything else to do?

Quartermaine Oh yes, yes, I was fine, don't worry, tell Nigel, because just after he phoned, old Henry phoned, to invite me around.

Anita What luck. For dinner?

Quartermaine No, to baby-sit, actually.

Anita To baby-sit. But their oldest – Susan isn't it? – must be nearly fourteen.

Quartermaine Yes, but apparently she's working away for her O-Levels – she's very bright – taking it years in advance and all that, so they wanted her not to have to worry about the young ones, you see – in fact, they really hadn't meant to go out, and then they discovered that there was some film they wanted to see at the Arts, some old German classic they seem to be very fond of, about – about a child-murderer as far as I could make out from what Henry told me. So that was all right.

Anita You enjoyed it, then?

Quartermaine Oh Lord yes – well, children, you know, are such – such – it took me a bit of time to get them used to me, of course, as the smallest one, the one they call little Fanny – very charming, very charming – cried when she saw me – she hates it when Henry and Fanny go out, you see – and then the boy – my word, what a little devil, full of mischief, told me little Fanny had drowned in the bath and when I ran in there she was – lying face down – hair floating around – and I stood there thinking, you know – (*Laughs.*) – Lord, what am I going to say to Henry and Fanny particularly when they get back, especially after seeing a film like that – but it turned out it was only an enormous Raggedy Anne doll, and little Fanny was hiding under her bed – because Ben had told her I was going to eat her up – (*Laughs.*) But I got them settled down in the end, in fact it would have been sooner if Susan hadn't kept coming out of her room to scream at them for interrupting her studying – and anyway Henry and Fanny came back quite early. In about an hour, as a matter of fact.

Anita Well, at least you had a bit of an evening with them, then.

Quartermaine Oh rather – except that Fanny had a terrible headache from straining to read the subtitles, that's why they'd had to leave, a very poor print apparently – then Henry got involved in a – an argument with Ben, who'd got up when he heard them come in, so I felt, you know, they rather wanted me out of the way –

The sound of the door opening, during the above. Footsteps.

Oh hello, Mark, top of the morning to you, have a good weekend?

Sackling appears on stage. He is carrying a briefcase, is unshaven, looks ghastly.

Anita (*looking at him in concern*) Are you all right?

Sackling Yes, yes, fine, fine. (*He drops the briefcase, slumps into a chair.*)

Anita Are you growing a beard?

Sackling What? Oh Christ! (*feeling his chin*) I forgot!

Anita But there must be several days' stubble there.

Sackling Haven't been to bed, you see. All weekend.

Quartermaine Ah, been hard at it, eh?

Sackling What?

Quartermaine Hard at it. The old writing.

Sackling grunts.

Terrific!

Anita Oh, I've got a message from Nigel, by the way, he asked me to ask you to hurry up with an extract, they're desperate to get it into the first issue, he says don't worry about whether it's self-contained, they can always shove it in as 'Work in Progress' or something.

Sackling Right.

Anita You look to me as if you've overdone it – are you sure you're all right?

Quartermaine I say, how's old Camelia?

Sackling (*barks out a laugh*) Oh fine! just – fine!

Quartermaine Terrific, and little Tom too?

Sackling Tom too, oh yes, Tom too.

Quartermaine The last time I saw him he was teething, standing there in his high chair dribbling away like anything, while Camelia was sitting on old Mark's lap making faces at him with orange peel in her mouth –

> *Sackling bursts into tears. Anita goes to Sackling, puts her hand on his shoulder.*

What? Oh – oh Lord!

Sackling Sorry – sorry – I'll be all right – still – still digesting.

Quartermaine Something you had for breakfast, is it? Not kidneys – they can give you terrible heartburn – especially with mushrooms –

> *Anita shakes her head at him.*

Mmmm?

Anita Do you want to talk about it?

Sackling I don't want anyone – anyone else to know – especially not Thomas or Eddie – don't want them dripping their – their filthy compassion all over me.

Quartermaine What?

Anita We're to keep it to ourselves, St John.

Quartermaine Oh Lord, yes. Of course. What, though?

Sackling She's left me.

Quartermaine Who?

Anita Camelia, of course.

Quartermaine What! Old Camelia! On no!

Sackling Taking Tom – taking Tom with her.

Quartermaine Oh, not little Tom too!

Sackling Tom too.

Anita Well, did she say why?

Sackling (*makes an effort, pulls himself together*) She –
she – (*He takes an envelope out of his pocket.*) I was
upstairs in the attic – writing away – as far as I knew she
was downstairs where she usually is – in the kitchen or –
ironing – with the television on. And Tom in bed, of
course. So I wrote on and on – I felt inspired, quite
inspired, a passage about – about what I'd felt when I
saw Tom coming out of her womb – so shiny and whole
and beautiful – a wonderful passage – full of – full of
my love for her and him – and when I finished I went
downstairs to her – to read it to her – as I always do
when it's something I'm burning with – and she wasn't
there – the house was very still, empty, but I didn't think –
never occurred to me – so I went up the stairs and into
our bedroom and – all her clothes – the suitcases
everything – gone – and this – this on the pillow.

> *He hands the note to Quartermaine. He takes it,
> opens it, makes to read it. Stops. Shakes his head.
> Anita makes a small move to take it from him.*

Quartermaine (*not noticing*) No, we can't – can we,
Anita? Really – I mean it's from her to you so – so – (*He
hands it back.*)

Sackling (*takes it back*) 'I'm sorry, darling, so sorry, oh
my darling, but it seems after all that I wasn't cut out to
be a writer's wife. I can't stand the strain of it, the lonely
evenings, your remoteness, and most of all the feeling
that your novel means more to you than Tom and I do.
Perhaps that's what being an artist is. Not caring about
those who love you. I'm going back to mother's, I'll
take the car' – yes, taken the car – she'd take that all

right, wouldn't she? – 'as you don't drive, and begin
proceedings as soon as I've got a lawyer. Take care, my
love, look after yourself, I wish you such success and I
know that one day I'll be proud to have been your first
wife, just as Tom will be proud to be your father.'

There is a pause.

Quartermaine Um, son, surely.

Sackling What?

Quartermaine Um, Tom's your son. Not your father.
You read out that he was your father. Not your son.

Sackling Oh, if only I'd been able to read her that
passage – she would have understood my feelings, she'd
have known – but what do I do? I can't give up now, not
when I'm so close to finishing – my fourth draft – my
penultimate draft – I know it's the penultimate – then
one final one – and – and – so what do I do – I can't
think – can't think –

*Loomis enters through the French windows. He walks
awkwardly, has thick glasses, is carrying a file.*

Loomis Good morning, good morning, Anita my dear,
Mark. I trust you all had a good weekend?

Quartermaine, Anita *and* **Sackling** Yes, thank you, Eddie.

Loomis I'm just on my way through to do my little
welcome speech, with a small dilation this time on the
problems of our Cambridge landladies, we've just heard
that our faithful Mrs Cornley is refusing to take any of
our students except what she calls traditional foreigners,
all over some dreadful misunderstanding she's had with
those three really delightful Turks we sent her, over the
proper function of the bathroom – such a nuisance,
Thomas has been on the phone to her for hours – but
still, I suppose the problems of a flourishing school –

nine Japanese have turned up, by the way, instead of the anticipated six, and as it was three last time we can hope for a round dozen next – Mark, is it these fast-fading old eyes of mine, or did you forget to shave this morning, and yesterday morning, even?

Sackling No, no – I'm thinking of growing a beard, Eddie.

Loomis Alas! And what saith the fair Camelia to that?

Sackling (*mutters*) I don't think she'll mind.

Loomis Mmmm?

Sackling I don't – I don't think she'll mind, Eddie.

Loomis Good, good – Anita, my dear, may I pay you a compliment?

Anita Yes please, Eddie.

Loomis I like your hair even more that way.

Anita Well, thank you, Eddie, actually I put it up for a dinner party we had last night – and thought I'd give it a longer run – it was a sort of editorial dinner, you see – (*realising*)

Loomis Ah! And the magazine's progressing well, or so we gathered from Nigel. We bumped into him on the Backs, on Saturday afternoon, did he tell you?

Anita No. No, he didn't.

Loomis He was having a conference with one of his co-editors, I suppose it was.

Anita Oh. Thomas Pine.

Loomis No no, I don't think Thomas Pine, my dear, but co-editress I should have said, shouldn't I? One can't be too precise these days.

Anita Oh. Was she – blonde and – rather pretty?

Loomis Oh, very pretty – at least Thomas was much smitten, you know what an eye he's got.

Anita Ah, then that would be Amanda Southgate, yes, I expect he was trying to persuade her to take on all the dogsbodying – you know, hounding contributors, keeping the printers at bay – she's terrifically efficient. She's an old friend of mine. I used to go to school with her sister.

A little pause.

She's smashing, actually.

Loomis Good good – now, St John, what was it Thomas asked me to tell you? Or was it Henry and Melanie I'm to tell what to? Oh yes, this of course. (*He hands him a postcard from the file.*) We couldn't resist having a look, postcards being somehow in the public domain, one always thinks. At least when they're other people's. (*He laughs.*) Do read it out to Mark and Anita, don't be modest, St John.

Quartermaine Um, I must writing to thanking you for all excellent times in your most heppy clesses, your true Ferdinand Boller. Lord! (*He laughs.*)

Loomis And which one was he, can you recall?

Quartermaine Oh. Well, you know a – a German –

Loomis Postmarked Zurich, I believe, so more likely a Swiss.

Quartermaine Oh yes, that's right, a Swiss, a – a well, rather large, Eddie, with his hair cut *en brosse* and – round face – in his forties or so, and –

Loomis – and wearing lederhosen, perhaps, and good at yodelling, no no, St John, I don't think I quite believe in your rather caricature Swiss, I suspect you must have made rather more of an impression on Herr Ferdinand

Boller than he managed to make on you, still I suppose
that's better than the other way around, and his sentiments
are certainly quite a tribute – would that his English
were, too, eh? But do try to remember them, St John,
match names to faces. (*He laughs.*) And on that subject,
you haven't forgotten Mr Middleton begins this
morning, have you?

Quartermaine Who, Eddie?

Loomis Middleton. Dennis Middleton, St John, Henry
told you all about him at the last staff meeting, he wrote
to us from Hull expressing such an intelligent interest in
the techniques of teaching English as a foreign language
that Thomas invited him for an interview, and was so
taken by the genuineness of his manner that he offered
him some teaching – only part-time to begin with, of
course, until we see how things go – anyway, he should
be here any minute, so whilst I'm making the students
welcome perhaps you would be doing the same for him,
and tell him that either Thomas or I will be along before
the bell to introduce him to his first class, which is, I
believe, Intermediary Dictation – Mark?

Sackling Mmmm?

Loomis Middleton, Mark.

Sackling (*blankly*) Yes. Yes. Right, Eddie.

Loomis See you all at the bell, then – (*He walks off,
stage left. Then sound of him stopping. A slight pause.*)
Oh Mark, there is one other thing – if I could just have a
quick private word –

Sackling What? Oh – oh yes –

He gets up. As he goes over:

Loomis (*takes a few necessary steps to be on stage. In a
lowered voice*) Nothing important, Mark, merely Thomas

wanted me to mention, in a by-the-way spirit, one of our French students Mlle Jeanette LeClerc, do you recall her?

Sackling Oh. Yes. I think so. Yes.

Loomis She's written complaining that you forgot to return two or three pieces of her work, an essay and two comprehension passages I believe she listed, as I say, not cataclysmic in itself, but as Thomas always points out, so much of our reputation depends on Jeanette passing on to Lucien what Lucien then passes to Gabrielle, so do make a note of which students are leaving when and make sure of getting every item back before they go. Mark? (*Sackling tautly nods.*) Good, good, and may I put in my personal plea against the beard? I do think they make even the handsomest chaps red-eyed and snively-looking, I don't want to end up begging Camelia to be Delilah to your Samson, eh, and think of poor little Tom, too, having to endure Daddy's whiskers against his chubby young cheeks at cuddle-time – (*Sackling rushes past him out of the door.*) But – but – what did I say? A little professional criticism – it *can't* have been about the beard, I couldn't have been more playful.

Quartermaine Oh, it's not your fault, Eddie, is it, Anita? You see the poor chap's had a – a horrible weekend –

Anita (*warningly, cutting in*) Yes, up all night, working at his novel. I'll go and see if he's all right. (*She goes off, left.*)

Loomis I see. Well that's all very well, after all, nobody could respect Mark's literary ambitions more than Thomas and myself, but we really can't have him running about in this sort of state, what on earth would the students make of it if he were to gallop emotionally off in the middle of a dictation –?

Meadle appears at the French windows.

Meadle Um, is this the staff room, please? (*He is hot and flustered, wearing bicycle clips, carrying a briefcase, and mopping his brow.*)

Loomis Yes, what do you want – oh, of course, it's Mr Middleton, isn't it? Our new member of staff.

Meadle Well, yes – well, Meadle, actually, Derek Meadle.

Loomis Yes, yes, Derek Meadle, well, I'm Eddie Loomis, the Principal. One of two Principals, as you know, as you've met Mr Cull, of course, and this is St John Quartermaine, who's been with us since our school started, and you've come down to join us from Sheffield, isn't it?

Meadle Yes sir, well, Hull actually.

Loomis Hull, good good – and when did you arrive?

Meadle Yesterday afternoon.

Loomis And found yourself a room?

Meadle Yes, yes thank you, sir.

Loomis Good good, and found yourself a bicycle too, I see.

Meadle (*who throughout all this has been standing rather awkwardly, keeping face-on to Loomis*) Yes, sir. My landlady – I happened to ask her where would be a good place to buy a second-hand one, not being familiar with the shops, and she happened to mention that her son had left one behind in the basement and I could have it for two pounds so I –

Loomis (*interrupting*) Good good, most enterprising – at least of your landlady. (*He laughs.*) But Mr Meadle, I've got to have a little talk with the students, and Mr Cull is still looking after enrolment, but one of us will be back at the bell to introduce you to your first class – Intermediary Comprehension, isn't it –?

Meadle Dictation, sir.

Loomis So I'll leave you in St John's capable hands –

Meadle Yes, sir. Thank you.

Loomis Oh, one thing, though, Mr Meadle – sir us no sirs, we're very informal here – I'm Eddie, Mr Cull is Thomas, and you're Dennis.

Meadle Oh, well thank you very much –

Loomis (*as the sound of students' voices is heard off, crossing the garden*) Ah, and here they are – (*He goes off, left.*)

Quartermaine Well, I must say – jolly glad to have you with us – I think you'll enjoy it here – the staff is – well, they're terrific – and the students are – well, they're very interesting, coming from all quarters of the globe, so to speak – but look, why don't you come in properly and sit down and – and make yourself at home?

Meadle Yes, thanks, but – well, you see, the trouble is, I've had an accident.

Quartermaine Really? Oh Lord!

Meadle Yes, I didn't want to go into it in front of Mr Loomis – Eddie – not quite the way to start off one's first day in a new job – but – well – here – you'd better see for yourself. (*He turns. His trousers are rent at the seat.*) How bad is it, actually?

Quartermaine Well – they're – they're – a bit of a write-off, I'm afraid. How did it happen?

Meadle Oh, usual combination of unexpected circumstances, eh? (*He laughs.*) For one thing the bicycle – I suspected there might be something wrong with it for two pounds, but I checked everything – the brakes, the mudguards, the wheels, the inner tubes, even the pump and the dynamo. The only thing I didn't examine meticulously was the seat. There was the minutest bit of spring sticking up, and I suppose it worked its way into my trousers as I was pedalling here. The worm in the apple, eh? (*He laughs.*) But even so I'd probably have been all right if it hadn't been for a little pack of Japanese coming up the school drive. They were laughing and chattering so much among themselves – not the usual idea of Japanese at all – you know, formal and keeping a distance from each other – (*Laughs.*) Didn't hear my bell until I was almost on top of them, and then a big chap with a bald head – I didn't realise they came in that sort of size either – stepped right out in front of me – I was going pretty quickly, I have to admit – wanted to be in good time, you see, for my first day – and of course I lost control on the gravel and skidded and had to leap sideways off the bike. But with my trousers snagged I only half-made it. They were very tactful about it, by the way. Averted their eyes to show they hadn't seen it, and went on into the office. What they call saving face, I believe. My face, in this case. Oh, except for the big bald one. I had the impression he found it rather amusing – but of course the question is, what do I do about it? I mean I don't really want to spend my first day going about like this, do I? People might get the impression it's my normal attire.

> *He laughs. But this speech should be delivered to convey a simmering rage and desperation behind the attempt at an insouciant manner, and of a natural North Country accent held in check under stress.*

Quartermaine Well, you know, old chap, I think the best thing would be to go back and change. Don't worry about being late – I'll explain what happened –

Meadle Ah, yes, but into what, is the question.

Quartermaine Well – into another pair of trousers, I –
I suppose.

Meadle Yes, but you see, I haven't got another pair is
the problem. An elderly gentleman on the train yesterday
spilt his chocolate out of his thermos right over the pair
I happened to have on, so the first thing I did when I got
in – irony of ironies – was to take them to the cleaners.
And my trunk, which I'd sent on from Hull and which
contained my suit and my other two pairs, hasn't arrived
yet. So there it is. Hot chocolate, a broken spring, a pack
of unusually gregarious Japanese and British Rail, all
working together in complete harmony to bring me to
my first day of my new job looking like Oliver and
Hardy. What do I do? Any suggestions? I mean if I pull
them really high – like this – (*pulling them up*) – and
leave my clips on – does it still show?

Quartermaine Well, just a little – well, not really – well,
I say, I'll tell you what – if you can get your jacket down
just a fraction –

Meadle (*he pulls it down*) – but if I keep my hands in –
(*putting them in the pockets, and pushing down*) what
about it?

Quartermaine How does it feel?

Meadle (*laughs*) Well – unnatural. Extremely unnatural.
(*taking a few steps*)

Quartermaine Actually, you look rather – rather formid-
able actually.

Meadle (*taking another step or so*) No no – (*exploding
into a violent rage*) Bloody hell, I'm meant to be teaching,
I can't go round like this all day, everybody will think I'm
some sort of buffoon – this is the sheerest – the sheerest –

Windscape enters through the French windows. He is carrying a briefcase, wears bicycle clips, smokes a pipe.

Windscape Hello, St John.

Quartermaine Oh – oh, hello, Henry – um, come and meet our new chap – (*to Meadle*) Henry's our academic tutor – syllabus and all that –

Windscape (*comes over*) Oh yes, of course, very glad to have you with us, Merton, isn't it?

Quartermaine Middleton, actually.

Meadle Meadle, as a matter of fact.

Quartermaine That's right. Sorry. Dennis Meadle.

Windscape Well, whatever yours happens to be –

Meadle Derek. Derek Meadle.

Windscape – mine is Windscape. Henry Windscape. How do you do?

Meadle (*he gets his hand out of his pocket, they shake hands, Meadle replaces his hand*) How do you do?

Quartermaine I say, how were they in the end, Susan, little Fanny and old Ben – and Fanny's headache?

Windscape Oh, fine thank you, St John, fine – I didn't get Susan to bed until midnight of course. (*to Meadle*) She's studying for her O-Levels – a couple of years in advance – and – and Fanny had rather a bad moment when she went into the lavatory because of Raggedy Anne sitting there – and dripping – she thought it was little Fanny, you see – (*laughing*)

Quartermaine Oh Lord, I forgot –

Windscape St John was good enough to come over and sit with our three last night – we went to see *M*, you

know – such a fine film – so delicate and human in its
treatment of a – a sexual freak and Peter Lorre –
unfortunately the print was a trifle worn – but still –
memorable – memorable – but isn't it interesting – on
another subject – this English thing about names, how
we forget them the second we hear them? Just now, for
instance, when St John was introducing you. Unlike
Americans, for instance.

He puffs and pulls on his pipe throughout this speech.
Meadle nods and chuckles tensely.

I suppose because we – the English, that is – are so busy
looking at the person the name represents – or *not*
looking, being English – (*laughs*) – that we don't take
in the name itself – whereas the Americans, you see,
make a point of beginning with the name – when one's
introduced they repeat it endlessly. 'This is Dennis
Meadle. Dennis Meadle, why hello, Dennis, and how
long have you been in this country, Dennis? This is
Dennis Meadle, dear, Dennis was just telling me how
much he liked our fair city, weren't you Dennis . . .?' (*All*
this in an execrable imitation of an American accent.)
And – and so forth, and in no time at all they've learnt
what you're called by even if not who you are –
(*Laughs.*) – while we, the English, being more empirical,
don't learn your name until you yourself have taken on
a complicated reality – you and your name grow, so to
speak, in associated stages in our memories, until what
you are as Dennis Meadle and the sounds Dennis
Meadle are inseparable, which is actually – when you
think about it – a radical division in ways of perceiving
that goes back to the Middle Ages in the Nominalists –
the name-callers – calling the name preceding the object,
so to speak, and the realists –

During this, Melanie has entered through the French
windows. She puts her briefcase on the table.

– who believed the object preceded the name – but one could go on and on; there's Melanie, Melanie come and meet our new chap –

Quartermaine Hello, Melanie, have a good weekend?

Melanie Yes thanks, St John, you're in top form for a Monday morning, Henry, how do you do, I'm Melanie Garth.

Meadle Meadle. Derek Meadle.

Melanie And you've come to reinforce us. Well, we certainly could do with you, Thomas was just telling me about the enrolment chaos, you'll be getting a lot of overspill from my groups, I can tell you.

Windscape Melanie's our Elementary Conversation specialist, by the way.

Melanie Oh, I don't know about specialist, Henry. Henry's our only real specialist here, he specialises in – well, everything, doesn't he, St John? From pronunciation to British Life and Institutions, but what I enjoyed most about the sight of you two philosophising away here was that you both still had your bicycle clips on – as if you'd met on a street corner –

Windscape (*laughing*) Good heavens, so they are. Thank you for reminding me, my dear, whenever I forget to take them off I spend hours after school hunting for them –

He bends to take them off. Meadle, grinning and distraught, makes a gesture towards taking his off.

Quartermaine (*taking this in*) I say – I say, Melanie, how's um, how's Mother?

Melanie Top form, thanks, St John, her left leg's still giving her bother, and the stairs are a dreadful strain, you know, because of this sudden vertigo, but yesterday she managed to hobble down to the corner shop all by herself, and was halfway back by the time I came to pick her up.

Quartermaine Oh, that's terrific! Melanie's mother's just recovering from a thingmebob.

Melanie Stroke, if you please, St John. She insists on the proper term, she hates euphemisms.

Windscape Not surprisingly, as Melanie's mother was Cambridge's first lady of philology – the first woman ever to hold the chair in it – I had the honour of being supervised by her in my second year as an undergraduate – and although she's retired she was still very much a behind-the-scenes force on the faculty until she had her – little upset a few months ago. And will be again, I suspect, as she appears to be coming to terms with her condition in a characteristically – characteristically indomitable –

Meadle I have an aunt who had a stroke a year ago. She was the active sort too. Of course not a professor but – very active. In her own way. She went in for jam.

Melanie And how is she coping?

Meadle Well, she was doing splendidly until she had the next. Now she's pretty well out of it altogether, my uncle has to do virtually everything for her. But then that's one of the usual patterns, they said at the hospital. First a mild stroke, followed by a worse stroke, and then, if that doesn't do the job – (*He gestures.*) But in a sense it's worse for my uncle, he's an independent old fellow, used to leading his own life –

Melanie Yes, well, Mr Meadle, I'm sorry for your aunt – and for your uncle – but sufficient unto the day, sufficient unto the day – if you'll excuse me, I haven't sorted out my first hour's Comprehension – (*She picks up the briefcase, goes to her locker.*)

Windscape Of course that's only *one* of the possible patterns – there are many cases of complete – or – or more than merely partial recovery – if I might – might just – Melanie puts on a remarkably brave front, but don't be led astray, she's an intensely feeling person who knows very well the likely outcome of her mother's – her mother's – she's deeply attached to her, as you probably gathered, isn't she, St John?

Quartermaine Oh Lord, yes!

Windscape I hope you don't mind my saying it?

Meadle No, no. Thank you. Thank you.

Windscape Good man! (*He puts his hand on Meadle's shoulder.*) Well, I'd better unpack my own –

    He goes over to his locker, looking towards Melanie, who is standing still by hers.

Meadle (*smiling tightly, and in a low voice*) Don't think I can stand much more of this. Hardly know what I'm saying – really put my foot in it –

Quartermaine Well, why don't you just tell them? I mean, it's only a torn pair of bags –

Meadle It's too late now, I've left it too late. I can't just clap my hands for attention, oh, by the way, everybody, come and look at my trousers, ha ha ha. What I need is safety pins – and then a few minutes in the toilet – can you get me some?

Quartermaine I'll nip over to the office –

Meadle Well, take me to the toilet first.

Loomis (*comes through the French windows*) Good morning, Melanie, my dear, good morning, Henry – good weekend, I trust?

Melanie *and* **Windscape** Yes thanks, Eddie.

Loomis All well with mother, I trust.

Melanie Yes thanks Eddie. Top form.

Loomis Good, good – and Fanny and the children?

Windscape Yes thanks, Eddie – all splendid.

Loomis Good good – (*as Anita and Sackling enter from the right*) Ah, and here you are, you two, and quite composed again Mark, I trust –

Anita Well, Eddie, actually I'm not sure that Mark –

Sackling feebly gestures silence to Anita.

Loomis And Mr Meadle, I don't know which of you have had the chance to meet him yet, but those who haven't can make their separate introductions, in the meanwhile I'll say a welcome on all our behalves, we're delighted to have you with us – I see you've still got your clips on, by the way, perhaps you'd better remove them or you'll create the impression that you're just pedalling through –

He laughs. Meadle bends to take them off.

– now as we're all here and there are a few minutes before the bell, I'd like to say a few words, if I may. As you've no doubt realised, we have an exceptionally high enrolment for the month, the highest in the school's career, as a matter of fact.

Little murmurs.

Quartermaine I say, terrific!

Loomis Yes, very gratifying. You all know how hard Thomas has worked for this. Though he'd loathe to hear me say it. But what he wouldn't mind hearing me say

is that in his turn he knows how hard you've worked.
I think we all have a right to be proud of our growing
reputation as one of the best schools of English – not
one of the biggest but one of the best – in Cambridge.
Which, when it comes down to it, means in the country.
Well and good. Well and good. But success will bring –
has already begun to bring – its own problems. (*He
gestures to Meadle.*) As Mr Meadle's presence here
testifies. But even with Mr Meadle – or Dennis, as I've
already told him I intend to call him – with Dennis to
help us, there is going to be a considerable strain on
our resources. Perhaps a few too many students to a
classroom, more work to take home and correct, more
difficulties in developing personal contact – that so
crucial personal contact – with students many of whom
are only here for a short time – well, as I say, you've
already become familiar with the problems, the problems,
as Thomas remarked 'midst the chaos this morning, of a
flourishing school – but please remember, I'm reminding
myself too when I say this, how important it is if we are
to continue to flourish –

*Sackling faints. Anita cries out, tries to catch him,
half-supports him, as Windscape gets to him,
Quartermaine attempts to.*

Windscape There – there, old chap – I've got you – out
of the way, everyone – while I lower him – (*He does so.*)
The thing is to keep his head up.

Quartermaine Yes, right.

*He makes to go round, as Anita runs over, takes
Sackling's head, then sits down, gets his head into her
lap.*

Windscape Mark – Mark – can you hear me? (*He slaps
his cheeks.*) He's right out. (*He puts his hand on*

Sackling's heart.) It's very faint. (*massaging his heart*)
Somebody better telephone for an ambulance.

Quartermaine Right!

*He makes to go to the telephone. Loomis goes to the
telephone, dials.*

Windscape And chafe his wrists – and something to put
over him – your coat – (*to Meadle*) Hurry, man!

*Meadle hesitates, takes off his coat as Quartermaine
struggles out of his.*

Come around – put it over him – over his chest –

*Meadle does so, as Quartermaine stands, jacket half
off.*

There – now – now – now –

*Loomis finishes speaking, puts the telephone down,
comes over, stands looking anxiously down. The bell
rings.*

Quartermaine (*also looking down*) Oh Lord! Oh Lord!

Lights.

SCENE TWO

*Some weeks later. Friday afternoon, a few minutes before
five p.m. The French windows are open. It's a sunny day.*
*Quartermaine is putting books and papers away. He is
humming to himself. He closes his locker, does a few
elegant dance steps, and then goes into a tap dance, at
which he is surprisingly adept. Loomis enters through
the French windows, watches Quartermaine.*

Quartermaine (*sees Loomis, stops*) Oh Lord! (*He
laughs.*) Hello, Eddie.

Loomis You're in sprightly mood, St John.

Quartermaine Yes, well, Friday evening and off to the theatre and all that – you know.

Loomis And what are you going to see?

Quartermaine Oh that – that Strindberg, I think it is. At the Arts.

Loomis I believe it's an Ibsen, *Hedda Gabler* I believe, but tell me – the bell's gone then, has it, I didn't hear it – but then these old ears of mine – (*He laughs.*)

Quartermaine Ah yes, well I let them out a little early, you see, Eddie.

Loomis Why?

Quartermaine Well, it was the special Life and Institutions lecture, you see, and I chose Oxford Colleges with slides – to give them the other point of view, for once – (*Laughs.*) – but of course the old projector broke –

Loomis It's the newest model.

Quartermaine Yes, I think that's the trouble, all those extra bits to master – anyway one of the colleges went in upside down and wouldn't come out so I had to – to abandon technology and do it all off my own bat – you know, reminiscences of my time at the House and – and anecdotes – and – you know – that sort of thing. The personal touch. But of course I ran out of steam a little, towards the end. I'm afraid. (*Laughs.*)

Loomis And how many turned up?

Quartermaine Oh well – about a handful.

Loomis A handful!

Quartermaine A good handful.

Loomis But there are meant to be twenty-three in the group that that special lecture's designed for.

Quartermaine Yes, well, I think, you know – it being Friday and – and the sun shining and the Backs so lovely and the Cam jam-packed with punts and – but the ones who came were jolly interested – especially that little Italian girl – you know, um – um – almost midget-sized, the one with the wart –

Loomis If you mean Angelina, she happens to be Greek. Her father's an exceptionally distinguished army officer. Thomas will be very disappointed to hear about all this, St John, he devised that lecture series himself, you know, it's quite an innovation, and if you can't keep attendances up – and then there's the question of the projector, I only hope you haven't done it any damage –

The sound of a door opening, footsteps hurrying.

– and you know very well how important it is to keep classes going until at least the bell – ah, hello, my dear, you've finished a trifle on the early side too, then?

Anita (*enters, slightly breathless*) Oh, isn't it past five?

Loomis Well, the bell hasn't gone yet, even in your part of the corridor – Intermediary Dictation, wasn't it, and how was your attendance?

Anita Oh, nearly a full complement, Eddie, they're a very keen lot, mostly Germans, in fact that's why I thought the bell had gone, one of them – Kurt – said he'd heard it.

Loomis Good, good.

He is not convinced, perhaps. Anita makes to go to her locker.

My dear, have I told you what I think about your sandals?

Anita No, Eddie.

Loomis Well, when I first saw you in them I wondered if they were quite *comme il faut*, Thomas and I had quite a thing about them –

Quartermaine I think they're smashing.

Loomis But I've been quite won around, I've come to the view that they're most fetching. Or that your feet are. Or both. (*He laughs.*)

Anita Thank you, Eddie.

Loomis And Nigel's still in London, is he, with his co-editress?

Anita Yes, he comes back on Saturday or Sunday.

Loomis Quite a coincidence Thomas seeing them on the train like that, he's scarcely been out of his office this many a month, as you know – and it's all working out all right, is it?

Anita Yes, she's been absolutely wonderful, quite a surprise really, because when I first met Amanda at a party a few years ago I thought she was – well, absolutely charming, of course, but rather – rather feckless, if anything. But the girl who gave the party's a great friend of mine and she's always said Amanda had a good tough brain. Her boyfriend's being a great help too. He's invaluable.

Loomis How odd, I had an idea you went to school with her?

Anita (*slight hesitation*) No, no – with her sister. Seraphina.

Loomis Ah yes – but I was really asking about the magazine itself, how that was coming?

Anita Well, they're still having to delay publication because of these printers letting them down, but now they've found a new one in London – and they're getting in some really decent articles and things and – oh, they've finally settled on a title. It's going to be called *Reports*.

Quartermaine Terrific!

The bell rings.

Loomis *Reports*, *Reports*, mmm, well, tell Nigel when he gets back that Thomas has decided to take out two subscriptions, one for ourselves and one for the student common room, so we'll be showing a great personal interest –

Anita Oh thank you, Eddie, Nigel will be so pleased –

From the garden, the sound of Windscape.

Windscape (*off*) I can't stay too long, I'm afraid, just to start you off and explain the rules – but first let's get the mallets and balls – (*The voices recede.*)

Loomis (*going to the window*) Ah, the croquet's under way again, good, good, – and who's playing – ah, Piccolo and Jean-Pierre, Gisela – Teresa – Okona – Liv and Gerta – you know, I always feel that if ever our little school had to justify itself, we could do it by showing the world the spectacle of an Italian, a Frenchman, a German, a Japanese, a Swedish girl and a Belgian girl, all gathered together on an English lawn, under an English sky to play a game of croquet –

Anita through this has gone to her locker.

Quartermaine Absolutely, Eddie, absolutely – croquet – I must try my hand again – haven't for years – my aunt had such a lawn, you know, and I remember, oh Lord, (*shaking his head, laughing*) Oh Lord, I say, I forgot, Thomas told me to tell you he was looking for you.

Loomis Thomas? When?

Quartermaine Oh, just at the end of my lecture – he popped his head in.

Loomis Really, St John, I wish you'd mentioned it straight away, it would have to be something urgent for Thomas to interrupt a class – was he going back to the office?

Sackling enters during this, carrying books, etc. He sports a moustache.

Quartermaine He didn't say, Eddie.

Loomis Mark, have you happened to glimpse Thomas –?

Sackling Yes. I think he and Melanie were going up to your flat –

Loomis Oh. Well, if he should come down here looking for me, tell him I've gone upstairs – and that I'll stay there so that we don't do one of our famous boxes and coxes – (*Goes out right.*)

Sackling Right, Eddie. (*going to his locker*)

Anita, during the above, has finished packing and is leaving. There is an air of desperate rush about her.

Quartermaine Phew! He'd pretty well stopped showing up in here before the bell – wasn't he in a dodgy mood? But I say, where shall we meet, Anita, shall Mark and I come and pick you up at your place, or shall we go to Mark's place, or the foyer, or – or we could go to The Eagle – or you two could come to my place –

Anita Oh, I'm sorry, St John, I completely forgot – you see I'm going to London. It suddenly occurred to me that

274

as Nigel can't get back until tomorrow or Sunday, why not pop down and spend the weekend with him?

Quartermaine Oh what a good idea, spend the weekend in London with Nigel, much more fun than some old Ibsen thing –

Sackling Shouldn't you phone him first? I mean, he may be going out or – you know.

Anita I haven't got time. Anyway, I don't mind waiting for him – look, I've got to dash if I'm going to make the five-thirty – damn Eddie!

Sackling Oh – Anita, would you apologise to him again for my letting him down, I'll really try for the second issue –

Anita (*rushing off*) Yes, right, I'll tell him –

Sackling Oh Christ! Poor old Nigel!

Quartermaine Mmmm?

Sackling Well, surely you know?

Quartermaine What?

Sackling About Nigel and Amanda Southgate. They're having a passionate affair. He only started the magazine because of her – she's got literary ambitions.

Quartermaine Oh Lord – oh, Lord, poor old Anita! But they always seemed so happy –

Sackling You know, St John, you have an amazing ability not to let the world impinge on you. Anita's the unhappiest woman I know, at the moment. And has been, ever since she met Nigel. Amanda's his fifth affair in the last two years, even if the most serious. But she covers up for him, pretends it isn't happening, or tries to protect a reputation he hasn't got and probably doesn't

want anyway, she's had three abortions for him to my
knowledge, three, although she's desperate for children –
haven't you had the slightest inkling of any of that?

Quartermaine No, but good Lord – how do you know?
I mean –

Sackling Well, Nigel told me most of it, as a matter of
fact. But I'd still have thought it's perfectly obvious there
was something amiss – but what I don't understand is
why she's suddenly gone down to confront him. She's
only survived so far by not daring to have anything out
with him – she's never once mentioned even the most
blatant of his infidelities, actually that's one of the things
about her that drives him mad. But perhaps the thought
of the two of them in London while she has to spend the
weekend here – anyway, there's nothing we can do about
it, is there? I haven't even got his number, so I can't warn
him.

Quartermaine Don't you like Anita?

Sackling Of course I do. Far more than I like Nigel, as a
matter of fact.

Quartermaine Oh. Oh well it all seems – all seems –
I mean these things between people – people one cares
for – it's hard to bear them – but, but I say, what about
this evening then? I wonder if they'll take her ticket back
or – anyway, how would you like to play it? Eagle or –

Sackling As a matter of fact, St John, I'm going to have
to bow out of the theatre, too.

Quartermaine Oh. Oh well –

Sackling To tell you the truth, I couldn't face it. You see,
last night I went back to it again. My novel. The first
time since Camelia left. And there was the old flame
a-flickering as strongly as ever. And if I don't get back to

it again this evening – I'll – I'll – well, anyway, I'll have a rotten evening. And give you one, too, probably. Look, you haven't actually bought the tickets, have you?

Quartermaine (*makes to say yes, changes his mind*) No, no, never any need to at the Arts, so don't worry about that, but – but it's terrific, that you've started writing again, that's far more important than going to see some – some old Ibsen thing.

Sackling Thanks. And St John, thanks also for your companionship these last weeks. It must have been bloody boring for you, having me grind on and on in my misery.

Quartermaine Lord no. I've enjoyed it enormously. Not your misery I don't mean but your – your – I say, did you get that letter, though?

Sackling Yes, this morning. She's allowing me a few hours tomorrow afternoon. With my son. Which is another reason I must spend this evening at the typewriter –

Quartermaine But that's wonderful, Mark. A breakthrough at last – look, when will you be back?

Sackling Tomorrow evening, I suppose.

Quartermaine Well, perhaps we could have lunch on Sunday or dinner or meet for a drink – and you could tell me how things went with little Tom – I'd really love to know.

During this, the sound of a door opening and closing, followed by a yelp.

Meadle (*off*) Blast!

Quartermaine You all right, old man!

Meadle (*he is wearing a blazer and flannels, and has a bump on his forehead covered by a piece of sticking* *plaster*) Yes, yes – (*rubbing his hand*) It's that doorknob, a bit too close to the door-jamb – at least for my taste – (*He laughs.*) I'm always scraping my knuckles on it – hello, Mark, haven't seen you around for a bit, I suppose because you're usually gone before I finish.

Sackling Don't worry, I do my time. Right to the bell.

Meadle Oh, I didn't mean any reflection – (*He laughs.*) Good God, I only meant that I always seem to get caught by students who want to practise their English after hours too – of course it doesn't help to be carrying a conversation piece around on your forehead – 'What 'appen 'ead, Mr Mittle?' 'Whasa matter weet de het, Meester Meetle?' 'Mister Mittle, vat goes mit der hed?' (*laughing*) Up the corridor, down, in the classroom, in the garden – by the time I'd gone through all the details, with pantomime, landlady calling to the telephone, toe stubbing in cracked linoleum, body pitching down the stairs and bonce cracking down on tile I'd have settled for serious internal injuries instead.

Sackling (*smiles*) Goodnight, see you both Monday. (*He goes out through the French windows.*)

Quartermaine (*who has been laughing with Meadle*) Oh, 'night, old man, but oh, just a minute, we haven't fixed our meeting – (*Goes to the French windows and stares out.*)

Meadle (*who has registered Sackling's manner*) He's a hard chap to get to know, isn't he?

Quartermaine Who? Old Mark? Lord, no – oh, well, perhaps to begin with but once you do know him you can't imagine a – a better friend.

Meadle Oh. Well, I'll keep working on it then.

Quartermaine And of course he's been through a very bad time – and with his – his particular talent –

Meadle By the way, you haven't seen Thomas, have you? (*going to his locker*)

Quartermaine I think he's with Eddie, anyway they're looking for each other.

Meadle Oh. (*He nods.*)

Quartermaine I say, I've managed to get hold of some tickets for the theatre tonight. They're doing an Ibsen! Would you like to come?

Meadle To tell you the truth, Ibsen's not quite my cup of tea, thanks, but anyway, as a matter of fact, Oko-Ri's taking me out to dinner tonight with the rest of the boys.

Quartermaine Oko – what?

Meadle Ri. Oko-Ri. My Japanese chum.

Quartermaine Oh, old baldy, you mean? Taking you out to dinner – well, that's – that's – I didn't know you'd hit it off so well with them, after that business –

Meadle Well, I never thought they'd made me skid deliberately – and we've had lots of good laughs about it since – now that I'm on their wavelength – Oko-Ri's got a splendid sense of humour. Loves a drink too, I gather, from some of their jokes.

Quartermaine Oh, well, you'll have a good evening then –

Meadle It's really just to say thank you for all the extra hours I've put in with them. They left it to me to decide where we'd go, and I've chosen that French place that's just opened opposite Trinity, Eddie and Thomas were saying it's very good – I'm a bit worried about that, though, I hope it's not too expensive – I had a feeling

they hesitated slightly, or Oko-Ri did, he's very much the
man in charge. One has to keep sensitive to these things –
but of course once I'd asked for it, it was too late to
change – but I'd better get back if I'm going to meet
them later – did I tell you my landlady's just offered me
another room as a bedroom letting me keep the bedroom
I've got now as a study-cum-sitting-room, so I'm virtually
ending up with a little suite of my own, and all for just
another twenty-five shillings, for five pounds in all.

Quartermaine Good Lord. And to think I'm paying six
pounds for my pokey little room – how on earth did you
manage that, Derek?

Meadle I think it's because I remind her of her son,
being the same age almost, and he never bothers to write
or come to visit, as far as I can make out.

Quartermaine Golly, I should have a go at Mrs Harris,
see if I can remind her of her son, if she has one, although
if he's anything like her I hope I don't, eh? Anyway, you
certainly do land on your feet, old man, don't you?

Meadle Well – (*laughs*) – sometimes on my head, eh?
Anyway, I'd better get back. (*Putting on his bicycle clips.*)
I've asked Oko-Ri and his boys to initiate my suite, with
a bottle of whisky, before our dinner, and I've still got
some furniture to move – I'd ask you to come along too,
but it's not really my invitation –

Quartermaine Oh –

*He gestures. The sound of a door opening and closing;
feet.*

Meadle (*going out*) Oh. Here. Let me give you a hand
with those, Melanie –

Melanie (*off*) No, it's quite all right, I've got them –

Meadle (*off*) Well, let me just take this one –

Melanie No, no, really – there's no need –

The sound of books dropping on the floor.

Meadle (*off*) Oh, sorry, Melanie –

Melanie (*irritably*) Oh – really! I had them perfectly well – and Thomas has just lent me that one with great warnings to be careful, it's a rare edition –

Meadle comes onstage, carrying a distinguished volume. Melanie comes onstage, carrying a briefcase, exercise books and further books.

If you could just put it on the table –

Meadle What, here do you mean?

Melanie Have either of you seen Eddie? Thomas has been looking for him.

Quartermaine Now what did Eddie say?– Oh yes, that he was going to wait for Thomas in the – in the office, it must have been.

Melanie Oh, well that's where Thomas has gone – he took me down into the cellar to find the book – it took him longer than he thought and he got worried that Eddie would go into one of his panics, and be in and out of every room in the school – you know how clever they are at just missing each other – so you're the last two then, are you?

Quartermaine Yes, well, apart from old Henry, that is, he's playing croquet –

Melanie Is he? Jolly good! (*She goes to her locker.*)

Meadle (*who has been looking through the book*) No, no damage done, Melanie – (*He looks at his watch.*) So Thomas is in the office, is he?

Melanie Yes, why, what do you want him for?

Meadle Oh – well – well actually he said something about seeing if he could get me some extra pronunciation classes – my rent has just gone up, you see, so I really rather need the extra bobs. (*He laughs.*)

Melanie I wouldn't go disturbing him now, if I were you, he's had a particularly fraught day. He's got a dreadful headache. The only person he'll want to see is Eddie.

Meadle Oh. Well, in that case – goodnight, Melanie.

Melanie Goodnight – oh, that reminds me, I'd be very grateful if you'd stop putting your bicycle against the wall just where I park my car – there's not enough room for both.

Meadle Oh, sorry about that – right, Melanie – well, see you Monday, then.

Quartermaine See you Monday, old man.

Meadle goes out through the French windows.

Melanie I really think I'd get on much better with Mr Meadle if he didn't try so hard to get on with me. Still, I really had no right to stop him from seeing Thomas – not my business at all. It's just that he's spent the whole afternoon on the telephone because of that wretched Jap – the big, bald one, you know – apparently he got drunk and ran amok in that new French restaurant last night, and the owners are demanding damages and threatening to call the police if he shows up again, and then one of the other Japanese turned up at lunchtime to book a table for tonight – Goodness knows what's going to happen if the bald one appears too.

Meadle (*meanwhile, off*) 'Night, Henry, see you Monday.

Windscape (*off*) Oh. 'Night, Derek. Have a good weekend.

Meadle (*off*) Thanks, Henry – same to you.

Melanie (*listens alertly to this*) Still, apparently he works very hard at his teaching, from all accounts, Thomas and Eddie are both rather thrilled with him – well, St John, and what are your plans for the weekend? Something on the boil, I'll bet!

Quartermaine Oh, well I thought I might take in a show tonight – that Ibsen thing at the Arts –

Melanie Isn't it *The Cherry Orchard*?

Quartermaine Oh, is it? Well – something like that. And then a bite of supper, I suppose. I might try that French place, in fact. Might be rather – rather amusing. (*He laughs.*)

Melanie It must be jolly nice being a bachelor and having the weekend before you. Especially in Cambridge. Well, I'd better get on with this. I don't think Thomas really wants me to take it off the premises. (*She pulls book towards her.*)

Quartermaine Oh. Righto.

He begins to wander up and down, gaze out of the French windows, etc. Melanie is writing, glancing occasionally at him. She is, in fact, anxious for him to be gone. There are occasional cries and sounds of Windscape's voice from the garden, to which Melanie responds by lifting her head, or stopping writing.

Quartermaine I say, Melanie – do you like *The Cherry Orchard*?

Melanie Loathe it.

Quartermaine Oh. Why?

Melanie All that Russian gloom and doom and people shooting themselves from loneliness and depression and that sort of thing. But then Mother says I don't understand comedy. I expect she's right.

Quartermaine How is Mother?

Melanie Oh, top-hole, thanks. (*automatically*)

Quartermaine Well, if there's ever anything I can do – you know – if she wants company when you want to go out –

Melanie That's very thoughtful of you, St John, thank you.

Quartermaine No, no – I'd enjoy it. I say, that is an impressive tome old Thomas has lent you, what are you copying out exactly?

Melanie Recipes. This one's for roasted swan.

Quartermaine Oh. For a dinner party?

Melanie No, no, St John, it's for my British Life and Institutions lot, to give them some idea of a medieval banquet. Swans are protected birds, you know, these days.

Quartermaine Oh yes, of course they are. (*He laughs.*) Fancy thinking you'd give them for a – a – oh Lord! But aren't they the most – most beautiful creatures? I was looking at one – oh, just the other day, you know – on the Cam – drifting behind a punt – and they were all shouting and drinking champagne and – and it was just drifting behind them – so calm – and I remember there used to be, oh! a dozen or so – they came every year to a pond near my aunt's – when I was – was – and I could hear their wings – great wings beating – in the evenings when I was lying in bed – it could be quite – quite

frightening even after I knew what was making the noise –
and then there they'd be – a dozen of them or so –
drifting – drifting around the next morning – and it was
hard to imagine – their long necks twining and their way
of drifting – all that – that power – those wings beating –
I wonder where they went to. I'd like to know more
about them really. Where they go, what they – they –

Melanie St John, please don't think me fearfully rude,
but I must try and finish this and I can't write and talk at
the same time, you see.

Quartermaine What? Oh – oh sorry, Melanie, no, you're
quite right, I can't either. Anyway, I ought to be getting
on –

Melanie Yes, with such a full evening. I do hope you
enjoy it.

Quartermaine Well – well, 'night, Melanie, see you
Monday. And don't forget about your mother – any
time –

Melanie I won't, St John, goodnight.

Quartermaine goes. Melanie sits, not writing, as:

Quartermaine (*off*) I say, Henry, any chance of a game?

Windscape (*off*) Actually, I'm just finishing I'm afraid –
perhaps next week.

Quartermaine (*off*) Right, I'll hold you to that. See you
Monday. Oh, by the way, if you want any baby-sitting
done during the weekend, I'll try and make myself
available –

Windscape (*off*) Righto, I'll put it to Fanny – I know
she's quite keen to see the *Uncle Vanya* at the Arts –
perhaps tomorrow night –

Quartermaine *À votre disposition.* (*off*) 'Night.

Windscape 'Night.

Melanie, during this, has got up, and gone to the French windows.

(*off*) Oh, well played, Piccolo, well played, Jean-Pierre – beautiful lies both – I have to go now, I'm afraid, but you're obviously learning very quickly, all of you – don't forget to put the mallets and the balls back in the sheds – goodnight, goodnight.

Replies, in the appropriate accents, of 'Goodnight, Mr Windscape', etc. Melanie, during the latter part of this, hurries back to the table, sits down, pretends to continue transcribing. Windscape enters through the French windows. He stops on seeing Melanie, braces himself, then enters properly, jovially.)

Windscape Hello, Melanie, my dear, I thought everyone had gone.

Melanie How are they taking to the croquet?

Windscape At the moment they find it a bit sedate, I think, but another time or two around and they'll discover just how much – how much incivility is possible on our tranquil English lawns – but – but what are you up to? (*coming to look over her shoulder*) Isn't that Cussons' *A Culinary History of England*? I've only seen it in a library before, and what are you transcribing – roasted swan, for British Life and Institutions, is it? But you know, Melanie, that's rather a good idea – as a way of teaching them some social history I mean – you'll be able to compare dishes from different strata of society at the same period, and then at different periods – why, you could work through a whole chronology of meals, from medieval banquets of – of roasted swan and no doubt boar and venison and guinea fowls right up to – to the modern dinner of frozen hamburgers, frozen chips and frozen peas – and – and – thus illustrating one aspect of our culture's advance, eh, from a very few eating splendidly to almost everybody getting hideously fed – and – and – why good heavens, see where it takes you – a consideration of meals as symbolic functions and domestic rituals – you could bring D. H. Lawrence in there, as *Sons and Lovers* is a set text, isn't it – and – and not forgetting of course all the semantic fun, the differences in meaning between lunches, luncheons, teas, high teas, suppers, dinners – and of course what they indicate as a kind of code about class – and – and – the illustrations, not only literary, Shakespeare alone – Banquo's ghost – Antony and Cleopatra – Titus Andronicus! Almost every play, and the novels – but also paintings, lithographs, Hogarth – (*He checks himself from going on.*) Good gracious you've really hit on something there, Melanie.

Melanie (*who has been gazing at him adoringly*) And all I thought I'd hit on was a way of attracting a little interest – especially from those three rather scowly French girls – but then how like you, Henry, to take up my copying out an old recipe and turn it into an intellectual adventure.

Windscape (*laughs, embarrassed*) Oh, just a few – just a few thoughts – letting myself get carried away as usual, and I really ought to be sorting myself out – I promised Fanny I'd be home by six – now where's my briefcase? Ah, yes – and a pile of unseens I seem to remember – (*going to his locker*) – to be marked by Monday –

Melanie How is Fanny?

Windscape Oh, very well thanks, very well – a bit tired in the evenings, what with the children on the one hand

and her two hours voluntary with the OAPs – but she's enjoying every minute of her day –

Melanie Good! – And the children – all well?

Windscape Oh yes – they're fine! Susan's a little tense at the moment, actually, with her O-Levels – a pity she's taking them so early, I think, but she insists – she's in with a particularly bright lot and doesn't want to fall behind or let herself down so she works away until all hours. Quite often after Fanny and I have gone to bed. But she's developing quite an interest in – in – well, philosophical speculation, I suppose it is, really – the other evening – (*bending during this to put on his clips*) – she suddenly insisted – in the middle of supper – she'd been very quiet until then – she suddenly insisted that we couldn't prove that other people existed – and that perhaps when we thought about them or remembered them or saw and heard them even – we were actually just making them up – and of course I took her up on this and attempted to explain how it is we do know that other people exist, including people we don't even know exist, if you follow – (*laughing*) – and she kept saying 'But you can't prove it, Daddy, you can't actually prove it!' until I found myself getting quite tangled in my own arguments – and trying to remember whether there is an irrefutable answer to solipsism – Fanny had to rescue me in the end by calling me up to read to little Fanny and Ben –

Melanie I've always thought she was the one who takes most after you.

Windscape Yes, yes – perhaps she does, perhaps she does – I'm afraid I rather like to think so anyway. (*Laughs.*) But you haven't seen them for ages, have you? You really must come over sometime soon – Fanny would love to see you again. We all would.

Melanie That would be lovely.

Windscape I'll get Fanny to give you a ring over the weekend or –

Melanie Good.

Windscape Right – well, oh, by the way, I've been meaning to ask – how is the day-nurse working out? Nurse – Nurse – with the name out of Dickens.

Melanie Grimes. Well enough so far – she seems a very efficient, cheerful little soul – a little too cheerful for my taste perhaps, as apparently she belongs to one of those peculiar revivalist sects that seem to be springing up all over the place now – you know, meeting in each others' homes and chanting prayers and dancing about in their love of God – at least that's how she describes it – but Mother seems to like her.

Windscape Well, that's the main thing, isn't it?

Melanie Yes. Yes it is.

Windscape Well, do give her my – my very best – see you Monday, Melanie, my dear.

Melanie See you Monday, Henry.

> *Windscape, carrying papers, books, etc., goes off left. The sound of the door closing. Melanie sits. She lets out a sudden wail, and then, in a sort of frenzy, tears at the page of the book from which she's been copying, sobbing. She checks herself at the sound of the door opening.*

Windscape (*laughing*) What on earth can I be thinking of – going off with all these in my arms and leaving my briefcase behind? I do that sort of thing more and more now – perhaps it's premature senility – (*entering, going to the briefcase, shovelling the papers and books in*) or did I get switched on to the wrong track and think I was going off to teach a class? I must have, as I went out that way – (*Looks at her smiling. A little pause.*) Melanie – Melanie – (*He hesitates, then goes to her, leaving the briefcase on the desk.*) Is something the matter?

Melanie I'm sorry – I'm sorry – but I've got to talk – talk to someone –

Windscape What is it?

Melanie She hates me, you see.

Windscape Who?

Melanie Mother.

Windscape Oh, Melanie, I'm sure that's not – not – why do you think she does?

Melanie She says I've abandoned her. Betrayed her. When I come back in the evenings she won't speak to me. She sits silent for hours, while I prepare supper and chatter at her, and then when I've got her to the table she refuses to eat. Since that second attack she can only work one side of her mouth, but she can eat perfectly well. She says Nurse Grimes feeds her and so I should too, but when I try she lets the food fall out of her mouth, and – and stares at me with such malevolence, until suddenly she'll say something – something utterly – last night she said, 'It's not my fault you've spent your life in my home. I've never wanted you here, but as you're too stupid to make an intelligent career, and too unattractive to make any reasonable man a wife, I was prepared to accept the responsibility for you. And now you refuse to pay your debt. Oh, sharper than a serpent's tooth . . .' And coming out of the side of her mouth, in a hoarse whisper, like a – like a gangster in one of those films. And she wets herself too. From spite. She never does it with Nurse Grimes, of course. Only with me. She says that as I'm behaving like a neglected parent, she'll behave like a neglected child. The only child I'll ever have. And she gives Nurse Grimes things – things that belong to me or she knows I love that we've had for years – the buttons from Daddy's uniform or the other day a silly lithograph of a donkey that's hung in my room since I was ten – of course Nurse Grimes gives them back, but – but – and the worst thing is I'm beginning to hate her, to hate going home or when I'm there have such dreadful feelings – because the thought of years – it could be years apparently – years of this – and so wishing she would have another attack and die now – too dreadful – too dreadful – almost imagining myself doing something –

Windscape You mustn't blame yourself for that, Melanie, you mustn't. It's only natural – and healthy, probably, even. But I'm so sorry she's – I had no idea – what can one say? I know – we both know – what a remarkable woman she was, and I suppose that the indignity of finding herself increasingly incapacitated and the – the fear of what's going to happen to her – I suppose when it comes to it, when we come to our ends some of us are – well, all the anger and despair turn to cruelty – and of course you're the only one –

Melanie I know. But I can't give up my teaching, Henry, I can't. Your getting me this job was the best thing that ever happened to me – of course she always despised it – even when she was well she thought it – thought it – having been a professor herself – but I love it and – and I've got to think of myself now. Haven't I?

Windscape Yes. Yes, of course you have. Finally, one always must. I wish I could give you some comfort, my dear.

Melanie You do, Henry. Your just being here and my knowing that you – that you care about me makes all the difference. All the difference. It always has. (*She begins to cry*.) Oh what a fool I was not to – not to marry you when you asked me – all those years ago – I keep thinking of it now – and what Mother said about your being too young and not knowing what you were doing – and – and blighting your career – of course I'm happy that you're so happy – I wouldn't have been able to make you as happy, but even then she was my enemy – my real enemy – I'm sorry, I'm sorry – (*sobbing*)

Windscape (*hesitates, then with reluctance puts his arms around her*) There there, my dear, there there – mustn't think of the past – it's the – the future – the future – there there –

The telephone rings. After a moment:

Perhaps I'd better – perhaps I'd better – um – (*Releasing himself, he picks up the telephone.*) Hello. Oh, hello, Nigel, yes it is! No she's gone, I'm afraid – at least I think she has – Have you seen Anita in the last half hour –?

Melanie, now handkerchiefing her tears, shakes her head.

Melanie hasn't seen her either so I'm fairly sure – yes, of course I will. (*He listens.*) You're phoning from Liverpool Street and you're about to catch the 6.13 so you'll be home before eight, right, got that, but as I say, have you tried her at home? – Oh, well, if she's going to the theatre perhaps she's gone straight there, eh? But if Melanie or I do see her by any unlikely – yes, right, goodbye – and oh, Nigel, good luck with your first issue, Fanny and I and everybody we know are so looking forward to it – have you decided what you're going to call it, by the way? Really? Well, that sounds – that really

sounds most – most – yes – goodbye. (*He hangs up.*)
That was Nigel – for Anita – as you probably realised
and – and anyway she's certainly left, hasn't she? Nigel
says she said she was going to the theatre – so – so –
I suppose the Arts – *The Three Sisters,* isn't it? – such a
beautiful play although not – not my favourite – which
will always be *The Seagull.* Apparently they're going
to call the magazine *Reports,* by the way, I'm not sure
I care too much for *Reports,* do you?

> *He stares hopelessly at Melanie, who has somewhat
> recovered herself.*

You must come round, Melanie, and have a real – a real
talk with Fanny – take you out of yourself – away from
your problems –

Melanie Thank you, Henry.

Windscape No, we'd love to see you, I'll get her to ring
you. All right? And now I must – I really must – (*looking
at the clock*) I promised Susan I'd help her with her maths,
and then I've got to listen to Ben doing a Chopin piece,
he's going to perform it at the school concert, really
rather too advanced, but still, and there's little Fanny's
bedtime read – I'm trying to get her on to Walter De La
Mare but he hasn't really taken yet – so – so –

Melanie Yes, you must get back.

Windscape Yes. See you Monday, my dear.

Melanie Monday, Henry.

> *Windscape looks around vaguely for a moment, then
> goes out through the French windows. Melanie stands
> for a moment, then sees the briefcase, registers it,
> takes it to Windscape's locker, puts it in, goes back to
> the book, looks down at it, tries futilely to sort it out,
> pressing the page flat with her hand, then goes to*

*collect her briefcase, etc. As she does so, the sound of
violent quarrelling, in assorted tongues, off, over the
croquet: 'No, you cannot – Mr Windscape said . . .'
etc. Melanie pauses to listen, then, as the voices
continue, then fade, the sound of the door, off left,
opening.*

Oh, hello, Eddie! (*brightly*)

Loomis He's not here then – I can't make it out – I've
been everywhere, everywhere, up to the flat, all the
classrooms and in the office – and the phone going all
the time about some of our Japanese and that French
restaurant, and they're not even French, it turns out,
they're from Wiltshire – and I don't know what Thomas
has said to them, I didn't even know about it – he knows
I can't deal with that sort of thing – and he's booked a
table for the two of us tonight at their request, forcing us
to take responsibility, I don't see what it's got to do with
the school if a few Japanese can't hold their drink, I don't
know why he agreed – it really is all too –

Melanie Now, Eddie. Now. (*going to him*) You mustn't
worry. You'll make yourself ill, and it's not worth it.
Why don't you go upstairs to the flat and have a rest?
I'm sure it'll all sort itself out. You know Thomas, he'll
get it completely under control, he always does, in the
end.

Loomis Yes, yes, of course you're right, my dear, thank
you, thank you. And a little rest – and I'll try and make
Thomas have one, too –

Melanie That's right, Eddie, you both need it – oh, and
would you give this back to him when you see him, and
tell him I'm terribly sorry (*as she collects her briefcase
and hands Loomis the book*) a page of it seems to have
got torn? Our Mr Meadle insisted on snatching it out of

my hands and then dropped it – he was only trying to be helpful, of course – but you know how clumsy he is –

Loomis Oh – oh dear, Cussons – one of our favourite books, Thomas will find it hard to forgive Meadle – well – have a good weekend, my dear, and bless you.

They go off.

Melanie (*off*) Thank you, Eddie.

Loomis (*footsteps off, then he stops*) Oh, and by the way, how's Mother?

Melanie Oh, top-hole, thanks, Eddie.

Loomis Good, good.

*The sound of the door shutting. There is a pause.
Quartermaine enters through the French windows.
He looks around him, stands for a moment, then
sweeps his left leg, vaguely, as:*

Lights. Curtain.

Act Two

SCENE ONE

The following year, towards summer. It is a Monday morning, about nine-thirty.

There have been a few improvements, different perhaps; a record player, with a record rack consisting of poetry readings and Shakespeare plays. There is also a large new tape recorder, sophisticated for the period.

Quartermaine is seated, with his feet up, staring ahead.

Windscape enters through the French windows, carrying a briefcase, smoking a pipe, wearing bicycle clips.

Windscape Hello, St John – (*He goes to his locker.*)

Quartermaine (*doesn't respond at first, then takes in Windscape*) Oh, hello – um – (*Thinks.*) Henry.

Windscape (*turns, looks at him*) Deep in thought?

Quartermaine Mmmm? Oh. No, no – just – just – you know.

Windscape Ah. Did you have a good half-term?

Quartermaine Oh. Yes thanks. Yes.

Windscape What did you do? Did you go away? (*going to his locker*)

Quartermaine Well, I – I – no, I stayed here.

Windscape Here!

Quartermaine Yes.

Windscape Oh, in Cambridge, you mean? Just for a moment I thought you meant actually here – in this room – I think perhaps because the last time I saw you, you were sitting in exactly the same place in very much that position – as if you haven't moved all week.

Quartermaine Oh. (*He laughs.*) But I say – good to be back, isn't it?

Windscape Well, I could have done with a little longer myself.

Quartermaine (*watches Windscape at the locker*) I say, Henry, what did you do for the half?

Windscape Mmmm? Oh nothing very exciting really, we packed ourselves into the caravan and took ourselves off to a spot we'd heard about in Norfolk –

Quartermaine That sounds terrific!

Windscape Yes – yes – well, the trouble was that it rained fairly steadily – all week, in fact – so we didn't get out as much as we would have liked – a shame really, as among other things we were hoping that a few jaunts would cheer Susan up.

Quartermaine Oh – is she a bit low then?

Windscape Yes, yes – well she's still brooding over her O-Level results – we keep telling her that at her age six positive passes – I mean Bs and Cs – is jolly good – but she seems to feel she's let herself down – but I'll tell you what we did see – it really was most – extraordinary – one morning at about six it was, I was up trying to plug the leak – it was right over little Fanny's bunk – and so she was awake and so was Ben – and Susan hadn't slept at all – so it was all rather – rather fraught. With tempers fraying – but Fanny she'd gone outside to the loo, as a matter of fact – and suddenly she called us – all of us –

told us to put on our wellies and macs and come out and look – and we did – and there – silhouetted against the sky was the most – the most –

Meadle enters through the French windows in bicycle clips, carrying a briefcase.

Meadle Greetings, Henry, St John.

Quartermaine Hello, old chap.

Windscape Hello, Derek. Have a good holiday?

Meadle Yes, thanks, Henry, very, very good indeed. What about you? (*Goes to his locker, taking off his clips, etc.*)

Windscape Yes, I was just telling St John, we went to Norfolk, a little wet, but there really was one very remarkable – well, moment is all it amounted to really. In temporal terms.

Meadle Sounds marvellous. Thomas isn't around yet, is he?

Windscape He wasn't in the office when I came through, have you seen him, St John?

Quartermaine Mmmm?

Windscape Thomas. Have you seen him?

Quartermaine No no – but I expect he's here somewhere. Up in their flat or – or down in their office, but I say – I say, Dennis, did you have a good holiday?

Meadle Who's Dennis, St John? (*He laughs.*)

Quartermaine Mmmm?

Windscape You said Dennis, instead of Derek. And he's already said he had a very good holiday.

Quartermaine Oh. What did you do?

Meadle I went to Sheffield, as a matter of fact.

Windscape Sheffield, I know it well, Fanny and I went there the year before Susan was born, we were doing a tour of out-of-the-way urban domestic architecture, I've got great affection for Sheffield, what were you doing there?

Meadle Um – oh. Attending my aunt's funeral, as a matter of fact.

Quartermaine What?

Windscape Oh Derek, I'm so sorry. How upsetting for you.

Meadle Yes, it was. Very. Very.

Windscape But actually when I asked you earlier, you did say – I suppose it was merely social reflex – that you'd had a good half-term –

Meadle Yes, well, actually I met someone there I used to know. And I managed to see quite a lot of her. That was the good part of it. Not my aunt's death, I need hardly say. (*He laughs.*)

Windscape Ah.

Quartermaine Who was she?

Meadle Oh, just a girl, St John, – we were at Hull University together, as a matter of fact, she was doing the library course but we – we lost contact, for various reasons. Although I hadn't forgotten her. And when I was in Sheffield I had to take back all my poor aunt's books. And there she was. Behind the counter.

Quartermaine What was she doing there?

Meadle Well, stamping the books in and out, of course. What do you think she was doing? (*with a mitigating laugh*)

Windscape Oh don't worry about St John, one of his absent days, eh St John, but how nice for you to bump into her like that, especially under those circumstances, eh?

Meadle Yes, I can't tell you what a – a blessing it turned out to be. As soon as she was off work she'd come over and sit with me and my uncle, and on a couple of evenings when I had to go out and console some of my aunt's friends, she came and sat with him anyway, by herself. He's very keen on football, but he can't follow it in the newspapers as his eyesight's nearly gone and they're too quick for him on the radio. So she'd read out all the teams and their scores. Which was very tiring for her, as she's got quite a serious speech impediment.

Windscape What a nice girl she sounds, eh, St John?

Quartermaine What, Henry?

Windscape What a nice girl Derek's friend sounds.

Quartermaine Oh – oh yes, terrific, terrific. Um, tell me – tell me – what – what are her legs like?

Meadle What!

Windscape Good heavens, St John, what an extraordinary question!

Quartermaine Oh yes – oh – I'm sorry – I was just trying to imagine – I have a sort of thing about girls' legs, you see. (*He laughs apologetically.*) I can't stand them if they're dumpy or – (*Thinks.*) – stumpy.

Meadle Well, let's just say, shall we, St John – (*manifestly exercising smiling control*) – that Daphne's legs happen to be my sort of legs. Will that help you to imagine them?

Quartermaine Your sort of legs. (*He looks at Meadle's legs.*)

Meadle The sort of legs I happen to like. But I don't want to dilate on the subject of Daphne's legs – (*laughs*) – at least just at the moment – look, St John, I wonder if you'd mind, there's a matter I was very much hoping to have a conversation with Henry about. As a matter of fact, it's rather urgent.

Quartermaine Oh. No. Sorry. Go ahead.

Meadle Well the thing is, St John, it's – it's of a confidential nature.

Quartermaine Oh – oh well, I'll go and have a little stroll then, in the garden. (*getting up*) To tell you the truth my head feels a little – a little – as if it could do with some air.

Meadle Thanks very much, St John, very decent of you.

Quartermaine (*going off*) Oh, not at all – but I say – I say – (*going out*) what a beautiful morning! (*He goes.*)

Meadle (*smiling*) You know, I can't help wondering sometimes about old Quartermaine. I can't imagine a more charming fellow but from the students' point of view – do you know what one of the advanced Swedes was telling me just before half-term –?

Windscape (*interrupting*) I think it would be better really – really much better – if we didn't find ourselves talking about a colleague and a friend – I know that your concern is entirely – entirely disinterested, but – but – these little confabs *can* do unintended harm. I hope you don't mind my – my – pointing it out.

Meadle Not at all, Henry, you're quite right, one can't be too careful, needless to say I meant no – no slur on St John –

Windscape I know you didn't, I know you didn't. But now. You said you had something urgent –

Meadle Yes, well, the thing is – well look, I've been here a year now, Henry, and Thomas said when I started that it wouldn't be long before I was made permanent – and yet here I am, you see, still on part-time. The only one of the staff on part-time, as it happens. (*He laughs.*)

Windscape And part-time isn't really very satisfactory for you, then?

Meadle Well, no, it isn't, Henry, frankly. I get paid one pound two and sixpence for every hour I teach.

Windscape But surely, Dennis –

Meadle Derek. (*He laughs.*) Quartermaine seems to have started you off on Dennis –

Windscape Oh, good heavens, I'm so sorry, Derek – but one pound two and sixpence an hour isn't such a bad rate, is it?

Meadle Ah yes, Henry, but you see I don't get paid during the vacations, you see. I only get paid by the hour for the hours I'm allowed to do, while the rest of the staff get paid an annual salary. So even though I'm currently doing twice as many hours again as everybody else, I in fact get slightly less than half of what everybody else gets, over the year. I mean, take this half-term we've just had, Henry, a week of paid holiday for everybody else but a week of no money at all for me, it was just luck that my aunt died in it, or I might have had to miss an earning week to go to her funeral and sort out my uncle, you see – And last Christmas, well, I've kept this very quiet, Henry, but last Christmas I had to be a postman. (*He laughs.*)

Windscape Oh dear!

Meadle Yes, and let me tell you it wasn't simply the work, Henry – being up at six, and trudging through the snow and sleet we had the whole of those three weeks – it was also the sheer embarrassment. Twice during my second round I nearly bumped into some students. I only got away with it because I kept my head lowered and once Thomas himself went right past me in the car – it was a miracle he didn't see me, especially as I'd slipped on some ice and I was actually lying on the pavement with the letters scattered everywhere – and now the summer holiday's looming ahead – I simply don't know how I'm going to get through that. Or at least I do. I've already sent in my application to be an Entertainments Officer at one of those holiday camps in Hayling Island.

Windscape Oh dear!

Meadle Yes. And now that Daphne's back in the picture – well you probably gathered from what I said that we're pretty serious about each other – and I don't want to keep her waiting around with a long engagement – there's been a lot of tragedy in that family, Henry.

Windscape Oh dear!

Meadle Yes, I won't go into it, if you don't mind. Not that Daphne tries to conceal it. She's too straightforward for that.

Windscape Well, she really does sound a most – a most remarkable –

Meadle Yes, I consider myself a very, very lucky man. So what do you think, Henry? I know how much Eddie and Thomas respect you – I'm going to try and nab Thomas for a few minutes this morning – how should I go about it, with him?

Windscape Well, Derek, I think there's no doubt that you have a very strong case. Very strong. And as we all know, Thomas and Eddie are very fair, always. I know they'd respond most sympathetically – most sympathetically – to all that you've told me about yourself and Deirdre –

Meadle Daphne, actually. (*smiling*)

Windscape Daphne – I'm sorry, Daphne of course –

The sound of the door opening: footsteps.

Sackling (*off*) 'Morning. (*He enters somewhat jauntily, his moustache now accompanied by a beard.*) Henry – Derek –

Windscape Oh hello, Mark, good holiday?

Meadle You didn't notice if Thomas was in his office as you went by, did you?

Sackling Yes, he was. Just come down. I like the chin. A comparatively unexplored area, isn't it, if we exclude the puffy nose from falling over the croquet hoop just before summer. How did you come by it, not shaving, I trust?

Meadle (*who has been getting up*) Oh, I'd forgotten about that – no, no, not shaving, don't worry – (*attempting a chuckle*) I'll tell you all about it later – and thanks, Henry, for your advice. It was most helpful –

Windscape Oh, not at all, I'm glad if – if –

Meadle goes out, during this, and as the door closes:

Oh – oh, good heavens – Derek! Oh –

Sackling What's the matter?

Windscape I think we had a slight misunderstanding – he's under the impression that I was advising him to go and see Thomas about being put on a more – a more

permanent basis – and the truth is I was going on to
explain to him that in spite of the – the strong claim he
has – he should – well, in my view anyway – hold his
horses for the moment – Thomas is under a bit of strain,
you see, with all the recent renovation expenses and now
the sudden drop in student intake – this business of the
Japanese suddenly deserting has really hit us very hard –
so in fact it's the worst possible moment for Meadle – I
was going to try and divert him to Eddie – I do sometimes
feel, strictly between ourselves, that it is hard on him as
the only part-time teacher – and we must be careful in
the staff room not to show any – any – well, make fun
of him more than is perhaps – under the circumstances –
if you see, Mark.

Sackling Oh, I shouldn't worry about Meadle. (*He's
been at the locker during all the above.*) Even St John's
observed that he's one of those people who always lands
on his feet – even if he damages a toe in the process. The
thing is to make sure it's his and not yours. Well, Henry,
peacemaker, apostle and saint, what sort of half did you
have?

Windscape Oh, we did the usual sort of thing, took the
caravan to a spot near the Broads. The weather wasn't
too splendid but as I was telling – St John, I think it was –
there was one rather exceptional experience. To tell you
the truth I've never seen anything quite like it. Fanny
actually wrote a small sort of prose poem about it.

Sackling Really? I didn't know Fanny wrote! But on that
subject – listen – I must tell you. I've finished.

Windscape Finished?

Sackling My novel, old cheese.

Windscape Oh Mark – well, congratulations,
congratulations!

Sackling Thanks, Henry. I knew *you'd* know what it means to me, I'd rather you kept it to yourself for the moment – for superstitious reasons, as it's still only the first draft. But the point is I feel – in my guts – that it's the first draft of the final version and damned near the thing itself, actually. Because of the way it happened, you see. What I did was – I put everything I'd previously written – a total, by the way, of 3,643 pages – into a box and lugged it into the cellar and started again. Completely from scratch. Just me, the typewriter and a carton of paper. I was actually quite – quite frightened. But it was all perfectly simple. No strain. No effort. Almost no thought. Just a steady untaxing continuous flow of creation. For a whole week. It was the nearest I've come, will probably ever come, to a mystical experience.

Windscape I envy you. I once tried to write a novel – but as Fanny said my forte – if I have a forte – (*He laughs.*)

Sackling The thing is, though – the thing is – it proves to me that I'm a novelist. The doubts I've had since Camelia left – and worst of all, the envy! I'd read the reviews and see the photographs of other novelists – the real ones, who'd been published – some of them people I knew, had been up with – God, there's a man at Trinity – an absolute imbecile – his *second* novel came out last month, well received too – and when I saw his face in the middle of some interview he'd given – the same imbecile face, with a smirk added – that I used to see opposite me in Hall, I – I – well, I'd better not go into what I wanted to do to him. And all those women that are getting published everywhere – everyone, everyone but me, that's what I began to think – as if they'd got something, through some genetic accident – like an extra gland or double joints – that I hadn't. And so they could do it, again and again – while I was working away like some – some drudge – some lunatic drudge who'd given up his wife and child and hours and hours of his life – and would go on and on drudging, through thousands and thousands of pages, not one of them publishable, to the end of my life – so I suppose that what I've discovered at last is my – well, let's use the word – my talent. Perhaps it's been growing down there, in the dark, all this time – until finally it's strong enough to take over, eh? Anyway, now all I've got to do is a bit of pruning, no doubt some tightening up – correct the spelling and the typing mistakes, and float an extract or two in Nigel's currently fashionable little magazine – I've been promising him for years – (*He laughs.*)

Quartermaine enters through the French windows.

Quartermaine All clear, then? Hello, Mark!

Windscape What – oh good heavens, St John – yes, yes, I forgot that you were still out there.

Quartermaine Oh no – I enjoyed it – to tell you the truth it seems to have cleared my head – I was feeling a bit – a bit odd before – Hello, Mark!

Sackling Hello, St John, have a good holiday?

Quartermaine Yes – yes – terrific thanks! Terrific! And how were they?

Sackling Who?

Quartermaine Camelia. And little Tom, too. Weren't you going to see them over half-term?

Sackling Oh, that's right. Actually, as it turned out, they were unavailable. Tom was getting over mumps, or so at least Camelia claimed, so she decided to take him to a friend of her mother's, in Wales, to convalesce. They have a cottage by the sea, and of course I couldn't offer him that, could I? Even though this half-term was mine, according to the agreement.

Windscape, during this, goes to his briefcase, takes out books, puts them on top of the tape recorder, puts his briefcase and other books in the locker, etc.

Quartermaine Still, perhaps it did him some good – I mean, the beach and the valleys and hills and – and – I mean if poor little Tom's been ill –

Sackling St John, I'd be grateful if you'd stop referring to him as little Tom, and poor little Tom too, it makes him sound like something out of the workhouse, and he's anyway not so little any more, the last time I saw him he must have weighed in at a good five stone –

Quartermaine What? Oh – oh, right. (*A little pause.*) Five stone, eh? (*He whistles.*) Um – but what a pity I didn't know you were stuck in Cambridge over the half, we could have got together – but perhaps you got some writing done –

Sackling Yes – well some – as always –

Anita enters through the French windows.

Hi, Anita!

Quartermaine Hello, Anita!

Windscape Anita, my dear –

Anita takes off her coat. She is pregnant.

Sackling – you're swelling along pleasantly. Rapidly too.

Anita laughs.

Quartermaine But you look – you look – (*gazing at her in a sort of reverence*) I mean – (*He gestures.*) – in just a week, good Lord!

Anita Well, it's taken a bit longer than a week, St John.

Quartermaine No, no, but I mean –

Windscape Just like Fanny, nothing shows for ages and then one day there it is – for the world to see –

Sackling And how's Nigel getting on in New York?

Anita Oh, he decided not to go. He suddenly became convinced – had a dream, or something – that I'd spawn prematurely, so he stayed at home and mugged up on all the texts – Spock for practicals, and Blake and D. H. Lawrence and some Indian writer he's discovered and is going to publish, for significance – which was lovely for me as I didn't have to go to my parents, I spent most of the time in the bath reading thrillers. It was lovely.

Quartermaine Oh, I wish I'd known you were here, so was Mark, as it turned out, weren't you Mark? We could have got together – but I say, it's good to be back in a way, isn't it? I mean, after a good holiday, of course –

Sackling (*to Anita*) Tell him I'm going to give him a ring, will you –

The sound of the door opening, and closing, during this.

– there's something I've got for him. At last.

Anita Oh Mark, really! He'll be so thrilled – he keeps refusing to phone you because he says it's like soliciting –

Quartermaine Hello, Derek, have you had a good half –?

Meadle enters.

(*laughing*) But of course I've seen you already, I'm sorry if I was a bit – off-colour, don't know what was the matter with me – but oh Lord, what have you done to your cheek? I didn't even notice it before, you do get in the wars, though, don't you, old man? Was it shaving?

Anita Are you all right, Derek? You don't look –

Meadle Yes, yes thanks – well – (*Laughs,*) Apart from just finding out that I won't be joining you as a full-time member of the staff. In fact, my hours are going to be cut. By over a quarter. Which won't give me enough money to survive on. Furthermore, unless there's a sudden swing upwards in enrolment, I may not have any hours at all next month. So I'll – I'll probably be leaving you then.

Quartermaine Leave! Oh no! That's rotten!

Windscape I'm very sorry, Dennis. I blame myself. I should have explained more fully. But you were out of the room so quickly –

Sackling Look, we must have a word with Thomas, with Eddie – we can't allow Derek just to be chucked out – Henry, perhaps you could speak to Eddie and Thomas on behalf of us all –

Anita Yes. Henry, you will, won't you?

Windscape Of course I'll – I'll do my best. But, you see, the financial situation – it's not at all good, at the moment, is it? The school can only afford what it can afford. But whatever happens, Dennis – it's no reflection on your teaching. None at all.

Meadle Oh, I know that. It's Derek, by the way, Henry. (*laughing*) But that's life, isn't it? That's the joke. How hard I've worked. I mean, old Quartermaine here – well, according to one of the Swedes I'm not allowed to mention because it's a fraction on the unethical side to speak ill of a colleague – well, he sometimes sits for a whole hour not speaking. Even in dictation classes. Or if he does condescend to speak, goes off into little stories about himself they can't make head or tail of.

There is a pause.

Quartermaine What, a Swede, did you say? What does he look like?

Meadle Oh, what does it matter? Everybody knows that for you one Swede is like another German, one Greek is like another Italian, you can't tell them apart and you don't know what they're called – unlike me, you see – because do you know what I do? I memorise their names before their first class, and then study their faces during it, and then when I go home I close my eyes and practise putting the two together so that by the second class I know every one of my students *personally* and do you know what else I do, I keep a look-out not only in term time but also in my holidays – my *unpaid* holidays – for any item that might interest them for British Life and Institutions and actually make a note of them – here – in my notebook, which I always keep especially in my pocket (*wrestling with it with increasing violence, jerking it out of his pocket, tearing his pocket as he does so*) along with any of the out-of-the-way idioms and interesting usages I might happen across – and do you know what *else* I do? I – but what does it matter what else I do? That's what I mean by joke or life or whatever it is, because I'm the one that's facing the push, and you're the one that's on permanent. (*During this speech Meadle's accent has become increasingly North Country.*) Not that I begrudge you – it's just that I reckon that I've earned it. Look – look, I don't mean – I don't mean – the last thing I mean is –

He turns away, possibly in tears. There is silence, into which Melanie enters, through the French windows.

Quartermaine Oh hello, Melanie, have a good half?

Windscape Hello, Melanie, my dear.

Sackling Melanie.

Anita Hello, Melanie.

Melanie goes to the table, puts down her briefcase, takes off her coat.

Quartermaine Um – um – how's your mother?

Windscape Yes, how – how is she?

Melanie She's dead. She died last Tuesday.

There is silence.

Windscape Oh, Melanie – I'm so sorry – so sorry –

Murmurings from the others.

Was it another attack, my dear?

Melanie No. She fell down the stairs and broke her neck. We don't quite know how it happened as it was after I'd gone to bed. Nurse Grimes found her there in the morning, I still hadn't got up, the first I knew of it was Nurse Grimes calling me – and – and – that's really all there is to tell. I'd be grateful if we could dispense with condolences and that sort of thing, because what I really want most of all is to get on in the usual fashion, without any – any fuss. I shall tell Thomas and Eddie, naturally, straight away –

The sound of the door opening: footsteps, rather odd, though.

Loomis Hello, everybody, hello, all rested up I trust, welcome back, welcome back – but first, is Melanie here? Ah, there you are, Melanie my dear. (*appearing on stage. He has a stick, his glasses are tinted, and his voice and manner are frailer.*) There are a couple of policemen in the office with Thomas who want a word with you. They refuse to say what about, but not to worry, not to worry, because I asked whether it was illness or accident,

312

and they assured me it wasn't, so your mother's perfectly all right, my dear, which is the main thing, isn't it? It's probably some nonsense to do with your car, anyway if you'd go along to the office and flirt with them – and whatever you do, don't let Thomas lose his temper.

He laughs. Melanie stands for a moment, then braces herself and walks off, left, as:

Really! Our Cambridge bobbies, they always have to make such a solemn meal out of the most trivial business – pursuing their inquiries on information received, as they put it – goodness knows how they'd behave if they had something truly serious – Anita, my dear, how blooming you look, how blooming – and how did Nigel find New York?

Anita Oh fine, thank you, Eddie, fine –

Loomis Good good good, well tell Nigel how much we're looking forward to the first Anglo-American edition, and how sorry we are we've had to cut back to just the one subscription but *semper fidelis*. Henry, what sort of half-term did you have – one of your adventurous caravan treks, where to this time?

Windscape Yes, Eddie – to Norfolk.

Loomis Weather all right, I trust?

Windscape Oh yes, Eddie, yes, lovely thank you, except when it rained and – and even then we had one – one amazing moment at sunrise –

Loomis Good, good, especially for Fanny, little Fanny, Ben and Susan eh – and how did Susan get on with her O-Levels, results as expected?

Windscape Yes, Eddie, thanks, lots of – of Bs and – and – Cs and – and so forth.

Loomis I'm not surprised, with you and Fanny behind her, give her our congratulations do, and Mark – if that is Mark I see behind a week's further fuzzy-wuzzy, lots of tap, tap, tapping?

Sackling Oh, well, yes – yes, a little, thanks, Eddie.

Loomis Well, keep at it, we know that one day – ah, there's our Derek, but I've already said my welcomes to him, haven't I, Derek, in the corridor – I gather you found Thomas?

Meadle Yes, thank you, Eddie, yes yes.

Loomis And that you got whatever it was you were so anxious to get sorted out, sorted out, at least Thomas seemed very pleased with the fruits of your deliberations.

Meadle Well – well yes, thank you, Eddie, all sorted out, yes.

Loomis Good, good – and St John, now what was I going to say to you – oh, I remember – in spite of this tired old brain of mine – yet another postcard for you in the office, from that fervent fan your Swiss – I hope you don't mind my having a peek, but I always think postcards – what's his name?

Quartermaine Um, Muller, isn't it –?

Loomis Boller, I think it is. Ferdinand Boller. How lucky that you don't have to recall his name to his face, or he might not go on being so devoted to you. Anyway, he's hoping to see you when he's in England on business late this year, or next or some time or never, that is, if I understand him correctly, his English actually seems to get worse from postcard to postcard, though we can't hold you responsible for that, can we, at this stage? (*Laughs.*) Now, now there's something I'd like to take the opportunity of saying to you, just between ourselves, and a little behind Thomas's back, so to speak. I expect you've all noticed the very distinct drop in student enrolment these last few months. Thomas is slightly more worried than perhaps he's let any of you realize, we all know how dedicated he is to the future of the school – and to the future of the staff –

Quartermaine Hear, hear!

Loomis – we've long thought of you as part of a family, I think you all know that we do our best to care for you in that spirit –

Quartermaine Absolutely!

Loomis – and I'm sure you're all wondering what you can do to help us through this little rough patch – and the answer is, to go on giving of your very best to your teaching, and to show what students we've got that while we may not be as grand as some schools in Cambridge, we yield to no school in the country in the thing that matters most, our devotion to their devotion to their learning of our language.

Quartermaine (*amid murmurs*) Hear, hear!

Loomis That's how we can best serve our school at this time of slight crisis, and as I say, this is strictly *entre nous*, without reference to Thomas. Thank you, everybody, and bless you all – the bell will ring in a minute or so I believe, so –

> *He gestures. And as all except Quartermaine move to their lockers, etc.:*

Quartermaine Eddie, that was – that was terrific!

Loomis St John, a word of warning, I'm afraid there have been a number of complaints about your teaching – Thomas, I regret to say, received a round robin before half-term.

Quartermaine Oh Lord, that Swede, you mean?

Loomis What Swede?

During this, the sound of the door opening: footsteps.

Ah – Melanie, my dear, you've cleared it up, have you, what was it all about?

Melanie Oh yes, Eddie. All too preposterous. Apparently a group of French girls – from my intermediary Life and Institutions – got hold of the wrong end of the stick. They didn't realise my recipe for roasting swan was for a medieval banquet, and actually tried to kill one on the Cam, can you believe it! Club one to death from a punt, with the intention of taking it back to their rooms and cooking and eating it! And then, when they were reported to the police, blamed me. I'm glad to say that the swan, being a swan, survived. And gave one of them a badly bruised arm. Typically French.

She goes to her locker. Amidst laughter from all except Windscape the bell rings. They all move towards the door, with books, etc., except for Quartermaine, who goes to his locker, stands before it looking puzzled, takes out one or two books, slightly confused.

Quartermaine If it's not Dictation it must be Comprehension. Or – or – oh Lord!

Lights.

SCENE TWO

A Friday evening, some months later. The French windows are open.

Quartermaine is asleep in an armchair, papers and books on his lap. He is visible to the audience, but not to anyone on stage who doesn't look specifically in the armchair. Quartermaine suddenly groans. There is a pause.

Quartermaine (*in his sleep*) Oh Lord! (*A pause.*) I say!

A pause. He laughs, sleeps. The sound of the door opening, footsteps. Melanie enters from the left. She goes to her locker, puts her books in. Quartermaine, not heard, or half-heard, by Melanie, lets out a groan. Melanie takes an overnight bag out of her locker. Quartermaine lets out another groan, rises to his feet.

Oh, Lord!

Melanie (*starts, turns, sees Quartermaine*) St John! (*She goes towards him.*) Are you all right?

Quartermaine (*blinks at her*) Oh – oh, yes, thanks – um – Melanie – next class, is it?

Melanie Heavens no, we've finished for the day. For the week, in fact.

Quartermaine (*clearly confused*) Oh, I – I didn't hear the bell.

Melanie It hasn't gone yet. Don't worry, Eddie's having one of his very out-of-sorts days, poor lamb, and Thomas is in the office. We're safe.

Quartermaine Oh. Oh yes – I suppose I must have let them go early – always restless on a Friday, aren't they, and then sat down and – and –

Melanie St John, what are you doing tonight?

Quartermaine Oh – usual – nothing very –

Melanie Then I'd like to introduce you to some very special friends of mine. Would you like that?

Quartermaine Well yes – yes – thank you, Melanie.

Melanie I'm sure you'll enjoy it – we always end up with singing and dancing, the food's delicious and the people are – well, you'll see for yourself.

Quartermaine Well, it sounds – sounds terrific!

The sound of the door: footsteps.

Melanie Right, you wait for me here, and I'll come and collect you when I'm ready – Oh hello, Derek, you too – what a bunch of skivers we're all turning out to be, eh?

Meadle Yes, well, it's only a few minutes off – besides Daphne's coming down for the weekend, I don't want to miss her train –

Melanie (*going out*) Jolly good – give her my love –

Meadle Right, Melanie, right – but I had a bloody near one in the corridor, I can tell you. I was sloping past the office – terrible din coming from it, sounded like a gang of Germans all bellowing away and Thomas trying to calm them down – anyway I'd just got past the door when Eddie came round the corner.

Quartermaine Phew!

Meadle Yes. I began to mumble some nonsense about wanting to check on a student – you know – but thinking I'd better wait until Thomas was freer – but he didn't see me – went right on past – I mean, we were like that! (*showing*)

Quartermaine Oh Lord! (*laughing*) Still, I hope he's all right – I mean for him not to notice –

Meadle Oh, by the way, I've got an invitation for you. You know Daphne and I are engaged – not that we haven't been from the moment I walked into the library

318

and saw her again. But now that I've got my permanency, we might as well make it official. We'll get married on the first day of the summer vac, and I'm going to ask Thomas and Eddie to be best man. I mean, let them decide which – I don't want to upset one by choosing the other.

Quartermaine Congratulations! Terrific! And then off on your honeymoon, eh?

Meadle Yes. We've settled for Hayling Island. Not very exciting, I know, but there may be a way to pick up a little money as well as having a good holiday ourselves. Daphne's keen to start saving for a house – you know how it is, there's a very practical head on those little shoulders of hers. There's a good chance she might even come and do a bit of teaching here – to replace me as the part-time, you see. I've already dropped a little hint to Thomas – I think he was worried by her speech impediment, but I pointed out that in some respects that could be an asset – with the elementary groups, for instance, and especially the Japs – that she understands the problems of pronunciation from inside, so to speak.

Quartermaine Absolutely – and she'd be – a great asset here, wouldn't she, in the staff room, I mean – she's a wonderful girl, Derek.

Meadle Yes, well, I think you'll like her even more when you meet her. Because frankly she's – she's – (*He shakes his head.*) And I'll tell you something – I don't know whether you've noticed but since she came back I've stopped having all those ridiculous accidents. They were the bane of my life, even though I was always trying to make light of them. I suppose it's – it's something to do with needing – well, well, the right person, eh? Love. Let's face it. Love. Oh, I'd better get going. So see you at seven. It'll be nothing special, but my landlady wants to put on a celebration supper – she's already very fond of Daphne, by the way – and she said if I wanted to ask along a friend – and there's nobody I'd rather have –

Quartermaine Derek, I'm very – I'm very honoured –

Meadle Actually, you'd better make it six-thirty, as it'll be more on the lines of a high tea. And if you could bring along a couple of bottles of wine –

Quartermaine My dear chap, I'll bring – I'll bring champagne – and – and – oh Lord, I'd forgotten! Oh no! I've already accepted an invitation for this evening.

Meadle Oh. What to?

Quartermaine Well, I can't make out, quite – I was in a bit of a haze when Melanie asked me, but she said something about friends and singing and dancing –

Meadle And you accepted?

Quartermaine Well, yes. She seemed so – so anxious – and anyway –

Meadle But it's – it's – one of those evenings. What they sing is hymns and dancing is up and down and around and about and then that Nurse Grimes declares for Jesus – and then the rest of them follow suit, and then they all stand around and wait for you to do it – at least, that's how it went the night she got me along. She's trying to convert you.

Quartermaine Oh Lord – oh Lord –

The bell rings.

Meadle But I told you all about it –

Quartermaine Yes, but I'd forgotten – I mean, she didn't mention Jesus –

Meadle Well, she won't let you get out of it now.

During this, he has been getting ready to go, putting on his bicycle clips, etc. Off, from the garden, foreign voices, laughing, calling out, etc., some of them Japanese; among them Sackling's, calling out goodnights, in the distance. Then:

Sackling (*closer*) No, sorry, I really can't – I'm in a hurry – and anyway – most of the mallets are broken and there aren't enough balls – so goodnight – goodnight –

Sackling enters, as Meadle speaks.

Meadle Well, I'll get you and Daphne together very soon – don't worry – (*making to go*) Here, Mark, guess what St John's got himself into – one of Melanie's evenings.

Sackling (*in a hurry, with books etc.*) Christ, you haven't, have you? (*He is clean-shaven, by the way.*) You *are* a chump, St John, you must have heard her going on about her dark night of the soul, after her mother died, and how Nurse Grimes introduced her to her sect and redeemed her – she's talked about nothing else for months and – and anyway I remember telling you how she tried it on me – don't you take anything in?

Quartermaine Yes, yes I did, but – but –

Sackling But you didn't know how to say no. Which, if I may say so, is both your charm and your major weakness.

Quartermaine Well, you never know – it may be – may be quite interesting – one has to – has to have a go at anything really – and I wasn't doing anything else this evening.

Sackling (*who is now ready to go*) This evening! Yes, you bloody *are* doing something else this evening. You're going out to dinner.

Quartermaine What – where?

Sackling At my place – oh Christ! Don't say I forgot to invite you. Well, you're invited. So there you are, saved from salvation. All you have to do is to tell Melanie that you'd forgotten –

Quartermaine Oh, this is terrible. You mean I'd be having dinner with you?

Sackling You *are* having dinner with us. It's obligatory. For one thing, I told Camelia I'd asked you – she's counting on you – we all are – even Tom, I promised him he could stay up an extra half an hour to see you again – you're always going on about looking forward to seeing him – (*He is putting on bicycle clips. The first time in the play.*)

Quartermaine But what about Melanie? I promised her –

Sackling Oh, to hell with Melanie! It's all a load of pathetic nonsense – and probably blasphemous, too, if one believed in God. Look, speaking as one of your best and oldest and dearest etc. – it's *crucial* that you come. Of the greatest importance. To me. You see. OK? Look, I've got to dash, I'm picking Tom up from school –

The sound of the door opening: footsteps.

Make sure (*to off*) that he turns up tonight, won't you? He's got himself into one of his usual messes – see you both at eight.

He goes as Anita enters. She has a look of weariness about her, is subtly less well turned-out than in previous scenes.

Quartermaine Oh, don't say you and Nigel are going to be there too – oh – oh –

Anita Why can't you come?

322

Quartermaine Well, I fell into one of those dozes again –
you know how they keep coming over me suddenly – for
a minute or so – and – and when I came out of it, there
I was, right in the middle of this – this Melanie business.

Anita Poor St John.

Quartermaine But I can't just turn round to her now –
she was so – well her eyes – I can't explain – very – well –
and anyway I can't just turn round now and say sorry,
Melanie, something much better's turned up – oh, if only
Mark hadn't forgotten! – but I suppose he knows I'm
usually free – and – thought he had – or – but what do
I do, Anita? Mark seems so – so determined, too. What
do I do?

Anita I don't know. But come if you can. It's meant to
be a reconciliation dinner, and you know how they
usually turn out. So you'd be a great help, as the perfect
outsider.

Quartermaine Well, you know I'd do anything –
anything – to make sure that old Mark and his Camelia
and little Tom too, of course, stay together.

Anita Oh, it's not them that need reconciling. They
already are.

Quartermaine Oh.

Anita It's Mark and Nigel. Hasn't Mark told you
anything about that?

Quartermaine No. Nothing. You mean old Mark and
old Nigel – oh, Lord, but they're such friends, what
happened?

Anita Oh, it was all a couple of months ago. They had
the most appalling row, because Nigel turned down an
extract from Mark's novel. About seven extracts, actually.

Sackling Oh no. Oh, poor Mark!

Anita Well, Nigel made everything worse by deciding to be completely honest for once. I suppose he thought Mark, being an old friend, had it coming to him. What he said was that everything Mark had sent him was imitative and laboured, and anyway, who really cared any more about the mysteries of sex, the wonders of childbirth, the delicacies of personal relationships? It had all been done and done and done to death, there were far bigger issues.

Quartermaine Oh Lord, oh Lord! Are there?

Anita So of course when the magazine folded, and Nigel was going through his rough patch, with the printers threatening to sue and various other things, Mark wrote him a gloating letter saying how delighted he was as *Reports* had never been interested in serious literary values, only in pandering to the top names – or trying to – and added a PS about the old Amanda Southgate affair, claiming to be indignant on my account, I must say, I rather wish he'd resisted that.

Quartermaine But still – but still – he has asked Nigel to dinner –

Anita Oh, that was probably Camelia. She never took literature seriously, and now that Mark's sworn off writing – at least for the time – the important thing for her is that we had them to dinner just before she left Mark, and now she's come back she's realised she owes us the return. I loathe the thought of it – for one thing we haven't been able to find a baby-sitter, so we'll have to bring Ophelia in her carry-cot – she's still got six-weeks colic, after four months – so it would be nice if you came, St John, you'd make the whole thing more bearable.

Quartermaine Oh, I'd love to – and to see Ophelia – I've only seen her the once, in hospital – what hair she had!

Anita laughs. Is in fact crying slightly.

Oh, Anita – what is it? Oh, Lord, I hate to see you unhappy – more than anyone else – (*He makes a move towards her, checks himself, makes a move again.*) Oh Lord! (*He stands before her, helplessly.*)

Anita I'm all right, St John, honestly – it's just that – oh, the way things go, I mean. Or don't go. Nothing seems to come out right. All the years I adored him and he couldn't bear me. And now he adores me and I can't bear him. You see. (*She looks at him.*) What a – what a nice man you are. (*She begins to cry again.*) I'm tired, I expect, tired –

She turns away, blowing her nose, wiping her eyes, etc. The sound of the door opening: footsteps.

Quartermaine (*turning*) Oh – oh, hello, Henry, you've finished – finished late – um –

Windscape (*appearing rather heavily*) Yes, I got into a bit of a tangle with my Intermediary British Life and Institutions, over our parliamentary system. Usually it's perfectly clear to me but this time it all came out rather oddly. Or it must have done, as I had the whole lot of them dismissing it with contempt – the three or four from the Eastern bloc, all the ones from fascist countries, the Spanish, the Portuguese, the South Americans – the French were the loudest, as always – but even the Japanese – normally such a polite, reticent man – and I don't see quite how it happened or what I said, but it was rather hard being lectured at on – on political decencies – and shouted at by – by – still, I suppose it's better they should all join up for a wrangle with me than with each other – although to tell you the truth I found it rather hard to

keep my temper – (*sitting down*) – But I think I managed
to – with the result that I've got a – a slight headache.
After all, I was only *explaining* our constitution, not
boasting about it. I've got my own – own distinct
reservations – no system's perfect, as I kept having to
say to Santos. His father's a Bolivian cabinet minister.

Anita (*who has been discreetly composing herself during
the above*) It's awful when they get like that, isn't it? I
always make them explain our politics to me, and then
just correct their English, whatever they say – one of the
advantages of being female, I suppose – (*She attempts a
little laugh.*) Well, goodnight, Henry, see you Monday –

Windscape 'Night, Anita, my dear. Best to Nigel, and
little Ophelia –

Anita And St John, see you later, I hope. Do, if you can.

Quartermaine Yes, well – I'll – I'll – right, Anita. Right.
If I can.

> *Anita goes out through the French windows. There is
> a pause. Windscape is sitting in the chair, stroking his
> forehead. Quartermaine is standing in a state of
> desperation.*

I say, Henry – I say – I wonder if you could give me
some advice.

Windscape Mmmm?

Quartermaine I'm in a bit of a pickle, you see.

Windscape Oh. Oh good heavens, St John, that reminds
me – I'd completely forgotten – is there any chance you
could come over tonight?

Quartermaine What?

Windscape I'm sorry it's such short notice, it wouldn't
have been if I'd remembered. The thing is that Fanny's

really very down in the dumps, very down, she really
does need an evening out. So do I, come to that. It's
Susan, you see. She's taken a turn for the worse.

Quartermaine Oh – oh –

Windscape Oh, it's probably just withdrawal from all
the tranquillising drugs they put her on, in hospital, and
then her friends would keep coming over in the evenings
and talking about their plans and their blasted A-Levels
and of course there's no possibility that Susan – at least
for a few years – anyway, last night, she laughed at
something on television, a good sign, Fanny and I thought,
the first time she's laughed since her breakdown, so we
didn't realise until we were in the living room that what
we were laughing at was a news flash to do with some
particular hideous atrocity in – in – (*He gestures.*) and
what followed was a bit of a nightmare, especially for
Ben and little Fanny – it ended with the doctor having to
sedate her – almost forcibly, I'm afraid – so – so I noticed
La Règle du Jeu at the Arts, one of our favourite films,
so decent and – and humane – and then a quiet dinner
afterwards at the French place – just the two of us – if
you could manage it. You're the only person Susan will
allow to baby-sit, you see. She seems to feel some – some
reassurance from you. And of course little Fanny and
Benjamin love it too, when you come.

Quartermaine I'd love to, Henry – love to – but could it
be Saturday?

Windscape No, Saturday's no good – we have our family
therapy session in the afternoon and we all feel so – so
exhausted afterwards. Demoralised, really. I've still to be
persuaded that they serve a – a useful – though of course
one mustn't prejudge –

Quartermaine Sunday, then?

Windscape Unfortunately Fanny's mother's coming on Sunday. Rather against our inclinations as – as she's rather insensitive with Susan – advises her to pull her socks up – that sort of thing – you can't manage this evening then.

Quartermaine Well, I – I – you see the problem is – I can't –

> *The sound of the door opening, footsteps. Melanie appears. She has changed her dress, is wearing high-heeled shoes, some make-up, and has taken much trouble with her hair.*

Melanie Well, there we are then, St John – sorry to have been so long – oh, hello, Henry, I didn't know you were still here.

Windscape Hello, Melanie. (*slightly awkward*) Oh, I've been meaning to say all day how much I like that dress.

Melanie (*smiles*) Thank you. I'm taking St John to one of my evenings –

Windscape Oh. Oh yes. I'm so sorry that Fanny and I have been unable to come so far –

Melanie Oh, I know how difficult things are for you at the moment – as long as you both realise that any time you want to come along, I've been thinking that perhaps Susan might –

Windscape Yes, yes, thank you, Melanie. (*Cutting her slightly.*)

Melanie Are you all right, you look a little fraught?

Windscape Oh, just tired, Friday eveningish, that's all.

Quartermaine And a bit of a headache – eh Henry?

Melanie Oh? Where?

Windscape Well – in my head.

Melanie Yes, but which part?

Windscape Well, it seems to be – just here – (*Rubbing his brow.*)

Melanie Ah, well then, it's a tension headache, Nurse Grimes showed me a marvellous trick for dealing with that, let me have a go at it. (*She comes over to Windscape, behind the chair.*) Now put your head forward – right forward –

Windscape does so, with perceptible lack of enthusiasm.

Melanie There. Now. (*She proceeds to knead her fingers into the back of Windscape's neck.*)

Quartermaine So that's how they do it – looks jolly relaxing, anyway –

Windscape endures for a few seconds, then suddenly lets out a cry, leaps up. There is a pause.

Windscape I'm – Melanie, I'm sorry – I – don't know quite what –

Melanie I expect I hurt you, pressed the wrong nerve or – I still haven't quite got the trick of it, with my clumsy –

Windscape Well – well, actually it feels a little better. (*He tries a laugh.*) Thank you.

Melanie (*smiles*) Well, St John, we'd better be on our way. It's quite a drive. Goodnight, Henry, and rest yourself during the weekend, won't you?

Windscape Yes, yes – the same to you . . . (*a slight hesitation*) my dear. Goodnight, St John, see you Monday.

Quartermaine See you Monday, Henry, and – oh, if it turns out that Saturday or Sunday – well, I'm sure I'll be free –

Windscape smiles, nods. As they go out through the French windows there is the sound of the door opening and feet, a stick.

Windscape Oh, hello, Eddie, I didn't know you were about today.

Loomis enters. He is much frailer than when last seen.

Loomis Well, there was a frightful schemozzle in the office – and Thomas asked me to come down – but was that St John's voice I heard just now?

Windscape Yes. His and Melanie's –

Loomis Ah. Well, I would have quite liked a word with our St John. He's caused us quite an afternoon. He appears to have missed his class entirely. His students waited doggedly through the whole hour for him to turn up, and then went to the office and berated poor Thomas – they were mostly Germans, and you know what they're like if they think they're not getting their money's worth of syllabus.

Windscape Oh dear.

Loomis Though I doubt whether they'd get much more sensible English from St John present than from St John absent – as far as I know that Swiss Ferdinand Boller is the only student who ever felt he got value for money from St John, thank goodness he's stopped sending those postcards at last, they made Thomas quite upset – but I wonder what it was he enjoyed so much about St John's classes – perhaps the lack of – of – I don't know what we're going to do about him in the end, though, if we turned him out, where would he go, who else would have him? One does look after one's own, I suppose, when it comes to it I agree with Thomas on that, after all the school's our – our family, the only family Thomas and I have between us, so one has a responsibility for them – but a responsibility for the students too – (*There should be a slightly rambling quality in the delivery of this speech.*) It's so difficult to get the balance right – so difficult – St John forgetting to teach them, and now Melanie's starting up her missionary work amongst them – Thomas is going to have a word with her too – the Catholic countries won't stand for it, and why should they? And now our Meadle, taking to slipping away before the bell now he's got his permanency, trying to bluff his way past me in the hall as if I couldn't see him – ha – well, at least Mark's pulling his weight now he's got his Camelia back, I never thought for a moment there was a writer in that lad, did you? – and Anita – really I don't know how these modern young couples cope – but I gather Nigel's taken to it wonderfully, Thomas and I saw the three of them on the Backs the other day, a very pretty sight it was too – so – so – good, good – just the problems of a flourishing school, eh? (*He laughs.*)

Windscape Yes. Yes indeed, Eddie.

Loomis Well, I'd best get back up to bed, or Thomas will have a fit. Goodnight Henry, see you Monday, bless you, bless you.

Windscape Yes, see you Monday, Eddie.

Loomis (*goes off, stops*) Oh, I haven't asked for a while – how's our Susan?

Windscape Oh, I think responding – slowly – slowly responding.

Loomis Good, good.

The sound of the door closing.

During this, the sound of students' voices, young, distant, in the garden. They get closer as the scene concludes. Windscape stands for a moment, touches his forehead, then goes to his locker, puts away his books, gets his briefcase. The sound of students' voices, probably two girls, two boys, now laughing, calling out to each other in some sort of game. Windscape gets out his bicycle clips, bends to put them on. As he does so, he looks towards the French windows, smiles slightly, continues putting on the clips, as the sound of voices, still raised in laughter, continues.

Curtain.

SCENE THREE

Eighteen months later. It is around Christmas. Not yet dark, but darkening slightly. The French windows are closed, but the curtains are open. There is an atmosphere of chill. One table light is on.

Sackling, Quartermaine, Melanie, Anita, Windscape and Meadle are variously sitting and standing. Sackling is smoking a pipe. He has a beard. Windscape is also smoking a pipe. Anita is pregnant. Meadle has a plaster neck brace. Quartermaine is wearing a dinner jacket. Melanie is sitting, rather hunched, nervously smoking a cigarette. It is the first time in the play that she has smoked. She smokes throughout the scene, lighting one after another. After a pause:

Sackling It's always at Christmas, somehow, isn't it?

Windscape Yes.

Sackling Oh Henry, I'm sorry –

Windscape No. You're right. I was thinking much the same thing. Both my parents too, but – but of course in Susan's case I don't think the season was – was relevant. At least to her. The blinds were always down, you see. Because any brightness hurt her mind. Natural brightness, that is. She could tolerate artificial light. Until the last – last bit.

Anita (*there is a faint touch of querulousness in her voice*) Look. I'm sorry, but I'll have to go soon, I'm afraid. I promised the *au pair* she could have the night off, and Nigel's probably not coming back from London until tomorrow –

Meadle Yes, I've got to get back pretty soon. Daphne's not too grand, what with her morning sickness and all the redecorating – she's been overdoing it and I promised – I don't want to leave her alone too long.

Windscape Of course – of course – there's really no need for all of us when it comes to it – it's just that – that – as soon as I heard I had some idea that you would want – well – without perhaps enough consideration – it was a bad idea, perhaps –

Quartermaine Oh, I say, Henry – well, I'm jolly glad you got in touch with me – though of course I wasn't doing anything in particular –

Sackling Well, I must say, St John, (*smiling*) you do look as if you might have been about to be up to something –

Quartermaine What? Oh – (*Laughs.*) Well, no, no, not really – it was just – just –

> *During this, the sound of the door opening. They all look towards it: the sound of footsteps, dragging feet, a stick.*

Loomis (*in an overcoat, with a stick, and with a deaf-
aid attached to his glasses*) I saw the lights on so I
guessed that some of you – one or two perhaps – had
come. But I didn't expect all of you. Not at this time
of year, with your families and responsibilities. Thomas
would have been so touched. So touched. My thanks on
his behalf. My thanks. (*A little pause.*) He died an hour
ago. They did everything they could, right to the end,
but of course, as we've all known for some time, there
was nothing to be done. (*A little pause.*) You know how
much you all meant to him. He talked of every one of
you, every evening, until – (*He gestures.*) But you'll also
want to know what its future is to be, this school that he
loved so much. I know what his wishes are, we discussed
them quite openly once we both knew that he was bound
to leave us. I've also talked to Henry. I'm sure it will be
no surprise to all of you that I asked Henry some time
ago to take over the school as its sole principal. I've no
desire to take an active part in it, now that Thomas is no
longer here. I loved it for his sake, you see. I'll make no
secret of that. Not this evening.

  A pause, nearly breaks down, pulls himself together.

Not this evening. I shall be leaving the flat as soon as
possible – it has too many memories – and settle
somewhere by the sea. As we'd always hoped to do. I
hope that some of you will come and see me – (A *little
pause.*) Bless you. Bless you.

  *He turns and goes. The sound of his feet dragging
  slowly. The sound of the door shutting. There is a
  pause.*

Windscape I – I really don't want to speak at such a
moment about plans or changes. We'll have a meeting at
the beginning of term to go into those, but I should just
say that I've already talked to Mark – at Eddie's

suggestion and with Thomas's approval – a few weeks ago, when it became clear that Thomas was more than seriously ill – about his following me as the academic tutor. I am happy to say that he has accepted.

There are murmurs.

So until next term – which has a very reasonable enrolment, I am glad to report, let me merely assure you that I intend to do my best, as I know you will, to maintain our reputation as a – a flourishing school. I know – I know – Thomas and Eddie wouldn't want me to let you part without wishing you all a Happy Christmas.

Murmurs of 'Happy Christmas'.

Well, see you all next term!

They rise to go, putting on coats, etc.

Quartermaine (*comes over to Windscape*) Henry – I say, well, you and Mark – that's quite a team, you know.

Windscape Thank you, St John – I wonder if you could hang on a minute or so.

Quartermaine Absolutely. Oh absolutely, Henry.

Sackling (*coated*) Well, 'night, Henry – we'll speak. And St John – over the Christmas, eh? You must come round. (*Gesturing with his pipe.*)

Windscape Yes, we'll speak, Mark.

Quartermaine Oh, I'd love that – thanks, Mark. See you then. Love to Camelia and Tom and little Mark too.

Anita (*also coated*) Sorry if I was a little edgy earlier, Henry. Put it down to my current condition and Yugoslav au pairs! (*She laughs.*)

Windscape You get home to your Ophelia, my dear, and make Nigel look after you.

Anita Oh, I will, Henry – see you over Christmas, St John, I hope.

Quartermaine Oh Lord, yes – lovely – lovely – 'night, Anita.

Meadle (*coated*) Sorry Daphne couldn't make it, Henry. She wanted to, of course. But I'll fill her in, don't worry, she's very much looking forward to her courses next term –

Windscape And I'm looking forward to having her join us. Goodnight, Derek.

Meadle Drop around when you feel in the mood, St John. Lots of paintbrushes for you to wield – (*He laughs.*)

Quartermaine Terrific! I love the smell of paint – love to Daphne –

Melanie (*comes up, hunched, smoking*) 'Night Henry. 'Night.

Windscape 'Night, Melanie, my dear. And perhaps we can all get together after Christmas – Fanny was saying how much she'd like to see you, after all this time.

Melanie Love to, love to, and St John, if you're free, pop around and have a drink. (*She laughs.*)

Quartermaine Oh, yes please, Melanie – I'd like that –

As Sackling, Anita, Meadle, and Melanie leave, one after the other, the sound of their feet, and of the door opening and closing. Quartermaine and Windscape are left alone on stage.

Windscape Well, St John – (*He hesitates.*) Where were you off to, tonight, by the way?

Quartermaine Oh Lord, nowhere, Henry. (*He laughs.*) You see, there was a suitcase I still hadn't unpacked –

it's been down in Mrs Harris's cellar all these years. But suddenly she wanted the space, so she made me take it up, and of course I opened it and there was this – (*Indicating the dinner jacket.*) So I decided to try it on, to see if it still fits. And then you phoned, and Mrs Harris was doing her usual thing right beside me, glowering away. (*Laughs.*) So – so I came straight on out here, forgetting I had it on. Stinks of mothballs, I'm afraid, but not a bad fit, eh? Might come in useful sometime. But I say, poor old Eddie, poor old Eddie. Wasn't he – wasn't he terrific!

Windscape Yes. Indeed. (*A slight pause.*) St John. St John. I've been worrying about this for – oh, ever since I realised I was to take over from Eddie and Thomas. If I'm to be principal, I have to run the school in my own way, you see.

Quartermaine Oh, I know that, Henry. We all do.

Windscape And – and – I don't see, you see – however fond of you I happen to be – we all happen to be – that there's – there's any room for you any more. You see?

Quartermaine nods.

I thought it only right to tell you at the first – the very first possible moment. So that you can – well, look around –

Quartermaine No, that's – right, thank you, Henry. I – oh Lord, I know that I haven't got much to offer – never had, I suppose – and recently it's got even worse – it's a wonder – a wonder people have put up with me so long, eh? (*He attempts a laugh.*)

Windscape If I could see any way –

Quartermaine No, no – I mean, it's no good being all right in the staff room if you're no good in the classroom, is it? They're different things.

Windscape I can't tell you how much I'll miss you. We all will.

Quartermaine And I – I'll miss it. All of you.

Windscape Yes, I know. Would you like a quick drink – or – or – come back and see Fanny?

Quartermaine Oh, no – no, thank you, Henry, I'll stay here for a while – you know – and get myself used to – used to – and – I'll go in a minute.

Windscape (*hesitates, looks at Quartermaine*) Well, goodnight, St John.

Quartermaine Goodnight, Henry, see you next – (*He gestures.*)

> *Windscape goes off. The sound of feet and the door opening and closing.*

Oh Lord! (*He walks a few steps, stops, shakes his head, sits down.*) Well – oh Lord! I say – (*He sits in silence, shaking his head, gradually stops shaking his head, sits in stillness.*) Oh Lord!

> *Lights. Curtain.*

THE LATE MIDDLE CLASSES

For Victoria

The Late Middle Classes was first presented by the Palace Theatre, Watford, on 19 March 1999. The production then played at Brighton, Plymouth, Bath, Woking and Richmond. The cast was as follows:

Brownlow Nicholas Woodeson
Holly *in his forties* James Fleet
Holly *aged twelve* Sam Bedi
Celia Harriet Walter
Charles James Fleet
Ellie Angela Pleasence

Director Harold Pinter
Designer Eileen Diss
Lighting Mick Hughes
Sound Designer Dominic Muldowney

Characters

Brownlow
Holly *in his forties*
Holly *aged twelve*
Celia
Charles
Ellie

Act One

SCENE ONE

Brownlow's study/sitting room. Autumn. Early evening.
The present.
  A baby grand piano, a sofa, desk, table, an armchair.
  Brownlow, in his seventies, is sitting in armchair,
dozing, muttering.
  Doorbell rings.

Brownlow (*mutters in his sleep, gradually wakes up,*
listens) No, I couldn't have heard it – must be a dream –

  Doorbell rings again. Brownlow goes to window,
  peers out. Knocks on window.

Is there anybody there? Who's there? Mrs Jameson, is
that you? Mr Jameson? Surely you know not to disturb
me at this hour, I'm very busy –

  Doorbell rings again.

Who is it? (*Agitated. Attempts to compose himself, goes*
out of room.)

  Voices off, indistinct.

Brownlow (*off*) Yes? Can I help you?

Holly (*off*) I don't know if you remember me. I'm
Holliday Smithers.

Brownlow Smithers – Holliday Smithers – Yes, yes, of
course I remember you.

Holly I was just passing and couldn't help wondering
if you were still here.

Brownlow Yes, yes, still here. Well, please come in.

Holly enters Brownlow's sitting room, followed by Brownlow. Holly is in his mid-forties. He looks around.

And, um, where have you come from?

Holly Well, from Australia, in fact. Melbourne.

Brownlow And you're staying on the island?

Holly No, I'm staying in London. But I had to come down to Portsmouth for a few days.

Brownlow And so you decided to pay us a visit, after all these years.

Holly Well, I had the afternoon off, couldn't resist driving over – odd that, being able to drive over, all the way by road. I still imagined having to take the ferry. I'd have preferred that on such a beautiful day. Especially when everything turned out to be so familiar. (*Looks around again.*) As it is here. Except that it's all older, of course.

Brownlow Yes, yes, like myself.

Holly Like myself. Do you mind if I sit down?

Brownlow Oh – oh, yes, of course, I'm sorry – please. Where would you like? (*gesturing around room*)

Holly (*walks over to armchair, sits down, watched by Brownlow*) There is a change, though. No, not a change, an absence. Yes, something's missing. Oh yes, a cat. There was always a cat called Kitty-Cat. Kitty-Cat Number Seven. You explained to me that your mother always called her cats Kitty-Cat so it was always the same cat to her. When one died she'd go straight on to the next Kitty-Cat almost without noticing the pain of

346

loss or the treachery of replacement. But you numbered them in your head. So I knew Kitty-Cat Number Seven.

Brownlow They were called Catty-Kit, not Kitty-Cat.

Holly Oh yes, sorry. I must have let the chocolate bar get in the way. Well, what number did it get up to, Catty-Kit, before its sequence ended?

Brownlow Eleven. Number Eleven I had put down the day after I buried my mother.

Holly Ah. The end of the line then.

Brownlow It felt like the end of an era.

Holly Yes, I suppose it must have done. (*Little pause.*) But have you gone on keeping the same hours?

Brownlow Well, I keep the hours, yes. Yes, I do that.

Holly Every morning from ten to twelve and every evening from nine, was it? until midnight.

Brownlow Nine-thirty until midnight. Back then. Now, of course, my time's my own and I start earlier. Whenever I feel like it.

Holly You and your beloved talking to each other. (*Glancing towards piano.*)

Brownlow Yes.

Holly And what do the two of you talk about these days? Anything in particular?

Brownlow A concerto. We're working on a concerto. We've been at it for a long time. A long, long time. I hope to complete it before I die.

Holly Oh yes, you must. You'd want to hear it, after all. You used to say that you couldn't compose the opening until you knew how the piece would close. So first close, then open, and then on into the middle, which would look after itself.

Brownlow Well, of course one has these theories at different times of one's life. One's creative life. Perhaps it's to do with memories. The more memories you have, the more difficult it all becomes.

Holly You mean the memories teem about and get in the way?

Brownlow Well, no, not teem about. Not quite as lively as that. They bob up.

Holly What sort of memories?

Brownlow Well, just memories. Of days gone by. (*Little pause.*) You, for instance. You bob up now and then. Quite often, in fact.

Holly Do I?

Brownlow Do I ever bob up for you?

Holly Oh, yes. This afternoon, when I was walking about the island. I went to see the old house, well, the family house, and one thought led to another and that led to another and then finally up you bobbed again.

Brownlow Like a jack-in-the-box.

Holly No, not really like a jack-in-the-box. The thoughts were quite logically connected, I think. Though there was a bit missing – something I tried to remember and couldn't. The music. The music that seemed to run through it all. It wouldn't come back. It won't come back.

Brownlow Really? Can I offer you something? Tea? Coffee? And I do believe there's some sherry somewhere – but very, very old. From my mother's day. Quite a few bottles of it there should be in the larder. Mrs Jameson helps herself to it from time to time but – she's my cleaning woman, you know, she came long after your time – after my mother's too – in fact she's only been here about ten years, I think it must be, and her husband does the gardening. Sometimes I hear them down in the kitchen, laughing and talking, and it occurs to me that they're at the sherry, especially when they're being rather loud. May I ask a question?

Holly gestures. There is a pause.

Holly (*gently*) A question. You're going to ask a question.

Brownlow Are you real?

Holly Yes, quite real. Well, at least I think I am. One can never be completely sure on that point, can one? (*Gets up, goes over to Brownlow.*) But here, feel this. (*Holds out his hand.*)

Brownlow tentatively moves his hand, touches Holly's sleeve. As he withdraws his hand, Holly catches it in his.

There, you see. Not just the garments but flesh and blood.

They stand, hands clasped for a second. Holly removes his hand.

Brownlow Did you say yes? To the sherry, that is?

Holly A glass of your mother's sherry, yes, I'd love to try it at last. Thank you.

Brownlow Well, I'll see what I can find. (*Goes out.*)

Holly goes over to piano, picks along keyboard as if trying to work out a tune. Shakes his head in exasperation, goes back, sits in armchair, takes out cigarette, lights it. Sits back meditatively. As he does so:

Piano music, over, as:
Lights going down as lights coming up on Smithers'
sitting room.

SCENE TWO

Spring. Evening. Early nineteen-fifties.
Smithers' sitting room.
Holly, as a child of twelve, playing the piano.
Holly continues to play for a second, stops. He gets
up, goes over to sofa, sits down. Takes out exercise book
from satchel, extracts a loose sheet of paper, reads it very
intensely, then reaches urgently into satchel, fumbles
deeply, takes out magazine, begins to go through it,
studying pictures, occasionally reading to himself aloud
but inaudibly from sheet of paper.
Sound of front door opening and closing.
Holly scrambles to his feet, stuffs magazine and
exercise book back into satchel, hurries over to piano,
starts playing.
Celia Smithers, Holly's mother, enters, dressed in tennis
shorts, top, carrying tennis racquet and tennis balls.

Celia She's chucked! That bloody Moira woman has
actually chucked! She couldn't phone me before I left
so I could have got somebody else, no, she just stepped
out as I was cycling past, with her hand raised like a
policeman – I nearly pedalled straight into her and I wish
I had – she honked out some nonsense about coughs and
sore throats, running eyes, her cheeks were like apples,
my dear, great shiny apples, by far the healthiest thing
I've seen all week – oh, I could kill her! Kill, kill, kill!
(*Serves viciously with imaginary ball.*)

Holly It's because you keep beating her.

Celia Oh, don't be so silly.

Holly It's true. Every time you come back from playing against her you crow about beating her six-love, six-love. You do the same with me, so I know how she feels.

Celia She wouldn't be so petty. Yes, she would. Everyone on this bloody island is petty. That's why you've got to win a scholarship. To get us off it.

Holly That makes complete sense. That's perfectly logical. I understand that.

Celia You sound just like your father. (*Banging her racquet gently on his head.*) I. Won't. Have. You. Making. Fun. Of. Your. Father.

Holly I wasn't making fun of him. I just don't see why my getting a scholarship would get you off the island.

Celia Because if you win a scholarship to St Paul's or Westminster we won't have to pay the fees and we can all move to London where we belong. And if you don't win a scholarship you'll end up going somewhere local where you'll have to be a day boy so we can afford your fees. We've been over and over it.

Holly You haven't been over and over it with me.

Celia No. I meant your father and I have been over and over it.

Holly What's wrong with Portsmouth Grammar School? A lot of boys from around here go there – all my friends – and they say it's jolly good.

Celia It may be jolly good for them but it's not jolly good enough for us.

Holly Well, I don't think it's fair that everything you want comes down to me getting a scholarship. I probably haven't got a chance. We don't know anybody around here who's –

Celia Edwin Tomkins.

Holly Oh, *him*.

Celia 'Oh, *him*' won a full scholarship to St Paul's, as his wretched parents never stop boasting. And as you despise him so much you could surely do just as well. Now, do get on with your practice, and what about your prep, have you done that yet?

Holly Almost. I've just got a bit of French left.

Celia Then finish your practice and on with your French. I want it done before Mr Thing-me-bob comes. You're always too tired to do any prep after your piano lessons.

Holly starts playing piano.

(*Watches him.*) Oh, you do remind me of someone, you know, whenever you play.

Holly Do I? Who?

Celia One of the young chaps in the war, one of the fighter pilots. He had the same – same intensity – as if there was nothing else in the world but the music, even though everybody was singing around him.

Holly (*plays for a little*) What happened to him?

Celia He went for a Burton, poor young devil, like so many of the rest of them.

Holly Oh. (*playing on*)

Celia Tell me something. Something very important.

Holly Oh, Mummy, I'm trying to concentrate.

Celia You have to answer this. Do you love me?

Holly (*sighs*) Of course I love you.

Celia Why?

Holly Oh, Mummy, you know why. Because you're my mother.

Celia I do wish you'd once, just once, come up with a more flattering answer. What is that piece anyway – it's been driving me mad trying to remember – Beethoven, isn't it?

Holly Very nearly. It's Brownlow. Mr Brownlow.

Celia Golly, really, you mean he writes it too? (*Staring over Holly's shoulder.*)

Holly Oh, yes. Thomas Ambrose Brownlow.

Celia Ambrose? Thomas Ambrose Brownlow? Is that hyphenated? Thomas Ambrose-Brownlow?

Holly No, that's his middle name, I think.

Celia Rather precious to use your middle name. Especially when it's Ambrose. But I suppose if your name is Brownlow, Thomas Brownlow, and you want to add a little splash, if you're a composer – what's it called? (*reading*) Mio – 'A Bagatelle for Mio'.

Holly It's miaow. It's about their cat when it miaows.

Celia Doesn't sound at all like a miaow to me. Except it's soft and velvety so I suppose that's a bit like a cat. What does he do with them when he's composed them? Does he have them played by people – concerts, that sort of thing?

Holly He says they're doing this on the Third Programme.

Celia The Third Programme, golly. Well, perhaps they'll let you play it.

Holly Actually, Mummy, I don't want to do the piano any more.

Celia What on earth do you mean?

Holly I mean I don't like it. And I'm not very good at it.

Celia Nonsense! Your Mr Ambrose says you're the best student he's ever had. By far and away the best on the island anyway.

Holly Yes, well, he doesn't really mean it, he's just being polite.

Celia You need your music, you know you do. You put it down on your scholarship form that you played the piano as one of your main interests.

Holly No, I didn't. I put down music. And so if I change to the violin –

Celia The violin! How on earth do you think your father's going to afford a violin?

Holly Well, we could sell the piano –

Celia Sell the piano! It's your legacy from your god-mother. You don't just sell off legacies and buy something else you prefer.

Holly I know I'd be better at the violin, I know it.

Celia But you'd have to start from the beginning and you've gone so far with the piano and – well, you talk it over with him – (*gesturing to music*) – he'll know what's best.

Holly He won't want me to give up the piano. And he doesn't do the violin.

Celia Well, there you are. As he's the only music person on the island you'll just have to stick with what he wants.

Holly It's not what he wants, it's what I want.

Celia It isn't what you want, it's what will get you a scholarship.

Holly I'll give up the extra football training if you let me do the violin.

Celia Don't be silly, you're captain of the first eleven, they wouldn't dream of letting you. And quite right too.

Holly Can't you ask Daddy at least and he can explain to Mr Brownlow and if I only took half my pocket money we could probably find a cheap violin in Portsmouth and somebody there who can teach me.

Celia And who's going to ferry you there and back every time you have a lesson? Your father, I suppose, as if he hasn't got enough on his plate – oh, I haven't got time to stand here and argue about something so completely absurd, for one thing I've the evening meal to think about, all I've got is powdered eggs, a bit of lard and almost no butter –

> *Holly bangs his hands down on the keyboard in anger and despair.*

Celia Don't you dare do that! How dare you do that!

Holly (*after a moment*) Sorry. (*Little pause.*) Sorry, Mummy. It's just that – that I'd love to learn the violin, that's all.

Celia Well then, darling, if we get to London you shall, I promise you. And I'll tell your father, I promise. There. I can't say fairer than that, can I?

> *Holly nods. He picks up satchel, makes to leave the room.*

Celia Where are you going?

Holly To my room. To finish my French.

Celia You can do it down here at the table where I can keep an eye on you.

Holly Why?

Celia Because I never know what you get up to in your room these days.

Holly What do you mean?

Celia You're blushing.

Holly I'm not blushing. You were going to go out and play tennis so it wouldn't have mattered to you then where I did my prep.

Celia I've had enough arguments for one afternoon. I don't want to talk about any of it. That's your father's job.

Holly What do you mean?

Celia Nothing. It's just that some things are between fathers and sons.

Holly What things?

Celia I told you, I don't want to talk about it. It's all perfectly normal, I expect. Not that I'd know.

Holly I don't understand.

Celia There's nothing for you to understand, I keep telling you. Now you jolly well get on with your prep, young man –

Holly You mean when I was praying and you came in? Why are you against my praying?

Celia Holliday, not another word. Get on with it before your Mr Thing arrives.

*Holly takes his books over to table, opens books,
begins to work.*

    *Celia watches him, then goes over to sofa, lights
a cigarette. Lies on sofa, smoking, her leg jigging
irritably. Suddenly struck by an idea, she gets up, goes
to telephone, dials.*

Celia (*on telephone*) Oh, Bunty dear, it's Celia. It just
struck me, lovely afternoon, a bit of a breeze, what do
you say to a game of tennis? (*Little pause.*) Well, right
now really. I mean, as soon as we've changed. We can be
at the court in ten minutes – oh, don't be so silly, dear,
you're a very good *natural* player, all you need is practice
– and weight has nothing to do with it, many marvellous
players are as heavy as you – what? No, no, I don't
mean that at all, all I mean is something you said the
other day about being worried that you're getting a little
– a little – and what better way to get it off? (*Pause.*)
Oh, very well, dear, if you really feel I'm inviting you to
join a chain gang instead of a mild knock-up – what?
Moira? No, no, she's a bit under the weather, she says,
and anyway I don't fancy an hour with Moira, all she'll
talk about is how marvellous everything is and their
wretched holiday in Ireland with all the steaks and
butter and fresh cream. Which reminds me, my dear,
have you got any eggs from those chickens of yours,
I want to give Charles a surprise, he was saying last
night how much he yearned for an omelette, but with
fresh eggs, not powdered – oh – oh, well never mind,
Bunty dear, I was going to offer you some chocolate in
exchange but I expect that the last thing you want at the
moment is chocolate so it'll have to be dried eggs again,
they'll just have to put up with it – what? Wait? Oh,
somebody at the door – somebody at the window? Oh,
tapping on the window – well, I really haven't got
anything more to – (*Stands, waiting, lights another*

cigarette, taps her foot irritably.) Who is it? Moira!
Tapping on your window! What does she want? A cup
of tea! Moira taps on your window whenever she wants
a cup of tea – no, no, thank you, dear, really what I
want to be is outside, you see. Give Moira my – my –

> *She hangs up.*

Really, these people – these people on this bloody island,
I don't know how I put up with them. Always presuming
on one's friendship. If they didn't claim to be friends
they wouldn't dare to do the kind of thing they do do.
Of course it's easy for them, they've both got help, they
can play tennis or have their cups of tea with each other
whenever they like. While I – what on earth was the
point of our winning the war if you end up worse off
than before it started? No housekeeper, no maid, while
both of them have got both. And Bunty's even got a
gardener. Well, she calls him a gardener but really he
looks like a convict – pasty-faced and furtive and
smoking, and doesn't even know how to say good
morning. Doesn't speak at all as far as I know. He may
be one of those Eyetie prisoners of war who stayed on.
But if you've got an Italian prisoner of war in your
garden I suppose you do feel you've won the war and
everything's almost back to normal. In spite of Winnie
being thrown out.

> *She looks at Holly, who is bent over exercise book,
> writing. Celia sits on sofa, allows her lids to become
> slack, her eyes vacant.*
> *Holly glances towards her, then slides piece of
> paper out of his pocket, puts it into exercise book,
> begins to read. Becomes increasingly aware of stillness
> from sofa.*

Holly Mummy? Mummy? (*Stares towards her anxiously
as he closes exercise book, puts it into his satchel, goes*

across to Celia with increasing terror, stares down.)
Mummy – oh, Mummy, what is it? What is it? Oh –
(*Wrings his hands, looks around.*) Daddy, Daddy –
(*Runs to telephone, dials frantically.*)

Celia (*looks towards Holly*) What are you doing? Who
are you phoning?

*Holly puts down telephone, stares at her with relieved
disbelief.*

Celia Who were you phoning?

Holly Daddy.

Celia Why?

Holly Because – because I thought you were dead.

Celia Oh, don't be such a fool. I was just lying here
thinking about things. Concentrating.

Holly (*realising*) No you weren't. You were pretending.
You were pretending to be dead.

Celia I was doing no such thing. I – I –

Holly Yes you were, you were! Why were you? You're
always doing things like that – why? (*on the verge of
tears*)

Celia, suddenly upset, gets up, runs to him.

Celia Oh, darling, I was just being silly, just playing
games. I didn't think for a minute you'd believe – and –
and – I'm sorry, darling, I'm sorry, there, there. Just a
silly game, that's all. Between us.

The doorbell rings.

(*stepping away*) Oh, there he is, your Mr Thing, I'll let
him in, darling, you'd better blow your nose and – (*going
towards door*) what's his name again? Oh, I remember.
(*Goes out.*)

Sound of front door opening.

(*off*) Good evening, Mr Ambrose. He's in there waiting for you, he's been practising all afternoon –

Holly hurries to the piano. Celia enters, followed by Brownlow.

There, you see. Warming the keys and finger tips.

Brownlow Good evening, Holliday.

Holly (*getting up*) Good evening, sir.

Brownlow No, don't be up, put yourself back where you're going to be for the next hour.

Celia I'm so glad to have caught you for once, Mr Ambrose, I always seem to be out or dashing off just as you arrive, it's usually my tennis hour, you see, but I do hope Holly thinks to offer you a cup of tea, do you, Holly?

Holly What, Mummy?

Celia Do you think to offer Mr Ambrose a cup of tea, darling?

Brownlow Yes, he does, Mrs Smithers, unfailingly. But I always decline. One has to worry too much about the clinking of cup on saucer. It's Brownlow, by the way.

Celia (*momentarily confused*) What?

Brownlow Not Ambrose. Ambrose is my middle name.

Celia (*laughs*) Oh, of course it is, I'm so sorry, I know your name perfectly well, don't I, Holly? It's just that my eye caught Ambrose on the what's-it Holly's playing and it stuck. Well, Mr Brownlow, I'll get out of the way and leave you two to it, shall I?

Brownlow Mrs Smithers, may I ask a favour? I'd be grateful if you'd let me take the telephone off the hook. Its ringing can be very disruptive, we've discovered.

Celia The telephone? Oh, but there are sometimes calls for my husband. From the hospital, you see. When they want him urgently. He's the pathologist, after all. The only pathologist, you know.

Brownlow Indeed, I do know. And I'm sorry, I wouldn't have dreamt of asking if I'd known Dr Smithers was in the house.

Celia Well, he isn't, as a matter of fact. So I suppose, now I come to think of it – (*going reluctantly to the telephone*) – and I'm not expecting anything myself that can't wait.

Brownlow They always come, when they come, at the worst possible time. And once one has come, one expects others to follow. The hour becomes about whether the telephone is going to ring and not about the piano. Which is why I refuse to have one in my house.

Celia Yes, I do understand. But we must remember to put it back when you've finished. In case my husband needs to call me urgently – well, if he's going to be home late or –

Brownlow We will remember, I promise you.

Celia Thank you. Well, then. (*Goes out.*)

There is a pause.

Brownlow (*as if to himself*) Well, here we are again. Just the two of us, surrounded by the foe. And visible this time. (*to Holly*) But how nice to have had a proper little conversation with your mother. How have you been getting on with my what's-it?

Holly Sir?

Brownlow Mr Ambrose's what's-it. Have you come to love it yet?

361

Holly I like it a lot.

Brownlow You're developing a feeling for it then, are you?

Holly It gets easier and easier the more I get to know it.

Brownlow Ah. Then you're not developing a feeling for it. It should get more and more complicated the more you get to know it. You'll only know it completely when you come to realise that you're never going to find out its secret. Perhaps because there isn't one. (*Laughs.*) I'm teasing you, mio. That's the way I'd like people to talk about my music. As they don't, I have to do it myself, and so I make it preposterous to myself. Especially when I do it to that. It's merely a finger exercise to make you more agile. Your fingers, anyway. (*Surveys Holly.*) What a strange posture. You look as if you're crouching for a sprint. Waiting for the gun to go off. Turn around, if you please.

Holly turns around.

Back straight, if you please.

Holly straightens his back.

Arms out, fingers ready.

Holly stretches out his arms, hooks his fingers.

No, no, you're not going to savage the keyboard, you're going to caress it, if you please. There. (*Makes caressing movements with his own hands. Little pause.*) If you please, mio.

Holly begins to make caressing movements with his hands. For a moment they are both making caressing movements.

Now. Oh, one thing.

Holly Sir?

Brownlow Who is this 'sir' you keep referring to?
I thought we'd got rid of him weeks ago.

Holly Sorry, Lowly. (*In a mutter.*)

Brownlow You're quite safe. They may be all around us
but they're not actually with us. Nobody can hear you
except me. Say it again without the apology.

Holly Lowly.

Brownlow That's better. Once more. (*Puts his hand on
Holly's cheek.*)

Holly Lowly.

Brownlow Now explain to me why we decided you
should call me Lowly.

Holly Because you have low aspirations or why would
you be bothering with creatures like me?

Brownlow Did I say that?

Holly I think so. I think that's what you said.

Brownlow Well, now I shan't be able to remember
whether I said it or not. I'll just remember what you said
I said and hope that it was really I and not actually you
that said it.

Holly It was, Lowly, I promise.

Brownlow (*taking his hand from Holly's cheek*) Now,
mio, to Lowly's 'Bagatelle', if you please. Unless you
have a greater aspiration.

> *Holly turns to keyboard, begins to play 'Bagatelle'.
> Brownlow stands, listening to music. Lets out a
> groan. Stands in a posture of despair.*

Holly (*turns slowly*) Did I make a mistake?

Brownlow No. I did. (*Goes over, takes score off music stand, looks at it.*)

Holly Don't you like it any more?

Brownlow You play it as if I never liked it, mio.

Holly I'm sorry. I do like it. Honestly.

Brownlow Thank you. (*Stuffs score into his pocket.*) Play something more worthy of your gifts, if you please. (*riffling through scores on piano, picking one out*) Here, play this. (*Puts score on music stand.*) At least we'll know where we are.

> *Holly begins to play opening bars of the 'Moonlight Sonata'. Brownlow puts his hands in his pockets, walks around the room, nodding his head, staring at Holly. There is a sudden slight discord. Brownlow winces. Holly proceeds to play.*

(*hissing it out*) Stop! Stop, stop, stop!

> *Holly stops.*

Didn't you hear yourself?

> *Holly nods.*

Then why didn't you stop yourself? How do you expect to learn, mio, if you simply ignore your mistakes? Mistakes bury themselves into our natures. They become habits we don't even know we possess. So we must be alert to them, ready to correct them – turn to our teachers for help. That's what I'm here for, aren't I? To help. Answer, if you please. Without mumbling. And no, don't turn.

Holly Yes, sir. (*pipingly*)

Brownlow Yes who, mio? (*gently*)

Holly Lowly, sir. I mean Lowly, I mean.

Brownlow And to what, mio?

Holly To help, Lowly. (*Pause. Brownlow waits.*) That's what you're here for. (*Pause.*) To help with your mistakes. My mistakes I mean, sir. Lowly.

Brownlow (*lets out a little laugh*) Who can say whether the man is playing with the cat or the cat is playing with the man? Eh? (*Goes over to piano.*) Move over, mio. (*Sits beside Holly.*) Now watch my hands. (*Begins to play.*)

> He has a velvet touch, his head moves very slightly to the music. He stops, nods at the keyboard and at Holly. Holly starts again.
>
> Brownlow at first watches his hands, then, as if against his will, turns, stares at Holly's profile. With an effort, he gets up, walks softly around the room, and as Holly reaches the point of the previous discord, passes it successfully, Brownlow nods to himself. Stares towards Holly, rapt.
>
> Celia enters room, makes to speak. Brownlow puts his finger to his lips.

(*after a moment, gently*) Holly. (*Holly stops.*) I think your mother wants a word.

Celia I'm so sorry to interrupt, such lovely sounds and such a gorgeous piece of music, what a lucky cat! But I've got to make – I've really got to make one telephone call, very important or the whole evening will be a shambles, I'll be very quick, I promise. (*Going to telephone, lighting a cigarette as she does so. Goes through telephone book.*) M – M – M – M – M – here we are. (*Dials.*) Well, fingers crossed. (*Holds out her fingers crossed, smiles at Brownlow. On telephone*) Mrs Milton? It's Mrs Smithers here, Dr Smithers' wife – how are you? Oh dear, how unpleasant. I think there's

something going around the island, I was going to play
tennis with Mrs Authwaite but she had to call it off
because she's got exactly the same – runny eyes, sniffles, a
slight temperature – my husband always says that they are
just little upsets and there's nothing you can do about
them really, but you know the famous saying about
doctors and their families – um, what I'm phoning about
is that when I bumped into you in the village the other
day you very sweetly said that sometimes your chickens
did you really proud and if ever I were in desperate need
it's always worth giving you a ring, so you wouldn't by
any chance – oh, you have, how wonderful! Well, I was
hoping four – three, I see. Well, I can make do on three,
that's very kind of you, the doctor will be pleased, he's
been longing for a freshly made omelette. He'll pick
them up himself on his way back from the hospital, I'll
phone him and tell him straight away – thank you, Mrs
Milton. (*Puts down telephone.*) Isn't it revolting how
obsequious we have to be these days? Especially with the
Mrs Miltons of the world. They don't do you kindnesses,
you know, they do you favours – (*Dialling as she speaks.
On telephone*) Oh hello, Dr Smithers, Path Lab, please.
(*Pause.*) Laboratory. Pathological Laboratory. (*Irritated.*)
This is Mrs Smithers, Dr Smithers' wife – oh, Jean, hello,
Jean, Celia Smithers here, can I just have a word? Oh,
doing a post-mortem, I see – well, Jean my dear, would
you just give him this message – to stop off at Mrs
Milton's on the way home and pick up –

Sound of front door opening and closing.

Good heavens, who's that?

Charles Smithers enters.

My dear, what are you doing here? I'm on the phone to
you, I mean leaving you a message about picking up the
eggs –

Charles I tried to phone to let you know I was on my way but the line was constantly engaged.

Celia What? Oh yes – (*remembering telephone*) – well, Mr Brown, he likes to have the phone off the hook – (*on telephone*) it's all right, Jean dear, he's here –

Charles No, don't hang up, let me have a word.

Celia (*on telephone*) Hang on, Jean dear, he wants a word. (*Handing phone to Charles.*)

Charles (*on telephone*) Oh hello, Jean. Bad case of the Gremlins again downstairs, Greatorix says he'll have it sorted out by eight and knowing young Greatorix he will. Thank you, Jean. (*Hangs up.*)

Celia You're not going to have to go back tonight, darling?

Charles I hope not. Sounds clear-cut enough. A drowning. There shouldn't be any urgency.

Celia A drowning, oh dear. One of the fishermen, I suppose – oh darling, this is Mr – (*Gestures.*) Holly's piano teacher, you haven't met, have you?

Charles (*nods*) How do you do?

Brownlow (*coming forward, hand held out*) How do you do, Dr Smithers, how do you do?

They shake hands.

Celia (*sotto voce to Holly*) Holly, do turn around. There are people in the room.

Holly turns, gets up.

Charles Well, do stay and – and have a drink. (*Gestures.*)

Brownlow How very kind of you, but I really mustn't use up any of your valuable time being sociable.

Charles (*surprised*) My time isn't at all valuable. Anyway, now I'm at home.

Celia I think, darling, Mr Brown – um – is thinking about Holly's lesson. They're right in the middle, you see. Perhaps we should have our drinks in the kitchen – oh, but first could my husband hear Holly play the thing you wrote for your cat?

Brownlow It's not so much a thing as a bagatelle. (*Smiling politely.*)

Celia It sounds very advanced – at least to my ear – but then I've got a tin ear, as you've probably guessed.

Brownlow It is quite advanced. But then so is your son. (*Little bow.*)

Celia (*to Holly*) There, you see, what did I tell you? Straight from the horse's mouth – and all your talk about violins!

Brownlow Violins?

Celia Yes, yes, he was full of one of his nonsenses about giving up football and the piano so he could go to Portsmouth to take lessons with goodness knows who.

Brownlow looks at Holly. There is a silence.

Holly Oh, Mummy, I didn't mean I wanted to give up the piano exactly – I like the piano – but I'd like to know more about the violin.

Brownlow I can show you whatever it is you think you'd like to know about the violin.

Celia There you are, you see? Everything you want without giving up anything.

Charles I'm afraid I'm a little lost in all this.

Celia Oh, don't worry about it, darling, we'll just listen to Holly for a minute and then go and have our drinks in the kitchen.

Brownlow Well then, Holliday. Perform, please.

Holly begins to play the 'Moonlight Sonata'.

Ah, we forgot to change the sheets. (*Puts his hand in his pocket, checks himself.*) Why don't you try it from memory, make a little test out of it?

Holly begins to play the 'Bagatelle', then starts to encounter difficulties. Celia and Charles listen, smiling politely, unaware.

Thank you, Holliday. (*Unable to suppress sharpness.*)

Holly stops.

Brownlow (*recovering*) Just entering a very treacherous patch – unless you know it by heart – and even then –

Celia Still, it was lovely, wasn't it, darling?

Charles Very impressive, very impressive. And you wrote it yourself?

Celia (*to Charles*) They're going to do it on the Third Programme, Holly was telling me. We must make a point of listening, darling.

Charles Yes, do let us know when.

Celia Yes, please do. Well, I'll just pour us our drinks – (*going to drinks table*) – and we'll be off to the kitchen and – oh, darling, we mustn't forget this whole thing about Mrs Milton.

Charles Mrs Milton? What does she want?

Celia I'm afraid, darling, it's what we want – it's some eggs that I said you were going to pick up on the way back.

Charles Oh, I'll drive over in a minute.

Celia No, no, that's not fair, you want to put your feet up, especially if you have to go out again. (*Pouring drinks.*) I'll pedal over – or Holly even, won't take him a minute with his young legs – what was it you said the other day (*to Holly*) when I told you to go and fetch something and your legs were so much younger than mine – and you said – he said – (*coming over, putting drink in Charles's hand, drink in her own hand*) – 'Oh, Mummy,' you said, 'wouldn't it be more sensible to use up the old ones first?' (*Laughs.*)

   Charles grunts a laugh.

Brownlow (*laughs*) Very amusing, very amusing.

Charles Are you sure you won't –? (*Holding up drink.*)

Brownlow No, no, I think – I really feel that it would be best for me to leave you – (*Gestures.*) you want to be comfortable –

Celia No, we can do perfectly well in the kitchen, can't we, darling?

Charles What? Oh, yes. (*Struggles to his feet.*)

Brownlow No, I'll make up the lesson the next time. But what I think would be a very good idea – so that we're not in your way in the future –

Celia Oh, you're not usually, it's just that the doctor's been up since seven –

Charles Oh, don't worry about me.

Brownlow Still, one wants one's home to be one's home after a hard day's work, whatever hour one gets back. I don't generally allow my pupils to use my piano but Holly has got such an exceptional touch that he won't be a danger to it. Also I think it's time he got the feel of a – if you will permit me to say so – a more delicate instrument. A more responsive one.

Celia Well, that's awfully good of you, Mr – isn't it, Holly, darling?

Holly Yes. Yes. Thank you very much, sir.

Charles Will your prep be all right, Holly?

Celia Oh yes, his prep. He always has to do his prep before the lesson, it's an absolute rule.

Brownlow He can bring his prep to me. I'll make sure we don't start until he's finished it.

Celia Oh. Well, what about his tea?

Brownlow My mother can make him his tea. She'll enjoy having a boy to feed, and it'll only be once or twice a week.

Celia Twice a week?

Brownlow Oh – when we get into something special. An extra hour now and then might make all the difference.

Celia (*to Charles*) Is that all right, darling? I mean from the financial point of view?

Brownlow Oh, please don't worry about that. Whenever a bit of extra time comes up it'll be entirely my decision, entirely on my account.

Charles It's very good of you, but won't this interfere with other arrangements – your other pupils, I mean?

Brownlow I haven't got any other pupils, Dr Smithers. I go to a number of boys and girls because their parents feel that their offspring ought to have some piano lessons, even though they're musical clodhoppers – a social matter, really. Holliday, who has a gift – be assured he has a very considerable gift – is my only pupil in any proper meaning of the word. I consider it a privilege to teach him.

Celia And I know he feels the same. He feels it's a privilege to be taught by you. (*Looking at Holly.*)

Holly Yes. Yes, thank you, sir.

Charles Well, then. However, I would prefer to pay for all my son's tuition.

Brownlow (*does his odd little bow*) Well, we won't quarrel over it, will we, Doctor?

Celia Now that's all settled, do stay and have a quick drink.

Charles Yes, have a drink, do have one.

Brownlow No, I've still got time to get to the fishmonger's, they generally keep a few scraps for my mother. Well, for her cat, I mean.

Celia (*triumphantly*) Oh yes, Miaow.

Charles looks at her. There is a pause.

Miaow. Isn't that the name of your cat, the one you wrote the music for? Didn't you say, Holly?

Holly Yes – yes – mi-oh, really, more than miaow, isn't it, sir?

Brownlow Yes, mi-oh. Mi-oh is my cat's name. I mustn't forget to introduce you. (*to Holly*) I'll be off. (*Makes towards door.*)

Celia Holly dear, show Mr Burnham the door.

Holly runs ahead of Brownlow, opens door.

Brownlow Thank you, Holliday.

Celia Oh, Holly darling, why don't you nip on over to Mrs Milton for the eggs, see if you can't wheedle four out of her?

Holly Right, Mummy. (*Hurries out after Brownlow.*)

Charles (*settling back*) Thank God.

Celia Sssh, darling, he'll hear you. (*Closing sitting room door.*) I suppose it's all right Holly going over there.

Charles A bloody sight better than my coming home and finding him here.

Celia He's a very good teacher, everybody says so, lucky to have him on the island. I must be careful, though, with Moira – he does her two, you know – I'm sure she wouldn't enjoy hearing his view of their musical gifts – what did he call them, 'clodhoppers' wasn't it, 'musical clodhoppers'? (*Laughs.*) Just like Moira on the tennis court – she stood me up, you know.

Charles Still, I'm going to pay him for anything extra.

Celia But why, darling, if it gives him so much pleasure?

Charles I just feel easier, don't want to be beholden, something about the chap, odd – that handshake. (*Grimaces.*)

Celia You don't think he's a Jew, do you?

Charles Could be. Anyway, something slightly off about him.

Celia Well, of course, a lot of them are very artistic and musical. And at least he's not being a Jew on the money front.

Charles No, but that's another reason for making sure we're all square. All square and straight.

Celia Well, let's see what kind of bill he gives us, he hasn't asked for anything yet. (*Comes and sits beside Charles.*) Have you had a rotten day, my Chaps? (*Stroking his leg.*)

Charles It's beginning to go away a bit.

Celia lights a cigarette, offers it with her mouth to Charles.

May I? (*Takes cigarette.*)

Celia lights another for herself.

Celia We'll make it go away completely, Chaps, we will. (*Stroking his forehead.*) You mustn't think about going back tonight to do the drowned man. There's nothing you can do for him that you can't do tomorrow.

Charles (*sighs*) Yes, but it isn't a matter of doing for him, it's what there'll be tomorrow as well. Might be wiser to clear him off the decks tonight. As a matter of fact, Ceci, I could have done him this afternoon somehow, could have managed it, but I took advantage of Greatorix not being quite ready – he hadn't finished cleaning the body. So I just left.

Celia Well then, you needed to. You would never do that unless you absolutely needed to.

Charles Couldn't face it, you see. Now we're back in civilian life, getting used to things as they used to be, although they never will be quite as they used to be, will they? – it's much harder, the death of young men particularly – boys they were, almost, at the beginning, weren't they? – three, four, five a day, no time for post-mortems, no need for them, just being an ordinary doctor in an air base – broken bones, burnt flesh – so you think you could deal with the occasional corpse, don't even have to see the pain, hear it – nothing to try

374

to save, just cut it open, sort through the organs, water in the lungs and pneumonia, heart failure, stroke, diphtheria, polio, drowning – anyway, this afternoon quite suddenly I couldn't face it. (*Little pause.*) That's all I mean.

Celia Here, come here. (*Takes his cigarette, stubs it out, stubs out hers, puts drinks on table.*) Come on, my Chaps, lay your head.

> *Charles puts his head on her breast, she strokes the back of his head.*

You stay here tonight. You stay here in your family, safe and sound, where you belong. (*Rocks him gently.*)

> *Charles lifts his head. They stare into each other's eyes, caress each other's cheeks, kiss gently, then passionately. Celia puts her hand between his legs.*

Celia We'll go to bed early and we'll play.

Charles Oh, of course. You haven't had your tennis.

Celia Jolly good thing too. It's saved me for you. Mmmm – (*Feels him.*)

Charles I must try to be worth your saving yourself for.

Celia You're always that, Chaps. Oh, my man!

Charles Yes, your man. Completely and absolutely yours.

Celia That reminds me – *this* reminds me –

> *Laughs, putting her hand between his legs again. Charles puts his hand on top of hers.*

Holly.

Charles What?

Celia Well, he's started.

Charles Started what? Oh!

Celia Though actually, my dear, I don't think 'started' is quite the word. I sometimes wonder if he ever stops. His sheets every morning – I thought something was up when he began making his bed so tight.

Charles You've been carrying out inspections then, have you?

Celia I do change the sheets, you know, darling. Inevitably, as I do all the housework. Anyway, it's not a question of inspections, I couldn't avoid it even if I tried – the other day he shot into the house and rushed upstairs saying he had to get some prep done before tea, and when I put my head around the door to make sure he was really at it – well, there he was, on his knees, can you believe?

Charles On his knees? Well, that's rather bold.

Celia What do you mean?

Charles Well, on his knees in his bedroom and you likely to come in at any minute – that's rather bold in my book.

Celia Well, he wasn't actually unbuttoned, and he pretended he was praying, he had his palms pressed in front of his face like this – (*Does it.*) – and his eyes closed, but I could see some wretched-looking magazine under one knee and a piece of paper under the other one.

Charles What did you say?

Celia Nothing, of course. Well, except that I was sorry I'd interrupted him at his devotions. Then at tea I said, darling, if you're becoming religious there's always church, you know, on Sundays.

Charles (*laughs*) And what did he say?

Celia That at the moment he wanted to keep it between himself and his God.

Charles That's rather a fine way of putting it.

Celia But seriously, darling – I know it's silly but I can't help it – I do rather hate the feeling that it's going on, you see. Furtively. Shamefully. And lying about it. It makes it all so nasty.

Charles Well, it's better, surely, than having him doing it openly and publicly and boasting about it, darling.

Celia Oh, don't be a fool, Charles! (*Laughing in spite of herself.*) But don't you think you ought to have a little talk with him? Let him know that what he's going through is all perfectly natural and normal and – and nothing to be, well, ashamed of. That's what we're meant to do, isn't it, these days in the 1950s – or you, anyway, as a father – be open and honest? And – and natural.

Charles laughs.

Celia What?

Charles I'm just thinking of my father being open, honest and natural with me, just think of him! 'Charles, after a great deal of thought and consultation with your mother and my colleagues, I have decided that the time has come to discuss with you certain matters connected to the procreation of the species. Not just in general terms but in specific, indeed, personal ones. As you know, your mother and I always believed that both at school and at home it is of the utmost importance that you keep, in the eyes of the world, a clean sheet' – (*Bursts out laughing.*)

Celia (*laughing*) But he probably didn't know what you were up to, or if he did, pretended to himself he didn't. Darling, if we had a daughter I wouldn't think twice about doing it myself. Anyway, I've told him.

Charles Told him what?

Celia That you're going to have a talk with him.

Charles Oh, God, you haven't! What on earth got into you?

Celia Well, it was really the thought of those magazines, you see. They may be absolutely foul and corrupting for all we know. They may even be against the law. And whatever it is he's been writing, it's been getting in the way of his prep – that's the point, Charles, we don't want him getting muddled and confused and carried away with his scholarship coming up. (*Picks up Holly's satchel, begins to go through it.*)

Charles (*noticing Celia and satchel*) Really, darling, I'm not sure we have the right –

Celia Ah, here you are. (*Triumphantly produces magazine, hands it to Charles.*) Nature Today.

Charles (*taking magazine, looking at it*) 'A magazine for naturalists' – oh, I see, for nudists. (*Flicking through it.*) Photographs of nudists – rather fleshy – still, young – oh, here's one that's quite pretty – (*Shows picture to Celia, who has found exercise book, taken out loose pages.*) anyway, nothing that qualifies as corrupting or foul or illegal. A perfectly reasonable way of finding out what a naked woman looks like, surely.

Celia But there's this.

Charles What is it?

Celia I don't know, I haven't looked, I don't want to – here. (*Hands him loose sheet.*)

Charles (*takes sheet*) It really does seem wrong, quite wrong – (*Muttering, as he reads sheet of paper.*)

Celia lights a cigarette.

(*Shakes his head.*) It's just about some girl he's been peeking at, or imagining he's been peeking at, under water – describing her nipples – and trying to see between her legs. (*Looks up.*) I used to write stuff like this, though actually not as good – well, as literary – and I can remember a time when I didn't know what was between a girl's legs either. Actually, I think I supposed it was rather like what I had between my own legs, only much smaller and daintier, more feminine, in other words.

Celia Well, there you are. You can set him right about that, for one thing.

Charles (*bursts out*) Would you like to help? Be the demonstrator's model?

Celia (*genuinely shocked*) Charles! What on earth's got into you!

There is a pause.

Charles Sorry, darling, sorry, I – I – it's just the thought of – of –

Sound of door opening.

Charles Oh, God!

Celia Quick, here, give it to me!

Charles hands Celia magazine and page. She crams them into satchel, pushes satchel down as they assume unnaturally natural positions as Holly enters, holding brown bag.

379

Ah, here you are, darling, we were wondering where you'd been all this time.

Holly Mr Brownlow asked me to walk to the village with him. And then I went and got the eggs. Egg, I mean. (*Takes in that satchel is upside down in different place.*)

Celia Egg? What do you mean, egg?

Holly Well, that's all she had. Just the one left, she said.

Celia But didn't you tell her that we need four – at least four – and she promised me three anyway for the doctor's omelette? Didn't you say that, Holly?

Holly Well, no, I just said I'd come for the eggs and she handed me this. And I said I thought there'd be more and she said, well, she was very sorry, there weren't, that's all she had left. (*Hands bag to Celia.*)

Celia Really, this island, these people! And to think how I grovelled to her! You should have gone straight there, Holly, instead of going to the village with Mr – (*Gestures.*) well, we'll just have to make up with the usual powdered, I'm afraid, darling. (*to Charles*) I'll get started straight away and you two chaps have a little chat, why don't you? (*Gives a quick meaningful look to Charles, goes out.*)

Charles Don't tell your mother, but actually I've come to prefer dried eggs.

Holly So do I.

There is a pause.

Well, I ought to go upstairs with my prep. (*Going to satchel.*)

Charles Not finished yet, then?

Holly All but a little bit of French.

Charles Well, why don't you – why don't you sit down and – for a minute or two? I'm sure that can wait. (*Nods to satchel, realises, lets out a little laugh which he converts into a cough.*) For a minute or two.

Holly sits down, clasping satchel to his lap.

So what did you talk about?

Holly Daddy?

Charles You and Mr – your piano chap. On the way to the village.

Holly Oh, just about the piano, really. And music. And the violin. (*Little pause.*) Nothing.

Charles You obviously get on with him.

Holly Yes, well, he's very good.

Charles I often wonder where you get your musical gifts from. Not from my side of the family – at least as far as I know. Oh, there was a great-uncle, your great-great-uncle – Cedric, I think it was – is said to have played the fiddle – but only jigs, and that kind of thing, to please the ladies, I suspect. He was a shameless philanderer, you know. A bit of a gay dog is what that means. A gay old dog, your great-great-uncle Cedric. Well, that's the family mythology anyway. But on your mother's side – well, your mother says she doesn't know of anyone at all on her side to account for you – of course she's almost completely tone deaf, isn't she? Although I'm not actually tone deaf myself – I mean I can carry a tune – but the fact is, apart from great-uncle Cedric, if it was Cedric who fiddled and jigged, we don't know of anyone on either side – (*Gestures.*) but of course that's the thing about a gene, isn't it – just bobs up generations after it was last seen or heard of. So you're what is known as a sport.

Holly Oh.

Charles It's the word in genetics for what you are.
A sudden resurgent gene.

Holly Ah.

Charles Well, everything seems to be going well then?
You mustn't let this business of a scholarship weigh you
down, you know, if you do get one – but on the other
hand, if you don't, you don't.

Holly Mummy says if I don't get one we won't be able
to go to London.

Charles Does she? I think you must have misunderstood
her. Going to London depends on a great deal of other
things, not the least of which is whether I can get a job
in London. Besides, we may not want to go to London.
We may end up somewhere else entirely – here, for
instance – or Australia, or South Africa, Canada or New
Zealand. Or London.

Holly Oh.

Charles All I'm saying is that it's not the end of the
world if you don't get your scholarship, that's all I'm
saying. I'm sure your mother would agree. All right?

Holly Thank you, Daddy.

There is a pause.

Well then, I'll just – (*Makes to get up.*)

Charles There's one other thing. It's nothing very – it's
not at all – well, Holly, there are some things in life, you
know – well, there comes a time – well, of course there
are some things in life, what do I mean there are some
things in life? Life is full of some things or other things –
some things and other things fill our lives every moment

of the day, every second. The point is – well, there comes a time between people – well, father and son – when they need to be – (*Thinks.*) – talked about. Mmm?

Holly Yes, Daddy.

Charles I wish, you know, that your grandfather had found a way of talking to me. Of talking to me as I'm talking to you now. But then – of course you never met my father, did you?

Holly No, Daddy. Well, I suppose I did but he died when I was two, wasn't it, Mummy says?

Charles Somewhere about that time it would have been, yes. Anyway, before you were old enough to get a real sense of him. But then I'm not sure I ever got a real sense of him. And he died when I was thirty-three. (*Laughs ruefully.*) I don't mean he was mysterious or there was some dark secret – no, no, not at all. I knew what he did. Like me he was a doctor, though not a pathologist. A straightforward general practitioner is what he was, so of course he knew how to talk to his patients – naturally I don't have to know how to talk to my patients as they're usually dead, although they talk to me in what I discover in this diseased organ or that, samples of tissue – I hear them through my microscope. (*Little pause.*) I've never really discussed my work with you before, have I?

Holly No, Daddy.

Charles What do you know about it?

Holly Well, only that you find out why people died. Isn't that it?

Charles (*after a little pause*) Yes. That's it, old chap. Why people died. There's always a scientific explanation,

even if I can't always find it. If I had my time again
I'd go into psychiatry, all the patients alive and talking
for themselves, that's where the medical future lies –
financially anyway – and I wouldn't have to put up with
all this death – I mean death is – is – (*Frowns, looks into
his drink as if lost.*) Do you know what a psychiatrist is?

Holly Well, no, not really, Daddy.

Charles Well, let's hope you never have to find out, eh?
(*Laughs.*)

Holly laughs. There is a little pause.

Oh, by the way, that reminds me. Girls, old chap. Do
you ever find yourself, um, noticing them? Thinking
about them?

Holly No, Daddy. Not really. (*Shaking his head.*)

Charles Never?

Holly Well, sometimes – a little bit, I suppose.

Charles Well, I'm glad to hear it. Because otherwise
there would be – well, frankly, something odd. (*Takes a
sip of Scotch, tries not to look as if he's bracing himself.*)
Um, masturbation, old boy?

The telephone rings.

Oh, blast! (*Picks up telephone.*) Hayling 349? Greatorix –
oh hello, you're still there, are you, how are you getting
on?

*As Holly gets up, gestures tentatively as he goes out.
Charles lifts his hand in vague salute.*

(*on telephone*) Mmmhm. Ah. So you think I'd better come
over tonight?

Celia enters.

(*on telephone*) Well, I'd like to eat first if the deceased doesn't mind. (*Smiles at Celia.*) It's a damn nuisance, I was looking forward to an evening at home – (*Hangs up.*)

Celia Poor darling. (*Pats him on the cheek.*)

Charles Well, we had that little talk you wanted. And I'm happy to report it's all just as I said it would be – normal. Perfectly normal at his age.

Celia There, I knew it would be. So why you had to make such a fuss about a simple little father–son chat! (*Goes to door.*) Holly? Holly darling, it's supper – hurry, because your father's got to be off. (*to Charles*) I wish it wasn't mainly powdered eggs but there, I'll put the fresh one in your bit for being such a dear old Chaps.
    Lights.

SCENE THREE

Three months later. Late afternoon. Summer.
    Brownlow's study/sitting room.
    Holly is sitting at the table, satchel beside him, writing, consulting the dictionary.
    Mrs Brownlow (Ellie) enters, carrying a tray of tea, on which is also a bottle of sherry and a glass. Ellie drinks sherry steadily throughout the following scene.

Ellie (*has a Viennese accent*) Come on, Catty-Kit, come on, Catty-Kit, puss, puss, puss, come on – (*Puts tray down on table. Pours herself a glass of sherry. To Holly*) Are you finished?

Holly Yes, I have. I was just checking some words. (*Closing dictionary.*)

Ellie Good, good, once more I have the right time, I seem always to know, yes? (*Rumples Holly's hair, goes to door.*)

Catty-Kit, Catty-Kit, puss, puss – don't be frightened of him, he's a very kind boy, he will not hurt you. (*Bends down.*) Oh – ooh, Catty-Kit – ooh, come to Mama – oh, silly! Silly frightened thing! (*Stands up, shuts the door.*) It is no good, when you are here she will not come. You must not think it is personal with you, she is not in the habit of guests, you see. We don't have many guests so she thinks you are an intruder, come to take her place even. But still I should leave the door open in case she changes her mind and wishes to be a friend with you at last. Now, here, let us have our tea. (*Lifting lids.*) We have two boiled eggs, we have toast and we have – here, Sachertorte. This is a very special cake we make in Vienna. Before the war it was famous everywhere. Now of course I do not know whether they can still make Sachertorte, it is difficult enough to do it on the island with so little chocolate, but we do not complain because here we have our Sachertorte whether they have it or do not have it any more in Vienna. Eat, please. Eat, Holliday. (*Claps her hands.*) Why must I always tell you to start? Is it that you are shy eating alone with me? (*Pouring him a cup of tea.*) Here, your cuppa, your nice English cuppa. Now you will feel safe and comfortable with your nice English cuppa. You have such good manners, how is the egg?

Holly (*swallowing egg*) Very nice, thank you, Ellie.

Ellie My boy also has very good manners. But not with me. Never with me. He always makes fun from me – even as a baby he was making fun from me. Do you make fun from your mutter?

Holly Not really.

Ellie Then you have a father and he won't permit you. So lucky mutter. My boy was never with a father. Dead before he was born. Did he tell you that?

Holly No, Ellie.

Ellie He was not a young man, my Emil, but he was very big, very strong. He had a bad heart, you see. A man of good heart with a bad heart. And sometimes he was angry, very angry. I think he would have been angry with my boy quite often. He was not an artist, he was a banker. And a soldier. Brave. What is it like today outside? Catty-Kit, Catty-Kit – I thought I felt her, did you see her? Was she there?

Holly No, I didn't see her.

Ellie (*going to window*) It is beautiful outside, I can see that, but is it cold, is there a wind?

Holly Not very cold, Ellie, no. Don't you like going out then?

Ellie No, I do not go out.

Holly Never? I mean, don't you ever go out?

Ellie No. I stay here, inside, where I have trust, you see. Safety. When I arrive in this house I think, now I will never have to go outside again. It was very bad for me, you see, in Portsmouth, in the war. Because of my accent. Everybody thinks I am a Nazi from the Gestapo. Such silly they think. When I go to shops – it is very terrible for my boy, they think he is a little Nazi Gestapo when I speak. Or black market when I have coupons. Or a Jew even. You, Holliday, do you think we are Jews?

Holly No. I mean, I don't know, I've never thought about it, Ellie.

Ellie Of course you have. And your father and your mutter. I know you English, they are always looking very close. So?

Holly I don't think you're Jews, Ellie. Nor do my parents. Well, they've never said, honestly, and I expect they would have said something if they thought you were.

Ellie Well, it is true they have only seen my boy. They look at him and they say straight away, no, he is not a Jew. But if they hear my voice – me – my voice, you understand? Then they would be confused. But now you can tell them yourself everything about me. Yes, Holliday? You are the only one he brings back to see me, ever. Oh, Teddy sometimes – when we were in London – but he was not his pupil, he is grown up. Like him, poor soul. Grown-ups. Hah! Do you know what I mean?

Holly shakes his head.

That is good. I am glad of that. There must be no trouble. I cannot move again to another house. I will not move. This is my home. This is my last home. Do you understand?

Holly Not really.

Ellie That is good. There is nothing for you to understand. What we say is private, yes?

Holly nods.

You cross your fingers?

Holly nods.

Well then, cross your fingers.

Holly crosses his fingers.

You are a little gentleman. Now you shall have some Sachertorte. There. (*Cutting slice, putting it on a plate.*) Eat, please.

Holly makes to pick it up.

No, no, there is a fork. You must always eat Sachertorte with a fork, otherwise it is not Sachertorte, it is only chocolate cake. Now. (*Putting fork into Holly's hand. Stands, watching Holly as he eats.*) There. What do you think of Sachertorte?

Holly Oh, it's – very nice, Ellie.

Ellie Very nice! All you English, you say that about everything – everything is always very nice – I am very nice, you are very nice, we are very nice, the house is very nice, God himself is very nice – or it's a very nice bomb, nice gas, nice, nice, nice – England is very, very, very nice – what a pity it isn't also very, very, very kind, huh? Because kind is nicer. Much nicer.

There is a pause.

Holly It's delicious. Really delicious.

Ellie (*claps her hands*) Thank you. Thank you, thank you, thank you. For that you will have some more.

Holly Oh no, no thank you, Ellie – no, really.

Ellie Why not?

Holly Well, if I eat anything more I'll be too full to play the piano properly.

Ellie And my boy will not like that, huh? If you sit there with a big stomach, playing the piano – (*Does piano movements with her fingers.*) – your stomach – woof – all big – woof! He is a very good teacher.

Holly Yes.

Ellie He is very serious.

Holly Yes.

Ellie He is a genius. You don't think so?

Holly Oh yes, yes – I mean, I expect he is. I'm sure he is, Ellie.

Ellie One day you will see. I hope only that I live so long, it is my hope. No, it is not my hope. After I am gone, then he can be a genius to all the world. Now he can be my genius and your genius, we keep him to us. Our little secret, eh, Holliday? (*Goes to him, rumples his hair, kisses him.*) Ah, yes, my little English gentleman, we shall have our genius to ourselves, mmm? (*Laughs, caresses him on the cheeks.*) Is he nice to you, like me? (*Stares intently down at Holly.*) Sssh – (*Picks up bottle of sherry and glass, takes a quick gulp from glass, then puts them behind flowers on table, goes to door, opens it.*) Catty-Kit, Catty-Kit, puss, puss, puss – oh, there you are, back then, we didn't hear you come in.

Brownlow enters, carrying his coat over his arm.

Brownlow That wasn't me you were calling then, Mutti?

Ellie What's your name, Catty-Kit, suddenly? (*Taking his coat, putting it on back of chair.*)

Brownlow Ah, Number Seven, you mean. He or she was hurrying out of the kitchen when I came in, carrying something or other between his or her jaws. A mouse, do you think? A mouse, Mutti? A mouse, Mutti, for Number Seven?

Ellie You're teasing me, you're teasing me again, Thomas. (*Slapping at him playfully.*) It wasn't a mouse and it is a girl, you know very well. And her name is Catty-Kit. Why are you back so early? Look, he is still drinking his cuppa.

Brownlow The Merrivale twins had colds so I refused to teach them. I went for a walk by the sea and if I'm early – (*Glances at his watch.*) – it's only by five minutes. You haven't practised for me yet, then? (*to Holly*)

Holly shakes his head.

Brownlow Ah.

Holly I was just going to.

Brownlow Were you? (*Fixes him with a look.*)

Holly lowers his eyes, looks away.

Ellie Oh, you mustn't be unkind with him, it is my fault, I was talking and talking and talking.

Brownlow Now, Mutti, you can stop talking and talking and talking and let us get on with our work.

Ellie You be kind to him, he is a good boy.

Brownlow Yes, I know. A little gentleman, isn't he? (*Turning Ellie around.*) Go, Mutti, and do the washing-up.

Ellie (*as she goes out*) Ah, there you are, waiting for me, come –

Brownlow closes the door.

Brownlow Where did she put it this time?

Holly Behind the flowers.

Brownlow goes to flowers, takes bottle of sherry, raises it, studies it.

Brownlow (*still holding bottle of sherry*) I trust you keep all our little family secrets to yourself, mio.

Holly Of course I do, Lowly.

Brownlow Because never forget, they're your family secrets too now, aren't they? What was she talking and talking and talking about this time?

Holly The same as last time, really, and the time before. What she always talks about. Though I never quite understand it, really.

Brownlow (*sits in armchair, puts bottle of sherry on floor beside him*) And what do you tell them when you go home, about what transpires here – our transpirations here? Mmm?

Holly Nothing.

Brownlow They don't ask questions then?

Holly Well, only the first time. About what I had for tea, mainly, and what Ellie was like – what your mother was like. I said they were both very nice. That's all. They haven't asked anything since.

Brownlow Secrets, secrets. So much of our life is spent not saying who we are, what we really do, what we really think. (*Little pause.*) What we really feel. We live in secret almost all the time. When I was walking along the shore, I listened to the waves and the wind, the cries of the seagulls, and I thought – I thought – here, mio, here mio, come on. (*Pats his lap.*)

   Holly goes over, sits on Brownlow's lap, stiffly.

And I thought – what did I think? That if I were Bach or Brahms or Mozart or Beethoven, I would hear so many different sounds – the deep movement of the sea, the soft wind – how it can become a scream – and the seagulls, within their ugly shrieks I would hear other songs, sad songs, of restless souls, whatever, whatever, whatever – I thought I am not Brahms or Beethoven, I can only imagine what they might imagine, and do I even want to hear it, what their imaginings want to hear? Not Ludwig van Beethoven but Thomas Ambrose Brownlow – well, Thomas Ambrose Brownlow, what do you really want to hear? Do you want to know, mio, what I really wanted to hear?

Holly Yes, Lowly.

Brownlow Yes, mio – yes, Lowly. (*Little pause.*) That's what I truly wanted to hear. Your voice saying 'Yes, Lowly.' So. So. Perhaps you will have to be my muse. Perhaps you are already my muse. But then – but then we have a contradiction, haven't we? A paradox. Why – why, if you are my muse, do you make me feel impotent? Do you know what impotent means?

Holly It means not being able to.

Brownlow And of course you know what a paradox is.

Holly I think so.

Brownlow What is it, mio? What is a paradox?

Holly It's one of the ways you say things when you want to show off.

Brownlow (*laughs shakily*) You are very clever. Am I the only person who knows how clever you are, mio?

Holly I don't know. They think I am at school, I think.

Brownlow And do they ever punish you for it?

Holly No. Why should they?

Brownlow Ah, so another duty falls on me. I will punish you for your cleverness.

Holly (*after a pause*) Why?

Brownlow (*coldly*) Yours not to reason why, little Englishman. (*Pushing Holly off his knee.*) Go and stand there – there, by the piano. Now, you know what to do.

Holly But it's not – it's not –

Brownlow And you know what not to do. (*Stares at Holly.*)

> Holly stands to attention, raises his arms, facing Brownlow.

Brownlow It is through the punishment that we shall
find the sin. Another paradox. A paradox that will be
received this time in silent respect, not to say humility.
A becoming humility. (*After a pause.*) What am I to do,
mio, if the muse I need so much is a bad muse? A muse
who takes away my power. (*.taring fixedly at Holly
through this.*) You see, this is not showing off, this is
giving up my secret. That's what my bad muse makes
me do, give up my secret.

Door opens. Ellie enters.

Ellie Excuse me, please, I'm so sorry, but how can I wash
the dishes if I do not have dishes to wash? (*Crosses room.
Looks at Holly.*) What are you doing, is this a new
exercise? Is he teaching you a new trick? (*Groping
behind flowers on table.*) What is he doing? (*Sees sherry
bottle beside Brownlow.*) He mustn't stand like that too
long, the blood will leave his hands, then how can he
play the piano? (*Picks up tray.*) Put it on the tray, please.

Brownlow (*in German*) Go away, Mutti, no more for
you until tonight.

Ellie (*in German, hissingly*) And what about you? I know
what you're up to, you will cause us trouble again, you
will be in disgrace, we'll have to leave – give me the
bottle, give me the bottle!

Brownlow puts bottle of sherry on tray.

(*in English*) Thank you. (*in German*) But for God's sake
be careful, control yourself, you must. (*Goes out, leaving
door open.*)

*Brownlow gets up, goes to door, closes it. Looks at
Holly, goes over to him, takes handkerchief out of his
pocket.*

Brownlow That was very good. Well done, mio. You didn't move your eyes, even though they were running. (*Wipes Holly's cheeks.*)

Holly makes to lower his arms.

A minute more, that's all. Let's have a minute more. You can manage that, I know you can. And then you'll have earned your chance with my – (*going to piano, playing*) – beloved. As you stand there think how privileged you are and tell yourself (*still playing*) that you must talk to him as I talk to him. Then perhaps he will talk to you as he talks to me. Eh, mio? (*Turns, looks at Holly. Suddenly begins to wheeze.*) Quickly – quickly –

Holly runs to jacket, fumbles in pockets for inhaler. As he does so, doorbell over, not noticed by Brownlow and Holly.

Holly comes over, squirts inhaler into Brownlow's mouth in a practised manner as:

Ellie (*loud, over*) They're not playing the piano so it will be all right, I'm sure it will be all right – (*warningly*) Thomas! Thomas! (*Opening door.*) There's someone to see you, it's the mutter.

Brownlow breathes in, still wheezing, beginning to recover. Celia enters.

Celia What on earth is going on?

Holly Mr Brownlow, he's having an attack, Mummy.

Celia What of?

Ellie Oh, it's his asthma. I always tell him he must not get excited.

Celia Oh. Are you all right?

Brownlow (*squirting inhaler, breathing in, recovering*)
Yes – thank you. Thanks to your son's quick thinking.
I left this (*indicating inhaler*) over there. I should always
have it on me. (*Getting up.*) There. Mrs Smithers.

Celia Well, I just came – I couldn't resist coming, I
wanted him to have the news straight away. He's won a
full scholarship to Westminster. Congratulations, Holly.
(*Shaking Holly's hand.*)

Holly Thank you, Mummy.

Brownlow Indeed, indeed congratulations, my boy.
(*Shaking Holly's hand.*)

Holly Thank you, Lowly – Mr – Mr Br –

Ellie (*rampaging across*) Oh, how wonderful, what a
wonderful, clever boy! (*Clutches Holly to her.*) But
please – please, you will have some tea with us, you will
have a cuppa and some cake – but no Sachertorte, I'm
sorry, no Sachertorte left, we have finished it together,
haven't we, Holly? But there is cake – sherry, would you
like a glass of sherry?

Celia No, no, I won't, thank you very much – um, I've
got my tennis, you see. I just wanted to give the news.
See you later, darling. (*to Holly*)

   Ellie accompanies Celia out.

Ellie (*off*) Such a boy, such a boy you've got. And such a
little gentleman, such a little English gentleman. How
lucky you are.

Brownlow Well then. That means you'll be leaving us
for London, doesn't it?

Holly Yes. Well, I mean it's in London, Westminster, so
I suppose –

Brownlow A scholarship. To Westminster. In London. How proud you must feel. Are you feeling proud, mio?

Holly Well, I haven't had a chance to think about it yet. What it means.

Brownlow What it means is that you're on your way. The little English gentleman is on his way. Away from all this. (*Sweeps arm contemptuously around room.*) And back to his proper little England.

> *Sits down at piano, begins to play and sing 'Rule Britannia' savagely.*
>   *Holly watches him as Ellie opens door in state of excitement, joins in, makes encouraging signs to Holly. Holly joins in, sings more and more full-bodiedly. They sing through to end.*

Ellie Oh, that was so good! So good for the spirit! Such a grand song!

Brownlow Thank you, Mutti.

Ellie And such a lovely lady, Holliday, *dein Mutti.*

Brownlow She is indeed. Thank you, Mutti. (*Nods at her pointedly.*)

Ellie Well, I leave you, I leave you. And your clever, clever boy. (*Going out.*)

> *Brownlow laughs. Holly laughs.*
>   *There is a pause.*

Holly They're talking of coming back some time. In the summer. They say once they're away they'll probably miss it, really. And the beach.

> *Brownlow looks at him.*

I'm sure they will, Lowly. Honestly. And anyway it's not for three months and so we'll have lots of time.

Brownlow Time for what, mio?

Holly (*after a little pause*) Well, to teach me.

Brownlow I should like, if I may, to teach you now. This minute.

> *Gets up, moves away from piano. Holly goes to piano, sits facing Brownlow, stretches out his arms, does his finger exercises. Brownlow gives a slight nod. Holly turns around, begins to play a hitherto unheard piece of music. Chopin Etude?*

> *Lights. Curtain.*

Act Two

SCENE ONE

A few weeks later. Early evening.
Smithers' sitting room.
Holly is at the piano. Celia is lying on the sofa,
smoking.
Holly completes passage, gets up quickly, stuffs score
into his satchel, goes towards door.

Holly 'Bye, Mummy.

Celia doesn't answer.

Mummy? (*Goes over to Celia.*) What is it this time,
going dead again or gone blind again? Mummy, please,
I'll be late, what is it?

Celia (*as if coming out of a trance*) Sorry, darling. I've
been away somewhere, I think. A bit of a headache.

Holly Oh. Well, you must take some aspirin.

Celia (*patting sofa.*) Just give me one of your rubs. Just
for a minute.

Holly But, Mummy, I –

Celia Just for a minute, darling, please.

Holly He gets very fed up when I'm late. (*Going behind
Celia, beginning to massage her neck.*)

Celia Well, you can tell him you've been looking after
me for once. Or I'll write him a note, if you like.

Holly Oh, Mummy. (*Laughs.*) A note.

399

Celia Mmmm – mmmm – deeper, deeper – oh, you've got such a feel for it. You seem to know my neck like your piano, I suppose. Holly, do you love me?

Holly Oh, Mummy, of course I do. Because you're my –

Celia No, no, not that, not the usual. I'm being very, very serious. I just want you to say it and nothing more.

Holly Well, I've said it.

Celia Well, say it again. Think about it first and then say it. Holly, do you love me?

Holly (*after a little pause*) Yes.

Celia You don't know how lucky you are being a boy. Look at me – I may not be stupid but I'm almost completely uneducated, really. You're far more educated than I am already. And when you grow up you'll have your freedom, you'll be able to make all kinds of choices. Be what you want. But what am I good for? I can't do anything except what I do. And sometimes that just seems to be nothing. Nothing at all.

Holly But you used to teach girls gym, tennis – and lacrosse.

Celia I can scarcely go back to that now, can I? Do you know, I wouldn't even know how to go about getting a job any more.

Holly But you drove ambulances at the air base. You're always saying how much you loved it.

Celia Oh, they don't want women driving ambulances now the war's over. They don't need us to be anything except what we've always been now they don't need us for carrying wounded men about.

Holly Mummy, are you crying?

Celia (*sniffing*) No, not really. Just a little.

Holly But why? Just because you're not educated?

Celia (*laughs*) Yes, I expect that's it. And because I feel a little sad too, I expect.

Holly But why are you sad?

Celia Oh, things, darling, things. Things I wouldn't dream of burdening you with. You wouldn't understand and I don't want you to.

Holly What things?

Celia Grown-up things, darling. Which are just childish things, really, that happen after a certain age.

Sound of front door opening and closing.

Oh, there's your father. Early. So he'll be going out again this evening, won't he?

Holly has gone to pick up his satchel.
Charles enters.

Charles Oh, hello, darling. (*Sees Holly.*) Off already?

Holly Daddy?

Charles Well, it seems that every time I come in you're going out. Rather like a French farce. At least we've both got our trousers on, eh? (*Laughs.*)

Holly (*laughs*) I've got my piano.

Charles Well, yes, I assume that. It's been virtually every evening, hasn't it?

Holly He's teaching me some preludes – Chopin – and they're rather difficult.

Charles And you want to master them, do you?

Holly Yes, Daddy.

Charles Well, now your scholarship's in the bag I suppose your time's your own for a bit. After all, you've earned it. Earned your Chopin. So. Off you go then.

Holly Thanks, Daddy.

Charles (*slightly surprised*) Not at all, Holly.

As Holly goes to door.

Oh, Holly, there is one thing. You might ask your Mr – Mr – um – no, it's all right, it doesn't matter.

Holly goes out.

I was going to ask him to find out when I can expect a bill at last. I know he said he wouldn't charge me for the extra hours but I don't feel right about it. It's all a bit awkward, if you ask me. Still, mustn't complain, I expect his London tinkler will want it in cash and on the dot – but there's something about him, Mr – Mr – why can we never remember his name?

Celia You're going out again, I take it.

Charles A little girl just come in, four years old. We're all hoping to God it isn't polio that did for her, though from what Greatorix says – (*Looks at Celia.*) Are you all right?

Celia A slight headache, that's all.

Charles Have you taken an aspirin?

Celia Yes, I took two.

Charles When?

Celia About an hour ago.

Charles And you've still got it?

Celia Yes, I've just said.

Charles Poor Ceci, poor Ceci. (*Kisses her forehead, goes behind her.*) Here, let's see what I can do. (*Begins to massage her neck.*) You feeling it?

Celia Yes. It's making it worse. (*Walks around room, her hand to her head.*)

Charles Oh. Sorry. (*Little pause.*) Shall I get us a drink?

> *Celia nods.*
> *Charles goes and pours drinks, glancing anxiously at Celia, who lights a cigarette. Charles goes over, hands her a glass.*

There we are. (*smiling*) May I? (*Makes to take cigarette from between Celia's lips.*)

> *Celia moves cigarette away.*

Darling – (*Stops.*) Oh, isn't it your period about now, old girl?

Celia Don't you know?

Charles Well, not the precise date, how could I?

Celia So you're guessing. Because I've got a headache and I'm feeling low and miserable, it must be old girl's period.

Charles Well, if it's not, then what is it?

Celia I suppose people can feel low and miserable because they're actually low and miserable, even if they are women, wives and mothers and aren't allowed to be low and miserable, except when they've got their periods.

Charles Is it the island again? The gang getting you down? (*Little pause.*) Has Moira said something?

Celia What sort of something?

Charles Well, the sort of something she's always saying that upsets you.

Celia No, Moira hasn't said anything she's always saying that upsets me.

Charles Well, anybody else in the gang? I know how much you hate them but, darling, we're away from here soon – a new life. There'll be a new life.

Celia Yes. A new life. A new life. (*Walking about, smoking. Laughs.*) But there's no getting away from the old life, is there? Ever?

Charles No, I suppose not. But the old life merges into the new life and things change directions and – I don't quite know what you mean, Ceci.

Celia I'm trying to talk about the old, old life, not this that will be the old life when we get to London, but the old life that was before we came to the island. Do you remember?

Charles Yes, of course I remember. Well, there was quite a lot of it, wasn't there, quite a lot of life before we came here. There was the war, for example. (*Little laugh.*) I mean, which part of the old life?

Celia Well, there were certain special moments, I suppose, even in the war, special moments for us – there must have been, mustn't there?

Charles Yes. Yes, quite a few of them. Which ones are you thinking of? I mean, darling, what are you talking about, really?

Celia Well, Whitstable. I think I must be talking about Whitstable.

Charles Whitstable?

Celia Yes. Do you remember us in Whitstable?

Charles Yes, of course I remember.

Celia We went there for the oysters.

Charles Well, darling – yes, the oysters – but we went there to become lovers. Surely that's what you remember about Whitstable.

Celia Yes, yes. All that embarrassment over getting the room for the night.

Charles Rooms actually. We had to take a room each because of that ghastly little landlady – she knew perfectly well what we were up to – so all my shuffling up and down the stairs in the dark . . . (*laughing reminiscently*)

Celia Yes, that's how it began. You shuffling about in the dark, me waiting for you in that horrid room with the curtains that didn't close and the window you couldn't open.

Charles (*laughs*) Yes, well, I suppose quite a lot of couples got off like that. It was all we could get of romance.

Celia Yes, quite a lot of us. Quite a lot of others must have got off like that. Got off on the wrong foot. Deceiving people right from the beginning. Whatever we pretended to each other, we knew it was furtive and it was wrong.

Charles Furtive – wrong? It was just how we had to go about things before – before we were properly married. As far as society was concerned, our parents and – for form's sake. Discreet, we were being, that's all.

Celia But still, we were different, you and I. We wanted to be different from the others. And that's why we kept saying that whatever happened in our lives together we would always be straight with each other, at least. That was to be our rule. Unbreakable. That we would be straight with each other. We made that rule the very next morning. In Whitstable.

Charles Well – yes. And we always have been.

Celia shakes her head.

What? What do you mean?

Celia Oh, Chaps, not me. I haven't been straight. I haven't been straight with you, Chaps.

Charles stares at her.

Celia I had an affair, you see, Chaps.

Charles An affair? In Whitstable? We were only there for three days!

Celia Oh, don't be so stupid, Charles! Of course not in Whitstable. Afterwards. After we'd just got married. At the base.

Charles (*after a pause*) Who? Who, may I ask?

Celia It was Johnny.

Charles Johnny? You don't mean Johnny Miller!

Celia No, not Johnny Miller.

Charles Which Johnny then? There were several Johnnies, I seem to remember.

Celia Johnny Seafield.

Charles Seafield. (*Thinks.*) Johnny Seafield! The one who used to tinkle the piano and lead the sing-songs in the mess?

Celia That's right. Piano Johnny we used to call him.

Charles That's not what some of us called him, some of us called him *Pansy* Johnny – and worse.

Celia Oh yes, I know you did. That was part of the – well, the joke, really. You thought he was like that because he was boyish and delicate and had a gentle manner.

Charles He was effeminate and – and he had a kind of lisp. He made our skins crawl.

Celia (*laughs*) You were such stupid chaps. Blind, the lot of you. We women knew what he was really like. And he was brave. Brave and doomed.

Charles They were all brave, and a lot of them doomed. He wasn't the only one to buy it, you know.

Celia I know. Oh, how I know. He and Julian Lownes and Dickie Storbuck. All in the same afternoon.

Charles But it was him you had a fling with, was it? Or did you have a fling with all of them? All three?

Celia gives him a look.

Celia It wasn't a fling. It was a sadness. The saddest time in my life. I used to watch the skies for him and when I saw him coming back I'd think, well, that's one more time, one more time at least, God has given us.

Charles One more time God had given you – *God* had given you – for you and he to – to – where did you do it?

Celia Rose House.

Charles Rose House. But that was the vicarage! You did it in the vicarage!

Celia The vicar was Johnny's uncle. He was the only person who knew. And he understood. Understood everything. Sometimes he stood with me watching the skies. Both of us looking for Johnny's plane.

Charles Well, we watched the skies too, wondering who was coming back – how many we could patch up – how many we could send up again, knowing that the more often we sent them back, the more likely it was – and that went for your Johnny too. For all the Johnnies we had to put back in the skies. Pansies or not.

Celia It wasn't your fault.

Charles What do you mean it wasn't my fault? Of course it wasn't my fault that you and your Johnny –

Celia No, no, I meant it wasn't your fault that you weren't up in the skies with them. You did the only job you could do. Just as I did in the ambulances.

Charles Are you saying I should be ashamed? That while you were having your – your – with him up in the skies – I should be ashamed for being down there on the ground?

Celia No, I'm saying you shouldn't be. That's it, you see, that's what I'm trying to explain. You and I – well, we had a chance and a future. For us, we could hope it would be over one day, there'd be peace and our lives to live. But Johnny – and the others too, of course – didn't have that hope –

Charles Look – (*getting up*) I know – I know what sort of thing went on. I'd supposed you were exempt from all that panic and living-in-the-moment stuff. But if you weren't – well, God knows how many stories there are to tell that shouldn't be told – what on earth is the bloody point –?

Celia Of being straight, you mean? When we promised we would be. That was our rule.

Charles Well, it's a bit late, isn't it? A dozen years or so late.

Celia I couldn't have told you then, not while it was going on – and I couldn't have told you afterwards – after he'd gone. It would have been unfair on Johnny – to my memory of him – if he'd been the cause for unhappiness between us.

Charles Well then, why now? Why now, when he's been at the bottom of the sea for seven or eight years and it no longer matters? You don't have to be straight when it no longer matters, there's no point to it. No – no moral value even. I mean – I mean, for God's sake, woman, I come home from a day's work, this morning's post-mortems behind me, and tomorrow's – no, tonight's probably – a child of four – a little girl of four and it could be polio, here on this island – if so, God help all of us who have children – looking forward – just looking forward to being alone with you, having our usual drink, our usual – our usual – and this. I get this. Why?

Celia But you see, Chaps, you see, you talked about a new life in London and I'm afraid, you see. So afraid.

Charles Of London? But you've been begging to go to London! Everything I've done has been to get you to London! We're only going there because of you.

Celia But what I'm afraid of, Chaps – my dear old Chaps – is that it won't be a new life. Because we'll be taking our old life with us, you see.

Charles Taking what you've told me with us, you mean? So why did you tell me? Because if I didn't know there'd be nothing to take with us, would there?

Celia looks at him.

What?

Celia There's Holly to take with us.

Charles Holly? What do you mean?

There is a pause.

That's not true.

Celia He'll have to know. One day. One day soon.
We've got to be straight with him. Or at least I've got to
be. He can't grow up in a lie and find out somehow,
people always do, and that would be the worst. Going
on lying to him, going on pretending – (*Shakes her
head.*) We've got to be straight.

Charles has gone over, poured himself another drink.

Charles Everything's upside down. Just some minutes
ago it was right side up and now it's upside down.
Everything. (*Sinks into sofa.*) I never thought the day
would come when I'd – when I'd hate you. Have you
any idea what you've done? Do you realise what it'll be
like from now on for me to be me? How I'll look at you
and him? How I'll think of you and him? Every time I
look at you and him together I'll see you at Rose House
and I'll see him at Rose House and I'll see that pansy at
Rose House, the three of you at Rose House – how can
I hope to go on?

Celia Oh, you foolish man, how can Holly be anything
else but yours? I wanted to enjoy this, I really wanted to,
I wanted to let you stew away, I was looking forward to
it. I think I deserved that. And so did you. But the awful
truth is I love you and I can't get away from that so I
can't bear to see you hurt.

Charles You mean – you mean this is a joke? Is it a
joke? Is that what it is? One of your stupid games, like
pretending you've gone blind or that you're in a coma
or are having a stroke, one of your dramatising, one of

your attention-seeking silly games? Can it really be?
Something like this – something as dangerous as this?
God damn you, Ceci, God damn you!

Celia I have a right! Because I wanted you to feel what
I've been feeling. It was my revenge.

Charles Revenge? Revenge for what?

Celia Moira, damn you! Moira, Moira, Moira!

Charles Moira? What has Moira got to do with any of
this?

Celia You might as well be straight, Charles. She told
me herself, you see.

Charles (*after a long pause*) She told you.

Celia And how many others have there been?

Charles Never anyone. Only her. I swear, darling.

Celia Why should I believe you?

Charles Because you know me.

Celia No, I don't know you. We don't know each other,
that's what we're discovering.

Charles You do know me, Ceci. Everything about me
that matters. The whole me. You're the only person in
the world who knows the whole of me.

Celia I know the whole of you has been unfaithful – lied
to me – betrayed me – and with my best friend.

Charles Oh, now, darling, your best friend? You can't
stand her.

Celia She's still my best friend on this bloody island
anyway. My only friend. Well. Are you going to tell me
what happened and how it wasn't your fault really?

Charles Of course it was my fault. I accept that completely. Though it wasn't entirely my fault. I mean – I mean – look, darling, what happened was that she phoned me. At the hospital. She needed my professional advice.

Celia Your professional advice? Why? Was she dead?

Charles It was about Richard. She wanted to talk to me about something that was wrong with Richard. And she asked me not to mention it to anyone. Not even you.

Celia Ahah.

Charles So I looked in on the way back –

Celia And when was this?

Charles I don't know – about two months ago it must have been, I suppose.

Celia Two months. Go on.

Charles I looked in on the way back and she gave me a cup of tea.

There is a long pause.

Celia (*helpfully*) She gave you a cup of tea.

Charles Well – then she told me about Richard.

Celia What did she tell you?

Charles Well, actually, darling, it's still – well, confidential. A matter of professional etiquette.

Celia Oh, I see. And it doesn't matter that she goes about blabbing about you and her because she hasn't any professional etiquette to worry about, has she?

Charles He's impotent.

Celia Oh, dear. Poor Moira. So you were called in as a replacement?

Charles (*in spite of himself, lets out a little bark of laughter. After a pause*) He absolutely refuses to discuss it with her so she wondered whether I could find some way to – to help him.

Celia And how had you planned to do it? Go up to him and say, 'Oh, Richard, old boy, I was rogering Moira the other afternoon and she happened to mention that you're having a little problem, so perhaps you'd like to pop in home and watch me when I'm at it.'

Charles You say you want to find out what happened but you won't let me tell you, tell you properly.

Celia Oh, I'm so sorry. Do go on. Please.

Charles Well, it seems things are pretty bad between them. In every possible way, really. Richard's not making out too well in his new job – well, like the rest of us, he was out of things for nearly five years and now there are much younger chaps coming into insurance straight from National Service and the universities – so he feels lost. Afraid of getting the sack, drinking far too much and – and – well, taking it out on Moira and sometimes quite violently. You see. Then she has to put on this front for the rest of the world – you know how she is, always cheerful and laughing – and suddenly there she was, breaking down in front of me. And I put my arms around her and she seemed to assume – and I didn't know how to refuse. Yes, that's what it comes down to. I was frightened of hurting her. You see, Ceci? I know it sounds feeble but that's what really happened.

Celia Where did you do it, by the way?

Charles Why?

Celia In their bedroom, was it?

Charles (*indignantly*) Of course not.

Celia Where then, darling? On the floor – on the sofa, perhaps?

Charles In the spare room. Spare bedroom.

Celia Oh, I don't think so, darling. I've seen that spare room, it hasn't even got a bed, it's got a cot, it wouldn't support Moira on her own, let alone the two of you. I should think you had to do it in their bedroom.

Charles It was in the spare room –

Celia And did you enjoy it, darling? Because that's the main thing, isn't it?

Charles Celia, really!

Celia Oh, don't be such a prude, Charles. You can tell your wife, surely?

Charles I don't know – I don't know – I did it because it seemed the right thing to do – that's what I'm trying to explain – even though I knew it was the wrong thing, at that moment – at that particular moment it seemed – (*Gestures.*) – the right thing. I don't think I was trying to enjoy it, I was just trying to – to do it.

Celia And the other times?

Charles shrugs.

How many other times have there been?

Charles Five, I think. Yes, five.

Celia And how did you manage them, your little visits? Oh, of course! When you have to go out in the evenings.

To the hospital. To visit your corpses. For their post-mortems that you hate doing, poor lamb.

There is a pause.

Charles Needless to say, there won't be any more – any more –

Celia So you'll be keeping the little polio girl for the morning after all, will you? Really, Charles, how sickening. (*There is a pause.*) But of course, in London, where there will be lots and lots of fat little Moiras laughing and cheerful with impotent husbands, it'll be so much easier for you. You won't even have to lie to me.

Charles Damn Moira – why did she have to tell you, why? I simply don't understand.

Celia She didn't have to tell me. She just couldn't help herself. After tennis the other day she suddenly started on Richard. She said she's fairly sure he has a floozy in London and that's why he'd lost interest in her and why he was drinking. And I said – I said – hah! (*Laughs.*) I said, '*Fairly* sure? But you must know. I mean, I'd *always* know if Charles had been with another woman – *fairly* sure wouldn't come into it. I'd just *know*. Just by looking at him.' And she said, 'Oh, how close you and Charles must be if you'd know about him just like that. That's what I call a real marriage, darling.' And I caught her look – a little gleam in her eye, a sort of grin in her eye. That's how she told me. The grin in her eye. I didn't know anything about it from you, however often I'd looked at you. Even now I wouldn't know anything about it just from looking at you. (*Pause.*) I could have had an affair with Johnny. He wanted me to. And I was so – so proud of myself for not. Because I was attracted to him. Very attracted. But then I could never do anything like that to you, could I? I couldn't stand the pain of the pain

415

I'd be giving you – knowing you as I do. But now – what difference would it have made? None at all. Except to me, of course. (*Smiles at him.*)

Charles (*attempts to smile back*) Everything's going to be all right. I'll make sure. (*Puts a hand out towards her.*)

Celia looks at him in sudden horrified bewilderment.

Celia But I don't believe you. It's true – I've never known you. Never really known you. So how can I live with you any more – in London or anywhere? (*Little pause.*) I'm not going to be like all those others. You've been like those other men but I'm not going to be like their women – standing by my man when I don't know what man I'm standing by. No, Charles, I've got to leave. I've got to take Holly and leave. Even though I've got nowhere to go because you've left me with nothing – there's nothing for me, nothing I can do in life, nowhere to go. But I'd rather nothing than be with you, just another man I don't know and can't trust. (*Gets up, goes towards door, collapses, sobbing.*) Oh, mama, mama, help me, help me – oh – oh!

Charles, appalled and distressed, goes to her.

Charles Oh, my Ceci, my poor darling Ceci! What have I done? Oh, please, Ceci, please – (*Attempts to put his arms around her.*)

Celia (*pushing him away*) No, leave me alone! Leave me alone!

Charles Ceci, Ceci – (*Forces his arms around her, holds her tightly.*)

Celia rocks and keens in his arms. Keening fades away. They cling together as if saving themselves. They become aware of a noise off, separate quickly, desperately trying to compose themselves as:

416

Door opens. Holly enters, followed by Brownlow.

Celia Oh, hello, darling, what are you doing back so soon? (*seeing Brownlow*) Everything all right?

Brownlow Oh, yes, indeed. It's just that I've had a rather exciting telegram from a friend of mine in London – a conductor. Teddy Schefflen. Apparently they're going to be playing a small piece of mine at his concert on Saturday.

Celia Oh, how exciting, eh, darling?

Charles Yes, yes, congratulations.

There is a pause.

Celia Would you like a drink?

Brownlow Thank you, if I may. But we mustn't stay long, we haven't begun our lesson yet.

Charles We're drinking gin and tonic. Will that do?

Brownlow Thank you.

Celia Do sit down.

Brownlow (*sitting down*) I wondered if you'd let Holly come with me. Stay over on Saturday night, coming back on Sunday evening. I think it could be very educative – there are a number of other concerts over the weekend – and I'd make sure, of course, that he would be well looked after.

Celia Well, that sounds – that sounds – what do you think, darling?

Charles Well – here, Holly, give this to Mr –

Hands Holly drink. Holly takes drink over to Brownlow.

Brownlow Wc studied music together, Teddy and I. And his wife. All three of us. She's a flautist. Now they have a delightful baby, very chubby. Their house is in Fulham – very convenient for the concerts. He's conducting two of them, the one with my piece and another on Sunday morning. He really is becoming something of a maestro, Teddy.

Celia It would be awfully good for him, darling. And I mean, as we're going to London, he'll already know something about music halls.

Brownlow We'll be visiting several. Concert halls. Though I'm not so sure about music halls. (*Gives a little laugh.*) Anyway, he'll learn a lot. We'll all conspire to make sure of it.

Celia And you'd like that, darling, would you? (*to Holly*)

Holly Oh, yes – yes. Very much.

Charles (*making an effort*) But you must let me know about the tickets, the train and any expenses. I insist on that. Insist on it.

Celia My husband is very pernickety about things like that, aren't you, darling?

Charles I just don't want Mr – um – anybody to be out of pocket.

Brownlow Oh, I shan't be, I'll make sure of it.

Charles Yes, please do.

There is a pause.

Celia How's the cat – Miaow – how's Miaow?

Lights.

SCENE TWO

The following Sunday. Nine p.m.
  Brownlow's study/sitting room.
  *Ellie is at the piano, accompanying herself as she sings
a Viennese folk song. She plays well, sings well. She is
drunk. She concludes song triumphantly and theatrically,
drinks from glass on piano.*
  Sound of doorbell.

Ellie (*in German*) What? Who is this now at this hour?
Has he forgotten his keys? (*Goes to window, taps on it.*)
Thomas? Thomas? Is that you there, Thomas?

  Sound of voice off.

(*in English*) Who is it? (*Obviously can't hear. In
German.*) Oh God, it's the police, it's the police, they've
come to take me, come to take us! (*Cowers.*) Thomas,
Thomas, why aren't you here?

  Doorbell rings again imperiously.
  Ellie goes out. Voices off.

Charles (*off*) Is my son here?

Ellie (*off*) Your son, *bitte*?

Charles (*off*) Yes, my son. Holly. Is he here, please?

Ellie (*off*) Oh, Holly, yes, yes, of course, of course! He's
with Thomas.

  Ellie holds door open. Charles enters.

(*attempting to conceal drunkenness*) So you're the father,
the father of Holly. I'm so sorry, I couldn't see you,
I thought it was the police, you see.

Charles The police? (*anxiously*) Why did you think I was
the police?

Ellie *Bitte?*

Charles Why are you expecting the police?

Ellie Oh, no, no, it's just that sometimes when it's late – so. You are the father of our boy.

Charles I'm Holly's father, yes. I thought you said he was here.

Ellie *Bitte?*

Charles My son and your son, isn't it, you said at the door they were here. Didn't you?

Ellie Ah yes, well, they were here before – for a long time – and then I went upstairs to rest and I came downstairs and you were at the window, no, you were at the door and – the kitchen, perhaps they are in the kitchen having a cuppa. (*Goes to the door, screams out.*) Thomas – Thomas – Holliday – Holliday, here is your father, are you there, are you there? (*Comes back in.*) No, there is no light, they are not in the kitchen, no. Well, they must have gone out for a walk, yes?

Charles A walk? At this hour?

Ellie Can I offer you a drink? It is only sherry but it is new, a fresh bottle.

Charles No, thank you. When did they get back?

Ellie Back? *Bitte?*

Charles When did they get back from London?

Ellie Oh, I don't know, let me think – back, back – this afternoon early, I made them some lunch, I remember, yes, soup and corn beef –

Charles But they were meant to be coming back on the last ferry, which was two hours ago – we've been getting worried, very worried – and you say they've been here all day virtually? Why didn't he phone us at least?

Ellie Yes, I know, so silly, I keep telling him he must have a telephone for his asthma but no, he will not –

Charles But why are they back so early?

Ellie I think my boy, there was some quarrel with his friend in London – Teddy – sometimes they have terrible arguments – shouting, anger, tears, you know with friends. Yes, probably there was a fight, I don't know.

Charles I see. A fight with his friend – Teddy. (*Little pause, thinks.*) But there's a wife, isn't there, and a baby?

Ellie Teddy, a wife, baby? (*Laughs.*) No, no. Not for Teddy a wife and a baby.

Charles But your son said – I remember distinctly – a wife, a baby – his friends, a husband, a wife and a baby.

Ellie Ah, that is Teddy's sister, Debbie. She has a baby, yes. But not husband. He ran away – poof! And no wife for Teddy.

Charles And what have they been doing here all day?

Ellie Doing? Who?

Charles My son and your son, what have they been doing since they got back? (*Just controlling anger.*)

Ellie Nothing. Playing like always. Always they play. Like children they are. Except when Holliday is at the piano and my boy is teaching him. Then goodness, my goodness, very serious, very strong. Yes, the music, that is always serious. But he is a genius. One day he will be a great artist, famous everywhere – oh, if I should live to see it, that's all I hope for! And your boy too, your

Holliday – my son, he hates to teach all the children
here – (*in German*) lumpen fingers – (*in English*) he calls
them, how you say? Yes, their fingers are lumps. They
have no music in their heads, their bodies, only English
stupidity and nice – all so nice. But his Holly, him he
loves and worships, he has a beautiful gift, a beautiful
soul – not English and nice but a free soul like his,
dancing, dancing – so they dance together. (*Wagging
her head, crooning.*) Like this, like this, they are, to
make you cry.

Charles Really. And you don't know where they are
now?

Ellie Oh, no. Perhaps on the beach. By the sea. They like
to hear the sea, to inspire them.

Charles Do they. And what sort of games do they play
when they're not at the piano?

Ellie Just ordinary games. They pretend – you know –
pretend they are at anger between them, and cruelty –
and then if he cries they are friends again. Like children,
you see. Playing, crying, holding each other – (*Stops.
Looks at Charles, suddenly worried.*) You are angry. Oh,
please do not be angry, do not be English – be nice, not
like English nice, there must be no trouble, no more
trouble – it is not his fault if he loves to teach, people do
not understand – we cannot move away, oh, we cannot
move away again – please, Mr Holly's father, please be
kind. (*Begins to cry, sags into a chair. In German*) Oh,
what have I said, what have I done?

> *Charles stares at her in disgust.*
> *Door opens. Brownlow enters.*

Charles What have you done with my son?

Brownlow I've just taken him home. To your home. Your wife told me you'd come over here so I hurried back.

Charles He's been here all afternoon, I gather.

Brownlow Yes, well, we came back early – the lunchtime concert was cancelled – and as I knew you weren't expecting him back until the last ferry –

Charles The last ferry is at six o'clock on Sundays.

Brownlow Oh, is it? I assumed it was the same time as in the week. I'm very sorry – but even so we're only an hour or so later than –

Charles That's not the point.

Brownlow What is the point?

Charles The point is – the point is that I've been talking to your mother. I think I have a fairly good idea – no, I won't call it a good idea – but an idea of the sort of thing that's been going on between you and my son.

Brownlow Indeed? What has been going on between your son and myself, may I ask? What is this idea you have of what has been going on?

Charles Let's just say that you are to have nothing further to do with him. Do you understand me?

Brownlow No – no, I don't understand. I've done nothing wrong. We did nothing wrong together. I would never do anything to harm your son. Never. So please, please don't stop his lessons – he will never find another teacher who understands him as I do, who knows his talents –

Charles If I catch you anywhere near him, I'll go to the police.

Ellie (*in German*) The police, the police – there, I warned you!

423

Brownlow I don't care – go to the police, I'm not frightened, I'm not ashamed, I have nothing to be ashamed of.

Charles Yes, you probably believe that, that's just it, isn't it, with a type like you? You don't know what decency is, you have no idea, no sense, no understanding even of what it is to be straight. You filthy, little – Jew.

Ellie No, no, we are not Jews! Not Jews!

Charles turns, goes out.

(*in German*) See? See what you've done? He'll go to the police and we'll be finished.

Brownlow What did you say to him? What did you tell him about me – about Holly and me?

Ellie (*in German*) Nothing – nothing – I said how good you were to each other, how happy, how you taught him and sometimes that you were strict, that you loved each other like children –

Brownlow Loved each other – loved each other like children –

Sinks into a chair, puts his face into his hands, his shoulders begin to shake. Ellie goes over to him, kneels beside him, strokes his head.

Ellie (*in German*) There, there, Thomas, my poor, poor Thomas.

Puts her arms around him, begins to rock him.
He rocks with her.
Lights.

SCENE THREE

The same.
    Smithers' sitting room.
    Holly's overnight bag by sofa. Holly is sitting at piano stool, facing away from piano, drinking cup of tea.
    Celia is lying on sofa, smoking.

Celia I must say, darling, it does sound all terribly Bohemian and hothousey. And what was it about, this ferocious row?

Holly Oh, a bit of music – well, that's what started it anyway, I couldn't follow the rest of it, it was all about people I don't know, but it was the Berg that did it in the first place.

Celia The Berg? What Berg?

Holly The composer, Alban Berg. They were trying to remember the first bars of some piano piece, I don't know which one, but they had a bet on it, you see – well, what happened was that Teddy began to play it and Lowly –

Celia Who?

Holly Mr Brownlow, that's what everybody calls him in London, Lowly. Anyway, he, Mr Brownlow, said that Teddy had got it wrong and it started like this and he showed him, and then they had their bet and then Teddy couldn't find the music and Mr Brownlow said he was hiding it because he knew he'd lost the bet and – and so, you know, that's when it went all over the place.

Celia But, poor darling, how embarrassing for you. What on earth did you do?

Holly Oh, I just went back to our room.

Celia Our room? Whose room?

Holly Well, the bedroom.

Celia Oh. So you and Mr Brownlow shared a bedroom, did you?

Holly Oh no, not really, I was on a sofa thing in the hall but I left my stuff in the room he was sleeping in so I went there and got the score for the lunchtime concert they'd given me.

Celia Then Teddy threw you both out, did he?

Holly No, no, he didn't throw us out, Mummy. It was all quite friendly after that, except it turned out the concert had been cancelled or something so he, Mr Brownlow, said let's go back and enjoy the weather and we said goodbye. It was all friendly and as if nothing had happened really.

Celia Well, I suppose musicians and people like that tend to have tantrums and melodramas. It's probably all quite fun in a way. And what was the little wife and baby doing during all this?

Holly Oh, she didn't pay much attention, as if she were quite used to it.

Celia Even so, you should have been more thoughtful, darling. He probably doesn't think about parental worries and fears when children are late – trains do crash, ferries do sink – so you should have popped in to let us know you were safe at least.

Holly Well, he didn't think you'd expect us back, he explained to you, Mummy, he just got the time wrong for Sundays, that's all.

Celia Well, the next time – (*Yawns.*) – you'll know what to do. Your father really was getting into quite a state.

Holly Well, I'm sorry. Do you mind if I just play something? It was in the concert last night and we've been practising playing it from memory this afternoon but I'm afraid it'll slip away if I don't do it once more before I go – (*Notices that Celia isn't paying attention, turns to piano, begins to play thoughtfully.*)

Celia goes on smoking, Holly goes on playing.
Celia, suddenly becoming aware of Holly, looks at him. She stubs out cigarette, looks at Holly again.

Celia (*sternly*) Holly, come here.

Holly goes on playing, as if unaware.

(*more loudly and sternly*) Holly. I said come here. This minute.

Holly sighs, gets up, goes over.

Holly What, Mummy? I was just –

Celia Sit down.

Holly (*going to sit down*) I was just getting to the bit I wanted to –

Celia Not there. Here. (*Pats side of sofa.*)

Holly sits on sofa.

Celia Now, look at me. Straight in the eye, my boy. I want the truth.

There is a long pause.

Holly Well about what, Mummy?

Celia You know what about. (*Pause.*) Do you love me?

Holly Oh, honestly, Mummy.

Celia I want an answer.

427

Holly Of course I do. You know I do.

Celia Why? Tell me why.

Holly Well, because you're my mother.

Celia That's not good enough.

Holly Why not?

Celia Because I'm not your mother. You're adopted. There. What do you say to that?

Holly stands, trembling and swaying, as if in shock.

Celia (*suddenly alarmed*) Darling – darling!

Holly (*holds up his hand*) Mummy, I think that's the most terrific news I've ever heard. I always knew it – well, I always hoped it anyway. Thank you, Mummy.

Celia grabs him, begins to tickle him. Holly squirms, giggling helplessly, pulls himself away.

Holly Now I've got to get back –

Celia Twiddle my toes. Twiddle my toes first, go on. They feel stiff and crampy. Just for two minutes.

Holly Ohh. Two minutes. Exactly two minutes. (*Looks at his watch, sits down.*)

Sound of front door opening, closing.

Celia Ah, there's your father.

Charles enters, taking in Holly massaging Celia's toes.

Oh, there you are, darling, and here he is, as I expect you already know.

Holly (*gets up*) Hello, Daddy.

Celia Darling, what is it?

Charles Holly, sit down, please.

Holly sits down.

Celia What is it, Charles?

Charles I've just been speaking to that creature.

Celia What creature?

Charles That creature and his mother. I know what sort of thing's been going on. What I don't know is exactly how far it went. (*Little pause.*) Holly?

Celia Charles, shouldn't we –

Charles Holly.

Holly I – I don't know what you mean, Daddy.

Charles I think you do. When you 'played' together, for instance.

Holly We just played Beethoven – Chopin –

Charles No, not when you played together on the piano. When you 'played' together like children. What did you do then, when you 'played' together like children?

Holly He – he – sometimes he pretended to get cross – that's all – when I went wrong on the piano. And – and it was just a game. He didn't mean anything. I didn't mind. It's just – just his way of teaching me, to make it more – to make me concentrate more.

Charles And your dancing together, was that to make you concentrate more?

Holly Dancing?

Charles Dancing.

Holly Well, we didn't – I mean – there's a bit of Handel he used to play and he taught me a few steps –

Charles Show me.

Celia Charles.

Charles Show me, please, Holly.

Holly, after a pause, takes a few steps, a pirouette, then a few more steps, bows.

Charles So he played and you did that for him. (*Little pause.*) When you were in London with his friend – Teddy – what then?

Celia There was Teddy's wife and the baby.

Charles In London with his friend, Teddy, and Teddy's sister and her baby by someone who's left her, what then?

There is a pause.

What did you do, you and Mr – (*Gestures.*) your dancing master. What did you do together in London?

Holly Nothing. We went to a concert in the evening and a walk and then there was a quarrel over music and then the concert was cancelled and then we came back and we didn't know you were waiting for us and – and that's all.

Charles And what were the sleeping arrangements?

Holly Well, I slept in the room with the baby.

Celia Yes, he was just telling me about it, Charles.

Charles You and the baby?

Holly Yes. And then the baby woke up and the mother came in and I slept in the hall on the sofa.

There is a pause.

Charles I told your friend that he's not to see you again. You will stay away from him, Holly. Is that understood?

Holly nods.

Good. If I had my way I'd drive him off the island. There's nothing I'd like better. But as we're leaving ourselves, it would probably just cause a lot of fuss and we don't want the fuss following us to London like a plague, and there'd be bound to be talk about you, what you let happen to you –

Celia Darling!

Charles You know this island, for God's sakes, better than anyone. Whatever the truth, there'd be gossip.

Celia (*turns to Holly*) All Daddy's saying is that people are so silly and nasty and quick to make silly and nasty things up – that you should – should, well, keep mum.

Charles (*as if ignoring her*) The point is, you're starting your scholarship with a clean sheet as far as everybody else knows, you'll just have to make sure you keep it that way. Now we won't discuss this any more ever again. All right, Holly?

Holly doesn't reply.

Now off you go.

Holly Where, Daddy?

Charles To bed, of course.

Celia Yes, darling, you should, you've had a – a long day – a nice hot bath and then tomorrow everything will be back to normal.

Holly But he didn't do anything wrong. He was always very nice – kind – kind to me. Honestly.

Charles I told you, we're not going to talk about this any more. And I told you to go to bed.

Holly sits for a moment, as if to speak, then gets up, goes to door, turns defiantly to the piano, sits down, begins to play a brief melange out of which 'Rule Britannia' emerges.

Charles, after a moment, gets up, goes to Holly.

Go to bed, I say. Go to bed!

Holly continues playing. Charles makes as if to strike him.

Celia Charles!

Charles just controls himself, looks from Holly to Celia, goes to door, turns.

Charles Pansy Johnny's boy. That's who you are. Pansy Johnny's boy. (*Goes out.*)

Holly continues playing, stops.

Holly What did he mean, Pansy Johnny's boy?

Celia (*gets up, goes to him*) Nothing really, darling. Just a grown-up sort of thing. One day you'll find out all about it, I expect. But there's no rush.

Puts a hand on his head, looks towards door, goes out. Holly sits for a moment, then turns to piano, continues playing 'Rule Britannia'.

    Lights going down as lights coming up on Brownlow's study, Holly still playing.

SCENE FOUR

The present. A few minutes after Act One, Scene One.
Brownlow's study/sitting room.
Holly is sitting in armchair, smoking, bowl as ashtray
cupped in his hand.
Brownlow enters, carrying tray on which decanter and
two glasses.

Brownlow And when are you planning to go back? To
Australia, I mean, Melbourne?

Holly Oh, when I've cleared up a few things, settled a
few things.

Brownlow has put tray on table. Picks up decanter,
holds it up, inspects it.

Brownlow I can't see any sediment, rather a lovely colour,
what would one call it? Tawny? No, no, of course not,
that's for port, isn't it? Topaz, what about topaz? Oh
yes, there are one or two black spots floating around,
I must try and keep them out of your glass. (*Pours sherry*
into a glass, brings it over to Holly, puts it beside him.
Gives a little cough.)

Holly Oh, I'm smoking, I'm sorry, I forgot.

Brownlow (*stepping away*) No, no, that's all right. As
long as I keep my distance. (*Pouring himself a glass of*
sherry.) So much dust in the room anyway, in the
corners, I'm always telling Mrs Jameson to get into the
corners but I don't think she ever does. There. (*Sitting*
down at table.) I'm quite safe over here.

Holly (*indicating bowl*) Is it all right to use this as an
ashtray?

Brownlow Oh, yes, yes, indeed.

Holly It's pretty. (*Looking at bowl properly.*)

Brownlow Yes, very useful, for little odds and ends. My mother used to have it by her bed. For her teeth, actually.

Holly puts bowl down beside him.

And your parents, how are they, are they still with us?

Holly Not my mother. She died fifteen, no, sixteen years ago. Cancer.

Brownlow Oh, I'm so sorry. She always seemed so – so vivid to me.

Holly Yes, she seemed vivid to quite a few people. Perhaps still does. I hope so, anyway.

Brownlow But your father, he's well, is he?

Holly Oh, yes. He's retired, of course. Lives on the Isle of Wight with his second wife and their two children.

Brownlow The Isle of Wight? That's – that's convenient. Now that you're here, you can just pop across –

Holly Yes, but I doubt if I'll have the time.

Brownlow But you found time for me.

Holly Yes. Yes, I did.

Pause.

Brownlow So. Life – life, um – and you? What has become of you, may I ask?

Holly I'm a doctor.

Brownlow Ah. And are you also a pathologist like your father?

Holly No, I'm a psychiatrist.

Brownlow A psychiatrist? Ah. So you abandoned your music then, after all?

Holly No. No, I think it abandoned me. My daughter has a gift, something of a gift. She's only ten but her mother keeps her at it. She's a professional cellist – my wife, that is.

Brownlow Oh. So it's the cello for your daughter, not the piano.

Holly The violin, actually. But her brother likes to play the piano when he's in the mood and can't find anything better to do.

Brownlow Well, it sounds a happy life. And a complete life. A happy and complete life that you've made for yourself in Australia.

Holly Yes, I suppose it does sound that. Though one never knows, does one, almost from minute to minute, what lies ahead – what memories lie ahead, even. Or don't lie ahead, as it turns out. Like the music. The music that won't come back.

Brownlow I'm sorry?

Holly I think I mentioned it before you got the sherry. Which is actually remarkably drinkable, by the way. It was a bagatelle.

Brownlow A bagatelle, was it?

Holly Yes. You wrote it especially for me. 'A Bagatelle for Mio' you called it. It was played on Radio 3. The Third Programme, I mean. Ring any bells?

Brownlow No, it doesn't, I'm afraid. But it was a very long time ago, wasn't it? Some thirty years.

Holly But might you still have the score somewhere?

Brownlow No, I've thrown everything out from those days.

Holly Oh. But could it still be in you, lurking – waiting to come out again? Perhaps if you tried on the keys for a few minutes, see if anything bobs up? I'll recognise it from just a few notes, I know I will. (*Little pause.*) Would you mind? Um, giving it a go? On the keys?

Brownlow gets up, goes across to piano, sits on stool, puts his hands out as if to play. Turns.

Brownlow I'd rather not. I'd really rather not. There hasn't been music for years – no concertos, no bagatelles, not even dreams of concertos, not even memories of bagatelles – nothing, for years and years. So why have you come here? You come looking me up like this, from so long ago, out of the blue, out of the darkness, remembering this, trying to make me remember that – what do you want? What do you want? To punish? To forgive? (*Laughs.*) It's too late – far too late –

Begins to wheeze, gropes for inhaler in his pocket, drops it to the floor. Holly, after a moment, comes over, picks up inhaler, puts an arm around Brownlow, supports him, puts inhaler in his hand, helps him to apply it. Steps away. Brownlow begins to recover.

Holly Are you all right?

Brownlow nods.

I'm so sorry. I just wanted to remember the bagatelle. You see, I remember everything else as clearly as I want to, I really do. But the bagatelle, not remembering it has been driving me mad. I shouldn't have been so pressing, I'm sorry. Though oddly enough – for what it's worth – I think – (*Hums.*) – isn't that it?

Brownlow shakes his head.

436

No, it isn't, is it? Oh well, it'll just have to nag away at me until I forget to try to remember it. (*Hums again, shakes his head.*) No. (*Laughs.*)

Brownlow laughs.

(*Looks at his watch.*) Good heavens, I'd better be on my way. Leave you in peace. Here –

Holds out his hand. Brownlow takes it.

There, you see. Still real, I hope.

Brownlow (*clutching Holly's hand*) No, stay. Stay and talk a while. We have so much to say to each other, we've hardly said anything – anything that matters.

Holly (*removing his hand, gently but firmly*) I can't, I'm afraid. I'm meeting somebody in Portsmouth. She's my what they call 'bit on the side', you see, so of course she doesn't like to be kept waiting. And nor do I. (*Smiles.*) But if I'm ever in the old haunts again – goodbye, Lowly. (*Goes out.*)

Brownlow (*stroking his hand*) Still real. Still real.

Brownlow goes to the armchair. Sits in it. As he does so, lights up on Smithers' drawing room. Holly at the piano. Plays 'Bagatelle' as lights go down.

Curtain.